D1733032

State and Local Government

State and Local Government

2008–2009

Edited by Kevin B. Smith
University of Nebraska–Lincoln

CQ PRESS

A Division of SAGE
Washington, D.C.

CQ Press
2300 N Street, NW, Suite 800
Washington, DC 20037

Phone: 202-729-1900; toll-free, 1-866-4CQ-PRESS (1-866-427-7737)

Web: www.cqpress.com

Cover design: Auburn Associates, Inc., Baltimore, Maryland
Composition: Circle Graphics, Columbia, Maryland

♾ The paper used in this publication exceeds the requirements of the American National Standard for Information Sciences—Permanence of Paper for Printed Library Materials, ANSI Z39.48-1992.

Printed and bound in the United States of America

12 11 10 09 08   1 2 3 4 5

ISBN: 978-0-87289-613-0
ISSN: 0888-8590

Contents

Preface

This edition of *State and Local Government,* like each of the editions that came before it, seeks to provide comprehensive coverage of important trends and policy challenges, and state and local governments currently are experiencing plenty of both. On the political front, Democrats continue to make inroads in state legislatures at the expense of Republicans, although the GOP continues to enjoy pockets of electoral success. Policywise, lawmakers of every partisan and ideological stripe are grappling with a wide variety of issues affecting the social, political, and economic life of citizens. The sheer breadth of these issues is astonishing: state and local governments are expected to deal with everything from potholes to pot, health care to home values, global warming to local property taxes.

Following the format of previous editions, this book samples the political and policy landscape of states and localities by drawing on the best writing from a wide variety of published sources, including *Governing* magazine, *State Legislatures, State News,* and *Campaigns and Elections,* publications that are probably familiar to many readers of this text. This edition also continues the precedent established in the previous edition of including several selections from academic publications that serve as outlets for the best state and local research. The latter include pieces drawn from *Publius* and *State and Local Government.* All of the readings are new to the current volume, and they are organized by key institutions, processes, and policy areas. Each introduction has been updated to reflect the content of the essays as well as to account for the political and policy changes that define the dynamic world of state and local politics.

Putting together this volume requires the efforts of many people. Thanks are owed to the excellent editorial team at CQ Press: Charisse Kiino, Dwain Smith, and Lorna Notsch—Charisse for putting together the train, Dwain for making sure it runs, and Lorna for making sure the chief engineer stays on the tracks. For seeing that the production process went smoothly, my thanks to Allyson Rudolph and Stephanie Guyaz. A special thanks is also owed to Amanda Balzer, who served as my graduate assistant as this volume was being compiled. Amanda provided invaluable assistance in helping to cast a wide net for source material. We hope that you find what follows informative and thought-provoking.

Federalism and Intergovernmental Relations

Relations between the federal government and states and localities have always been marked by conflict. At times the relationship has been outright adversarial. Rarely, though, has there been a period during which intergovernmental relations seem to be so marked by cynicism, distrust, and even outright contempt. In the last half of the George W. Bush administration, the partners in the federal system became a distinctly unhappy family.

There are historical and contemporary reasons for this state of affairs. Federal and state governments have been butting heads over who has the power to act in given policy arenas—and who is obligated to foot the bills—since the New Deal of the 1930s. More recently, residual acrimony from the multiple failures at all levels of government in the wake of 2005's Hurricane Katrina continues to inspire finger pointing. Wars in Iraq and Afghanistan consume the federal government's attention, which means that pressing issues for the states—immigration, transportation infrastructure, healthcare—get more inaction than action in Washington. And states and localities fume at the federal government's continued fondness for passing policies and then passing on a big share of the costs to the states.

While undoubtedly there are good reasons for the current strained relations between the different levels of government, there are even better reasons to look for solutions rather than assign blame. Put simply, the American political system cannot function without working cooperative relationships among federal, state, and local governments. On domestic policy issues, and increasingly on foreign policy issues such as trade and immigration, different levels of government have to work together to effectively address problems.

Yet over the past few, years high-profile issues have provided more lessons on how intergovernmental relationship should not work rather than the opposite: Hurricane Katrina, the Real ID Act, and illegal immigration are just some of the better-known examples.

Federalism in the United States is at an awkward place. New Federalism, the broad movement to devolve power from the federal government back to the states, has fizzled as states' rights and powers have slid down the federal government's list of policy priorities. The age of ad hoc federalism, the idea that the federal government supports or opposes state and local policy autonomy based on its own political and fiscal convenience, seems to have settled in, and states and localities are not happy with this development. Generally speaking, the federal government has been taking a larger role in a wide variety of issue areas traditionally considered the purview of state and local governments, including disaster response, public education, and issuing driver's licenses. But while it has been laying down the law, literally and figuratively, it has been much less eager to lay down funding, which has left states and localities on the fiscal hook, sometimes for billions of dollars.

States, however, are making sure ad hoc federalism works both ways. If the federal government cannot bring itself to deal with issues like illegal immigration or environmental threats, then the states seem increasingly willing to forge independent policy paths and work on local solutions to global issues.[1] These cross-pressured policy trends—the federal government moving into traditional state policy domains, and states moving into traditional federal government domains—are feeding more conflict, and no one is sure what it all ultimately means for the evolution of intergovernmental relations. Except for one thing: as always, there will be conflict and change.

NEW FEDERALISM BECOMES AD HOC FEDERALISM

Federalism is the central organizational characteristic of the American political system. In federal systems, national and regional governments share powers and are considered independent equals.[2] In other words, the states are sovereign governments. They must obey the mandates of the U.S. Constitution, but with that caveat, they are pretty much free to do as they wish. State governments primarily get their power from their own citizens in the form of their own state constitutions. At least in theory, they are not dependent on the federal government for power, nor do they have any obligation to obey federal requests that are not mandated by the Constitution.

In practice, the federal system established by the Constitution left the federal and state governments to figure out for themselves who must do what, and who has to foot the bill for doing it.[3] Initially, the federal and state governments tried to keep to themselves, pursuing a doctrine of dual federalism, under which federal and state governments had separate and distinct jurisdictions and responsibilities. Dual federalism was dead by World War II, a victim of the need to exert centralized economic and social power to fight two world wars and deal with the Great Depression.

These needs, and the general acknowledgment that the federal government shared overlapping interests in a wide range of policy areas with the state governments, gave rise to cooperative federalism. The core of cooperative federalism is the idea that both levels of government must work together to address social and economic problems. The basic division of labor that emerged was one in which the federal government identified the problem, established a basic outline of how to respond to the problem, and then turned over the responsibility of implementation to state and local governments, along with some or all of the money to fund any associated programs.

Cooperative federalism defined and described the basic relationship between state and federal governments for much of the twentieth century. This arrangement, though, always had critics who feared that the transfer of money at the heart of the relationship allowed the federal government to assert primacy over the states. The basic argument was that by becoming a central source of money for programs run by the states, the federal government would become a living embodiment of the golden rule: he who has the gold gets to make the rules.

This did indeed come to pass. The federal government began putting strings on its grants that required states and localities to pass and enforce certain laws or meet certain requirements as conditions of receiving the money. States and localities didn't like this much, but were faced with an uncomfortable choice. They could refuse to go along—as they were allowed to do as sovereign governments—but then they lost the money. Things got really bad when the federal government began passing unfunded mandates in the 1970s and 1980s, essentially ordering the states to establish programs and policies while providing either a fraction of their cost or no financial support at all.

All of this spawned a backlash that coalesced into a sustained political agenda known as New Federalism, which took as its explicit goals the reversal of the flow of power from the states to the federal government and the cutting of the federal government's fiscal responsibilities to the states. President Ronald Reagan openly embraced New Federalism in the 1980s, actively cutting and consolidating grant programs. President Bill Clinton, like Reagan a former governor, also supported key New Federalism initiatives in the 1990s. These included radically transforming welfare policy by turning over much of the responsibility to the states, and supporting passage of the Unfunded Mandate Reform Act, designed to stop the federal government from passing obligations on to the states without funding them.

When George W. Bush became president in 2001, it seemed as if New Federalism was about to hit a threshold moment. Bush was also a former governor, and his conservative political philosophy seemed naturally sympathetic to the notion of pushing power down from the federal government toward states and localities. Very early in his tenure as president, however, powerful forces aligned to slow, and even reverse, the trend of decentralization that had emerged during the previous two decades. A recession, the terrorist attacks of September 11, 2001, and drawn out conflicts in Afghanistan and Iraq created pressures on the federal government to again take the central role. Political scientists and historians have long noted that power tends to flow toward the states during times of peace and prosperity and back toward the federal government during times of war and economic stress (this is sometimes called the cyclical theory of federalism). The reason for power accumulating at the federal level during such times is simple: the federal government is better positioned to coordinate and implement responses to problems whose causes and consequences are beyond the borders of the states.

Yet the fading of New Federalism is not simply a product of unforeseen national and international events. The Bush administration has pushed for federal primacy across a wide range of policy areas. Key domestic initiatives have strengthened the federal government's hand

at the expense of the states. The No Child Left Behind (NCLB) Act, for example, requires states and localities to set up expensive new programs that are not fully funded by the federal laws that require them. It is one example of the ad hoc nature of federal-state partnerships that have evolved in recent years.

THE STATE OF FEDERALISM

Unlike ad hoc federalism, underlying cooperative federalism was a core philosophy of governance, a systematic notion of how federalism should work: the federal government would identify the problems and provide the resources (along with some constraints), and states and localities would actually address the problems. New Federalism had a different notion of how federalism should work, but one that was still relatively systematic: the federal government should allow the states to take less money in exchange for more policy-making discretion. Ad hoc federalism, however, seems to lack any such consistency or guiding idea. In this vacuum, states seem increasingly willing to impose their own ideas of good governance and good policy, even if it conflicts with federal perspectives.

This chapter contains a series of essays that highlight the current conflict in state-federal relations. The first essay by Alan Greenblatt details the deep concerns states and localities bear concerning their relationship with the federal government. These concerns range from hardnosed fiscal worries to more general perceptions about a lack of respect. Is it possible to repair this increasingly dysfunctional relationship? Greenblatt suggests the answer is yes, but it is going to take work on both sides. Carl Tubessing's essay points out why repairing the state-federal relationship is going to be hard. States feel enormous pressure to respond to a series of key policy issues that require action from the federal government. The problem is that the federation government is producing more heat than light, and not much in the way of forward progress.

Marc Landy's essay is a review of two federal reports on the Hurricane Katrina disaster, one produced by Congress and one by the White House. As Landy details, the lessons drawn by the federal government from Katrina have profound implications for intergovernmental relations, and he argues that the federal government may be reaching the wrong conclusions. Matt Sundeen's essay offers insight into the nitty-gritty details that bedevil state-federal relationships. The collapse of a bridge spanning the Mississippi River in August 2007 put a national spotlight on the need for investment in transportation infrastructure. That infrastructure is constructed and maintained by a partnership between all levels of government. Yet while all governments have a role to play, and all agree more investment is needed, all would prefer that some other level of government do the dirty work of raising the taxes to finance that investment. Here is a case in which cooperation is desperately needed, yet disagreement and conflict seem more likely.

The final essay by Katherine Barrett and Richard Greene takes a look at intergovernmental relations from a different angle. Much of the focus in federalism is on the state-federal relationship, but relations between states and localities are equally important. There is a big power imbalance between state and local governments, and the temptation is always for the more powerful partner to guard its authority jealously. As Barrett and Greene show, however, states that give localities the autonomy to match revenue tools with local economic conditions may be making a smart decision.

Notes

1. Kevin Smith, "Policy Challenges" in *State and Local Government, 2005–2006* (Washington, D.C.: CQ Press, 2004), 225–226.

2. Kevin B. Smith, Alan Greenblatt, and John Buntin, *Governing States & Localities* (Washington, D.C.: CQ Press, 2004), 26.

3. The U.S. Constitution does lay down a basic set of responsibilities for federal and state governments. See Lee Epstein and Thomas G. Walker, *Constitutional Law for a Changing America: Institutional Powers and Constraints,* 5th ed. (Washington, D.C.: CQ Press, 2004), 323.

1

Recipe for Respect

Alan Greenblatt

The relationship among states, localities, and the federal government is getting more dysfunctional. Is there a better way?

Each branch of the federal government is housed in its own palace in Washington. The White House—always surprisingly small to visitors—is lent grandeur by the open setting of the South Lawn, which hints at the expansive reach of an executive branch whose agencies are spread throughout the city and well into neighboring states. The long marble front of the U.S. Supreme Court stands careful watch, as often seems appropriate, over the Capitol dome that links the House and Senate chambers, located just across the street.

Tourists easily find these sites, even if visiting some of them has grown more difficult since 9/11. But they would be hard pressed to find any monumental building housing those other, equally important parts of the American system of government—the states and localities. States, cities and counties all maintain offices within close proximity to federal decision makers. But they are just that—offices in buildings shared with seafood restaurants, television networks and, of course, lobbyists for myriad private interests.

In some ways, this is understandable. Washington, after all, is the home of the federal government. It is a branch-office town for all other governments. Even so, the absence of a D.C. edifice to house state and local interests is more than a curiosity. It points up the inescapable fact that centralization of political power has left states and localities in a much-diminished political position. They have gradually come to be perceived by the Washington establishment as just another set of lobbyists, seeking favors and handouts whenever they can get them.

Increasingly, they don't get them at all: The amount of money coming their way out of Washington has remained essentially flat

From *Governing*, February 2008.

for two decades even as the number of federal mandates and preemptions continues to rise. This has become a matter of no small concern to state and local officials. The framers thought of federalism as one of the basic structural protections of government. Unless states and localities can regain some of the respect they once had in Washington, they won't provide much protection against the centralization of power.

Could they regain it? This may be the time to find out. January 2009 will bring Washington a new presidential administration working with a Congress dramatically changed from the institution of either the Clinton or Bush years. The nation's capital will be aching for new ideas. State and local leaders may be in a better position than anyone to provide them. While Congress and the president have been mired in stalemate for most of the past two decades, states and localities have been experimenting with new policies on subjects ranging from the environment to housing to higher education. They have something crucial to contribute at what may be a defining moment.

Many perceptive state and local leaders already are thinking about this. "We want the federal government to recognize that there are problems best solved at the state level," says Andrew Romanoff, speaker of the Colorado House. "Either give us the tools or remove the barriers so we can solve the problem. The worst thing the feds can do is say it's your problem and we're going to make it harder for you to solve it."

But to make their contribution, states and localities may need to rethink some strategies that have been second nature to them for a long time now. Not only are they saddled with a reputation as incessant supplicants, they often are considered complainers as well, more interested in blocking hostile initiatives than in laying the groundwork for significant change. Not that the complaints are always unreasonable. States and localities have had sound reasons to fight congressional proposals covering waterways regulation or challenging their taxing authority or imposing costly mandates. And sometimes they have managed, against formidable odds, to win their case.

In December, for example, the U.S. Department of Education opened up to all states the possibility of using a "growth model" to track student achievement under No Child Left Behind, which states and schools consider a more flexible approach than the one dictated by the original federal law. That same month, Congress gave back to governors clear authority over the National

Guard during times of emergency, overturning a law passed a year earlier that had given the president much more control.

Still, there is no denying that years of damage control have left states and localities looking like one more self-interested part of the forever-maligned Washington lobbying community. And the idea that they come to the Capitol only to prevent defeat is too negative. So it's worth asking what would happen if, instead of spending most of their energy asking for money and balking at mandates and preemption, state and local officials shifted their agenda to stress their competence to handle more of the implementation and creation of domestic policy themselves. They have been implementing much of it anyway, but with the federal government frequently acting as an obstacle rather than as a partner. Could a revival of state and local power become something for the feds to endorse, rather than hinder? Instead of favor-seeking, states and localities could build a new political relationship with the federal government around an entirely different idea. It wouldn't be easy. But it may be possible.

DYSFUNCTIONAL RELATIONSHIP

It's not as if the representatives of state and local government in Washington haven't been thinking about ways to recover some influence. Some organizations, led by the National Association of Counties (NACo) and backed by the broad-based National Academy of Public Administration, want to create a new formal institution that would give state and local governments an official and ongoing role in the federal policy-making process. It wouldn't have a grand new building or be a full-fledged cabinet Department of Federalism, but something akin to the old White House Advisory Council on Intergovernmental Relations, which—in the years before it became politicized and then abolished in 1996—provided a useful forum for top players from the federal branches to meet with governors, mayors and county officials to discuss which level of government was best suited to take on specific problems or needs.

Such a forum would be a start. There's no longer any congressional subcommittee concerned with the world of state and local government, and the White House Office of Intergovernmental Relations is mainly a political shop designed to sell administration policy to states and localities, rather than a conduit for taking their concerns into account. "Congress and the administration don't look at us as partners," says Larry Naake, executive director of NACo, "but as a political organization they can use or people trying to get handouts or money."

Both of the last two presidents had been governors, and both raised initial hopes that they would be sympathetic to state and local needs and concerns. George W. Bush, in particular, spent much of his six-year tenure as governor of Texas complaining about federal intrusion on states' rights. He appointed several of his former gubernatorial colleagues to cabinet positions. But any hopes for a new federal partnership under Bush have been systematically disabused. The No Child Left Behind education law and the REAL ID driver's license act are just the two most prominent examples of Washington placing new responsibilities on lower levels of government without providing adequate funds to support them. Congress has enacted more statutes preempting the powers of states and localities under Bush than under the previous three presidents, according to Joseph Zimmerman, a political scientist at SUNY-Albany. When Bill Clinton was president, the number of such laws averaged eight per year. Under Bush, the average has been 12.5.

The Bush years have represented not just increasing federal encroachment on state and local turf but a consistently adversarial approach to state policies the administration disagrees with. In a few instances, where the White House has supported a particular state policy, it has allowed federal waivers for experiment. Where there has been any dispute at all, however, the feds nearly always have tried to prevent states from acting. The most recent and best-publicized example was the Environmental Protection Agency's refusal to allow California and more than a dozen other states the authority to impose new regulations on vehicle emissions to curb greenhouse gases. But the administration also sued to block medical-marijuana statutes and physician-assisted suicide and sought to overturn the Florida Supreme Court's rulings in the case of comatose patient Terri Schiavo.

In addition to congressional action and legal challenges, there has been an onslaught of regulatory change that has caused headaches for states and localities. "What seems to be the case more and more in this administration is that preemptions and federal mandates may not just be coming out of Congress," says Texas state Senator Leticia Van de Putte. "Those may just be a preamble to rules and regulations that become egregious to the states."

SHARING THE CREDIT

During this presidential campaign year, many state and local officials are making familiar noises about trying to ensure that their issues are part of the national political dialogue. Cynthia McCollum, a member of the city council in Madison, Alabama, is president of the National League of Cities in 2008, and she is spending much of her time trying to persuade national candidates to pay attention to local issues. "We're not going to get everything we want and ask for," she concedes. But "if they at least understand the problems of cities and towns, we're ahead of the game."

Although presidential candidates make rote promises of inclusiveness and concern when seeking the endorsements of mayors and governors, these lower levels of government are no more likely to hear their issues raised as a serious part of the national debate than they have been at any time in the recent past. This is particularly true for cities. Republicans have little political reason to focus on issues affecting urban voters they know will not support them, and Democrats can win urban constituencies without making much extra effort to appease them. And it seems extremely unlikely that Democratic candidates will forsake the issues of Iraq and health care to deliver speeches on transportation funding. The states have a stronger claim on national presidential campaign attentions, but it may not be a sufficient one. "I shall redact mandates" is not a slogan destined to win a lot of votes for a presidential candidate.

But once the campaign is over, there will be a rare opportunity for state and local interests to seize the moment with a new approach. Call it credit-sharing. State and local leaders can make their pitch to members of Congress by offering a chance to cut them in on breakthrough initiatives being launched back home. Instead of asking for money or help with regulators, they can offer valuable publicity. They can make a legislator feel that her support was indispensable for getting a project underway—without asking her to do much more than make a supportive statement and show up for the press conference. Being able to claim authorship of a popular program in the district or statewide could make up for a lot of federal nay-saying on other issues. It might even help to level the playing field with private-sector lobbyists who are able to buy their way to access through campaign contributions.

State and local governments are constantly talking up innovative programs they've devised that are being imitated across the nation. Why not package themselves as true "laboratories of democracy," able to run meaningful experiments in public policy at no cost to the federal treasury—and able to offer Congress and the executive branch a chance to enjoy whatever degree of glory emerges?

Unorthodox as this approach might sound, it wouldn't necessarily be a hard sell. Intrusive as the Congress and the White House have been on many policy fronts, there has been little progress on some of the most important national issues, and this has left broad openings for states and localities to craft policy themselves. The absence of progress in Washington on immigration or health care, and the near-absence of it on environmental issues, has generated countless experiments in cities and state capitols across the country, typified, perhaps, by the decision of more than 700 local governments to abide by the Kyoto treaty despite its rejection at the national level. "I think there is the feeling among the governors now that they need to go it alone," says Ray Scheppach, of the National Governors Association, "because Washington has gotten so partisan and tied up in an international situation."

LABORATORIES AGAIN

But there's more than one way to go it alone. The way things stand now, for example, many states are reacting to REAL ID by simply threatening to ignore it. Under a credit-sharing approach, one state might take the lead in designing a model for much tighter state-driven security in the issuance of driver's licenses. It isn't hard to envision such a tactic winning congressional blessing in advance. It's true that governors and state DMVs had been working on new, less onerous standards before REAL ID became law, but it's also true that a single state acting alone could move much faster than all the states trying to act collectively. The designated pioneer state might have produced a workable solution that other states could be moving to implement right now, rather than continuing to fight a rearguard action against the costs and regulatory restrictions of REAL ID.

This sort of thing actually happens quite often; it just occurs by happenstance, rather than coherent strategy. New York State moves against shady student loan practices, other states decide to follow, and then Congress moves in to claim a piece of the action with investigations and legislative remedies. But a great deal gets lost in the translation to federal law. No Child Left Behind, for instance, was clearly based on programs and ideas that were already being tried at the state level. But when the White House and Congress put their own stamp on school testing and accountability, they came up with a law that left states feeling cut out of the process and burdened with an enormous cost. Things might have played out differently if states had arranged not only to present their own initiatives upfront but to work harder at making Congress part of them.

Dick Nathan, of the Rockefeller Institute of Government, suggests that the historical pattern is "innovation in leading states, spreading to other states and eventually morphing into national policy." That was the case a century ago, with railroad regulation moving from Massachusetts to other states and finally to Washington. It's the case today, with Massachusetts, Vermont and Maine offering model attempts at providing or requiring universal health insurance. "From my years in the U.S. House, I know Congress tends to act after states lead," says Maine Governor John Baldacci. "That's why in Maine, we keep working on the important issue of affordable health care, although we know a national solution is key." All that credit-sharing might require would be a conscious commitment by states and localities to get out in front and do these things systematically, rather than randomly.

If states and localities are willing to put their vaunted flexibility to work—while sharing pride of authorship rather than begging for federal dollars—they can go a long way toward being taken seriously again as important partners in Washington. Imagine a relationship in which federal officials know they can turn to states or local governments as real partners ready for a challenge, rather than having to impose mandates, or withholding waivers until some form of policy blackmail is paid up. "We hope for a process where we're involved," says Larry Naake of the counties' association, "rather than, 'We want X number of dollars for this project.'"

The bottom line is that states and localities are going to be given more and more responsibilities whether they ask for them or not. They can take advantage of the coming opportunity to shape those responsibilities by coming to Congress and the administration first whenever it's appropriate, winning not only a federal imprimatur but negotiating points for other battles that are bound to come up for them in Washington.

There's always the risk that their federal counterparts will not act in good faith, that they will accept the proffered credit for state or local ideas but continue to pour on the costly and unfunded mandates. Federal officials are never going to be shy about imposing their will on states and localities. There's no way to force public-spirited federalism. But if the states react to federal arrogance in the posture of victims or supplicants, the problem will only get worse. All the evidence suggests that the time to try a new approach has arrived. In the words of Cynthia McCollum, the National League of Cities president, "We can't sit back and wait for them to come to us. We're going to be on offense and help them to help us."

2

Federal (In)Action

Carl Tubbesing

It's hard to get much done in our nation's capital these days.

I f you've been frustrated by the gridlock in our nation's capital over the past 12 months—not to mention the bickering, posturing and partisanship—better re-stock your cache of Valium, because 2008 will be even worse. That, at least, is the word according to national political pundit Conventional Wisdom. Just tune in to any of the Sunday morning talk shows if you want to hear Mr. Wisdom pontificate about—whoops, we mean elaborate on—his prognosis. The shorthand version is this: We are now in 2008, with the presidency up for grabs and control of a closely divided Congress also at stake. President George W. Bush, confronting the dilemma faced by all of his lame duck predecessors, is determined to remain relevant and to leave a domestic policy legacy. Congressional Democrats, on the other hand, are equally determined not to give the president any victory or to do anything that might give an advantage to Republicans in the fall elections. Result? Stalemate. See you in 2009.

Fans of representative democracy, the legislative process, compromise and civil discourse find this scenario alarming and depressing. The incurable optimists in our midsts, though, see a touch of brightness in the public policy gloom. They see a particularly daunting set of issues on the country's domestic policy agenda. Some of these issues, such as health care, entitlement reform and immigration, so far have defied long-term, national solutions. In other cases, such as surface transportation and education, laws have been passed and solutions pursued, but there are questions about whether current approaches are effective, appropriate or workable for the long-run. Why not, say our friends who search for silver linings, use the next 12 months to examine these issues, explore alternative

From *State Legislatures,* January 2008.

approaches and even move toward consensus in time for a new administration and newly elected Congress?

FIVE BIG ISSUES

These "Big Five" of particularly vexing issues—health care, entitlement reform, surface transportation, education and immigration—have several things in common. Some observers would say that they must be successfully addressed to ensure the long-term viability of the country. At the very least, they are crossroads issues. Taking one path over another conceivably commits the country to an approach for a long period of time, perhaps a generation or longer. By their nature, these Big Five are complex and politically charged. They demand comprehensive, non-incremental, thinking outside the box, starting all over again solutions. They are state-federal issues, meaning the national and state governments share responsibility for them, and the states have a very substantial stake in how they are resolved.

Surface Transportation: Change in a Time of Crisis

"Often it takes a crisis to promote real change," said Washington Senator Mary Margaret Haugen speaking last fall during the initial meeting of NCSL's new working group on surface transportation.

There is little disagreement that the country's system of highways and mass transit is approaching crisis. The problem starts with money. The Highway Trust Fund, which supports highway construction and maintenance and mass transit, is running out of it. Spending is up and revenues are not keeping up. Spending has increased partly because the current highway law, the unfortunately acronymed SAFETEA-LU, authorized a lot of it and high energy costs have increased construction expenses. This accelerated the "spend-down" at a much faster rate than was originally projected. The revenue problem is probably more vexing. The trust fund is supported by motor fuel taxes and, according to a June report by Federal Funds Information for States, was "designed to run essentially on auto-pilot."

Revenues produced by taxes on gas consumption historically were more than enough to pay for the billions of dollars in highway and mass transit projects authorized by federal law. Altered driving patterns, more fuel efficient cars and resistance by federal lawmakers to raise the gas tax have substantially slowed the flow of revenues

into the trust fund. The result is that the trust fund could run out of money during the 2009 federal fiscal year.

The transportation crisis isn't just one of finances though. The collapse of the I-35W bridge in Minnesota has become a stark symbol of the nation's aging transportation infrastructure and has elevated fears about travel safety. Traffic congestion, which brings rush hour and even non-rush hour highway travel to a standstill, has a demonstrable impact on air quality and climate change. Congestion also has a substantial negative impact on the nation's productivity and mental health. Housing and land use patterns frequently exacerbate congestion and other transportation problems. Advances in technology, construction techniques and designs present opportunities for faster, but longer-lasting projects.

"We are treating the next examination of the federal transportation law as an 'authorization,' not a 'reauthorization,' " Susan Binder, executive director for one of two federal commissions looking at the future of the surface transportation system, told NCSL's working group last fall. That appears to be the underlying premise of each of the several recent efforts to address the crisis. When the current law expires in 2009, they say, there needs to be a fundamentally, perhaps even radically, different approach to funding and all of the other interrelated elements of transportation policy.

State officials, in the meantime, are laying the groundwork for this re-examination through a burst of transportation policy experimentation. The leasing of major toll roads in Indiana and Illinois has received nationwide attention. Texas officials have become known for encouraging public-private transportation partnerships; and Texas voters recently approved $5 billion in new transportation bonds. Oregon is trying out a tax on vehicle-miles-traveled, an alternative to the traditional method, which is based on consumption.

Education: Out of Stalemate, Opportunity?

Early in 2007, the stars appeared to have aligned to hustle a renewal of the No Child Left Behind Act through Congress. The chances for reauthorizing the law, widely thought to be the signature domestic policy achievement of President Bush's first six years, actually appeared to have been enhanced by the Democratic take-over of Congress in 2006. After all, Massachusetts Senator Ted Kennedy and California Representative George Miller had been instrumental in getting No Child Left Behind passed in 2001 when they were in the minority. When they moved into the majority last January and were chairing the committees with jurisdiction over the education law, they seemed at least as determined as President Bush to get a new version on the books in 2007 before the election year began.

It was not to be. On consecutive weeks in November, Kennedy and Miller announced they were giving up and would try again next year. If Mr. Conventional Wisdom is right, that really means 2009, after the presidential and congressional elections.

The key reason there was no agreement on a new law is that the current one is controversial. Although it has plenty of supporters, it has many detractors, among them members of Congress and state legislatures on both sides of the aisle. Before he gave up on moving legislation this year, Congressman Miller circulated draft amendments to the law. Weighing in at 600 pages, the amendments attempted to address many of the concerns that had been raised about No Child Left Behind. Critics of Miller's draft argued that its length alone—the current law plus the new language would total 1,600 pages—is an indication that it has added complexity without addressing the more fundamental concerns they have with No Child Left Behind.

Delaware Representative Donna Stone, NCSL's president, says Miller's solution does nothing to solve the fundamental problems of the federal act. "ESEA (The Elementary and Secondary Education Act) remains an admirable goal so wrapped in process and compliance that it fails to focus on outcomes and achievement."

There are members of Congress and other education experts who agree. Sixty-five House Republicans, including Missouri Representative Roy Blunt, the minority whip, have signed onto legislation that would allow states to opt out of No Child Left Behind and to receive their education funding through block grants. At the end of 2006, a national commission released a report calling for an even more radical overhaul of the education system. Sponsored by the National Center on Education and the Economy, the report, "Tough Choices or Tough Times," recommended such fundamental changes as funding schools by the state, not by local districts; having schools run by independent contractors; and providing a clear, early path for students to enter technical colleges.

Health Care: Show Me the Money

A few pretty simple statistics make the case for fundamental reform of the country's approach to health care. There are 46.5 million Americans who have no health insurance. The percentage of employers who provide health insurance is now 60 percent, down from 69 percent seven years ago. The costs of health care are high, rising an average of 7.4 percent per year over the past six years. There's also the competitiveness angle: health costs add $1,500 to the price of each car General Motors makes. And don't forget the 76 million baby boomers, many of whom are going to need long-term medical care.

Dealing with health care reform has been a dominant theme of the presidential campaigns so far. There have been plenty of reform bills introduced in Congress and even more national commissions and studies. Yet there has been no serious effort at comprehensive reform at the national level since the early months of the Clinton administration.

But there have been reforms—among the states. The most celebrated so far is the 2006 Massachusetts law, with its combination of individual mandates, subsidies to low-income individuals and employer requirements. Vermont and Maine have tried different approaches and California Governor Schwarzenegger has proposed a plan at least as ambitious as the one now in place in Massachusetts.

Reforms at the federal level often occur after years of experimentation by the states. The changes to federal welfare policy a decade ago happened after several years of efforts by Michigan, Wisconsin and a host of other states to revamp their approaches to welfare. The 1996 federal law was passed in large part because state legislators and governors realized there were limits to how much reform they could do within the constraints of the existing law. Health care reform almost certainly will follow a similar path.

The country's approach to health care is a three-cornered partnership involving the states, the federal government and the private sector. Many health experts predict that even the most ambitious state efforts will be stymied by their need to access significant amounts of money—either from federal sources, such as Medicaid, or the private sector. These would require changes to federal law—either Medicaid or ERISA (which prevents states from regulating or imposing state requirements on the health plans of large companies). That will only increase the pressure on the federal government to overhaul the country's health care system.

Immigration: Will NEXT TIME be the Charm?

During 2007, legislators in the 50 states introduced over 1,500 bills related to immigration and immigrants. Nearly 250 of these became law. At the same time, Congress tried to pass comprehensive immigration legislation. It failed three times. State ideas deal with education, law enforcement, employment, health and driver's licenses, to name a few. The federal bills covered border security, visas and quotas. Although the differences may seem subtle, they capture the tensions between the states and the federal government over this important area of public policy. Experts say that the states are looking almost exclusively at immigrant policy that deals with the lives of newcomers once they are in the country. The federal government's primary responsibility is for immigration policy, the terms and conditions for entry to the United States.

State legislatures clearly are acting in the absence of federal reforms. They are establishing criteria for accessing higher education. They are determining whether an unauthorized immigrant can obtain a driver's license. They are creating special programs for the victims of human trafficking. They are prohibiting unauthorized immigrants from obtaining professional licenses. But there are limits on how much legislatures can do. They can't legislate the number of doctors or computer specialists allowed in the country or how long they can stay. They can't establish a program for letting migrant workers in the country to harvest apples or work on construction sites. They can't enforce border security.

As much as President Bush wanted comprehensive federal legislation and as hard as a bipartisan group of U.S. senators tried to negotiate a bill that could pass, they couldn't quite muster the votes they needed. The question is whether the altered political landscape that will come after this year's elections will be more or less conducive to sweeping reforms.

Entitlement Reform: Saving the Worst for Last

David Walker, the comptroller general of the United States, is engaged in a crusade to educate the public and public officials about the fiscal dangers on the country's horizon. He and colleagues at several national think tanks will bring their "Fiscal Wake-Up Tour" to anyone at anytime. Their message is stark, sobering, daunting, vexing and a lot more, and it focuses on entitlement spending—the long-term costs of Social Security, Medicare and Medicaid. For them, the numbers tell the story. By 2034, Medicare and Social Security will constitute 20 percent of the gross domestic product, the equivalent of the whole current federal budget. In 75 years, the unfunded liabilities project to $50 trillion. (That's trillion, not billion.) Walker notes that is a $440,000 burden per current U.S. household.

The comptroller general is not shy about pointing out that the numbers cry out for reform of these entitlements, and they need to be addressed soon and not when one or more of the programs plunge into crisis. He and his colleagues also tell us that solutions have to involve both increasing taxes and limiting benefits. That has little immediate appeal for any elected official, Republican or Democrat. That's why most attempts to address entitlement reform have been done through bipartisan commissions and task forces.

North Dakota Senator Kent Conrad and New Hampshire Senator Judd Gregg, the chair and ranking member of the U.S. Senate Budget Committee, are the latest to propose such an approach. Their bill would create a 16-member task force, with seven Democrats, seven Republicans and two members of the executive branch. The task force would be governed by voting rules that would ensure bipartisan support for the task force's recommendations. It's the Butch Cassidy-Sundance Kid join arms and jump together approach.

Butch: Then you jump first.
Kid: No, I said.
Butch: What's the matter with you?
Kid: I can't swim.
Butch: Why you crazy, the fall will probably kill you.

With the armies of debt and bankruptcy rapidly approaching, Walker would say not jumping isn't an option.

WAIT UNTIL NEXT YEAR

There are, of course, no guarantees that waiting until next year to confront these and other challenging issues will find a new Congress and president reaching agreement and producing solutions. The current year, with its presumed federal policy paralysis, at the very least offers an opportunity for additional exploration and examination.

Review Essay: A Failure of Initiative and The Federal Response to Hurricane Katrina

Mark Landy

A Failure of Initiative: Final Report of the Select Bipartisan Committee to Investigate the Preparation for and Response to Hurricane Katrina (House of Representatives, February 15, 2006 www.gpoaccess.gov/katrinareport/mainreport.pdf) The Federal Response to Hurricane Katrina Lessons Learned (White House staff, February 2006 www.whitehouse.gov/reports/katrina-lessons-learned/)

Among the few predictable consequences of any major disaster is that the federal government will write reports about it. This is a tradition that dates back at least as far as the urban riots of the 1960s and has continued unabated to include the nation's most recent mega-disasters, 9/11 and Katrina. The entity issuing the report varies. It might be a blue-ribbon panel appointed either by the president, as in the case of the Kerner Commission, or by the president and Congress, as with the 9/11 Commission.[1] The two reports reviewed in this essay were written by the White House and by a bi-partisan committee of Congress, respectively.

These reports are themselves important political events. The amount of data assembly and analysis, drafting and review that went into them required large expenditures of money and human capital. The prestige of the sources from which they emanate ensures that they receive a good deal of public attention and comment. Therefore, it is worth asking whether or not they perform a useful public purpose. Do they serve to educate policy makers and the nation at large about the nature of the problems the reports address and do they propose useful instruments for addressing those problems?

The purpose of this review essay is to judge the judges. Its standards for evaluation are those that political science and economics has long employed when analyzing policy. How accurate and com-

---

The federal government publishes its analysis of what went wrong in the aftermath of Hurricane Katrina and draws the wrong lessons about state-federal relationships.

From *Publius: The Journal of Federalism*, October 2007.

prehensive is the fundamental definition of the problem they offer? Are the policy instruments chosen to address the problem capable of performing their assigned tasks? Do the proposed problem and policy definitions preclude the adoption of other, better problem and policy definitions?

THE REPORTS

The White House report was produced by a staff led by Frances Fragos Townsend, Assistant to the President for Homeland Security and Counter-terrorism. It included several members of her staff as well as staff from the Homeland Security Council and a staffer from the National Security Council. Their work was reviewed by an interagency group identified as the "Katrina Lessons Learned Review Group." The congressional report was prepared by the staff of the Select Bipartisan Committee to Investigate the Preparation for and Response to Katrina chaired by Tom Davis (R-VA). The committee was established by a vote of Congress on September 15, 2005. The House Republican leadership appointed ten members, but the Democratic minority leadership of the House refused to appoint any members claiming that the committee was a sham and demanding instead the appointment of an independent commission. Nonetheless, five Democratic house members did choose to respond to an invitation from the committee to participate.[2]

Both reports provide a comprehensive review of the events leading up to the storm, its impact and its aftermath. The focus of the congressional report is strictly on fact finding and fault finding. It offers no recommendations. It devotes a chapter to what it considers to be each critical aspect of preparedness and response, including: the levees, the evacuation, the national framework for emergency preparedness, FEMA, communications, command and control and law enforcement.[3] Its key findings are presented in the Executive Summary. Those include some positive evaluations especially as regards "the accuracy and timeliness of the National Weather Service and National Hurricane Center forecasts ... the invaluable role of the military ... and the contributions of charitable organizations."[4] But most of the findings are critical. The report criticizes: the inadequacy of levee protection; the incompleteness of the evacuations; the uneven and late execution of the National Response Plan; the insufficient preparedness

of DHS and the affected states; the failure of communications; the impairment of command and control; and the unevenness of military coordination; the collapse of local law enforcement; the lack of pre-positioning of medical supplies; and shortages of temporary housing and of commodities.[5]

The White House report covers much the same ground but in a terser fashion. It proceeds chronologically rather than by separating the question into its various functional parts. Sprinkled throughout its chronology are seventeen specific "lessons learned" which are then summarized and synthesized in a chapter by that name. These lessons provide the basis for more than one hundred specific recommendations presented in an appendix to the report. The lessons are designed to respond to what the report identifies as critical flaws in four specific aspects of national preparedness: (i) management of the national response; (ii) command and control structures; (iii) awareness and understanding of preparedness plans; and regional planning and coordination.[6] In order to repair these flaws and effectuate the changes which the "lessons" impart, the culminating chapter proposes a whole new federal disaster response framework, "a transformation of our homeland security architecture."[7] The model for this transformed approach is that provided by national defense.

PROBLEM DEFINITION

One would not expect a report issued by a White House under attack for botching its response to Katrina to sound like a report issued by Congress, and indeed it does not. The tone of the White House report is matter of fact. It presents its recommendations in the non-accusatory language that a consulting firm adopts when writing a report for the senior management of a corporation. In contrast, the Congressional report bristles with accusations and indignation. The Republican-dominated committee seems determined to show that the Democrats' charges of a cover-up are misplaced.

But, these differences in tone conceal a remarkable similarity in approach and in substance. The shared vantage point of Washington turns out to matter more than the Executive-Legislative divide in shaping their definition of the problem and their stance towards addressing it. Both reports make the requisite ritual obeisance to federalism by reporting on the behavior of state and local government. They acknowledge the importance of NGOs and are even willing to criticize the behavior of the citizenry. But none of this discussion enters into their framing of the problem. They unquestioningly accept the primacy of the federal government with regard to any serious domestic policy problem, regardless of its source or scope, and formulate their recommendations accordingly. The "failure of initiative" referred to in the title of the congressional report is a federal failure.

It may be argued that the reports had no choice but to take this D.C.-centric approach, since the president and the administrative apparatus he heads had already been singled out for blame and responsibility by that other great Washington-focused institution, the news media. If all one knew about national disaster policy was what one saw on CNN, one would have the impression that the national government was fully expected to run the show. The president was roundly and repeatedly criticized for not coming to New Orleans sooner. FEMA was denounced for not ensuring that the Crescent City had a ready supply of water bottles and that the Superdome was so miserably over-crowded.[8]

As these reports convincingly demonstrate, there is much to criticize about FEMA and also the president. But the idea that a federal agency should be responsible for local water bottle distribution or that the physical presence of the president is either useful or necessary in the aftermath of a hurricane is a sign of just how dismissive the news media is of state and local government. The sheer incessancy with which the media conveyed this attitude coupled with the inherent newsworthiness of the event ensured that hundreds of millions of viewers would come away with the impression that the White House bore the major responsibility for the suffering and death they were watching on their TV screens.

Thus, whatever their defects, the reports may well have been a political necessity, enabling a beleaguered White House and a Republican congressional majority to show their willingness to take responsibility for failure and to propose positive steps to remedy past mistakes. Seen in this light, it is all the more important for those of us who need not fear the adverse impact of media criticism and declining public opinion polls, to criticize these reports and the excessive, counterproductive, government centralization they promote. Such criticism is necessary to help create some political breathing

room for responsible congressmen and executive officials who do not want their policy agendas to be set by Anderson Cooper.

PUSH—PULL

Both reports use precisely the same "push vs. pull" metaphor to describe what they see as the essential flaw in the existing federal disaster response approach and the key change necessary to remedy the error. They deplore the reactive nature of the federal response to Katrina in which states were compelled to "pull" resources from the federal government. They advocate the creation of a proactive "push" approach. The congressional report urges the creation of "the operational imperative that federal agencies push assets to those who need them."[9] The White House report states that "…The system was biased towards requests and the concept of 'pull' rather than toward anticipatory actions and the proactive 'push' of Federal resources."[10]

The ability of Congress and the Executive to agree on the nature of the problem would be laudable, if it were correct. But, was the Katrina failure essentially due to a lack of federal government initiative? This conclusion becomes ever less convincing the further one travels away from the Capitol and the White House and the closer one gets to the Gulf. I have conducted interviews and toured along the Gulf Coast in both Louisiana and Mississippi. The lesson I learned from this experience is that success and failure can be found at *all* levels of government. In fact, the most heroic and effective response and recovery agents were local governments, churches and other NGOs. The egregious failures of the city government of New Orleans have caused investigators to under-rate the effective and often heroic initiatives taken by local governments elsewhere along the Gulf.

As one listens to the horror stories that local first responders have to tell about the tardiness and fecklessness of FEMA, the "push-pull" metaphor comes to seem woefully misplaced. New Orleans excepted, the locals did not need to be "pushed". They "pulled" hard at the federal government and received a tardy and halfhearted response. It is difficult to accept the idea that a federal government incapable of responding to initiatives from below can be so reconfigured as to initiate from above.

SEEING THE PROBLEM DIFFERENTLY: NEW ORLEANS

To provide a more compelling problem definition it is first necessary to re-examine the nature of the storm itself. One hurricane produced two separate and distinct disasters.[11] The eastern edge of the Louisiana coast and the bulk of the Mississippi coast endured the brunt of the storm. The sheer force of the wind and of the storm surge toppled houses, commercial buildings and power lines along that stretch of the coast and in many instances miles [inland] as well. New Orleans escaped the main force of the storm. Its misery resulted from the floods that took place when several of the levees protecting the city broke.

Although all parts of the Gulf Coast suffered dreadfully, the great bulk of the deaths took place in the city of New Orleans. Although New Orleans Parish accounts for less than half of the New Orleans Metropolitan area, it accounted for more than three quarters of the deaths. The population of New Orleans Parish is only about 25 percent greater than the combined populations of the three Mississippi counties that bore the brunt of the storm but its death toll was more than three times higher.[12] Neither report delves into these startling disparities. In fact, they do not even mention them. Is a flood inherently more of a killer than a windstorm that rips whole houses off their foundation? In the absence of clear evidence, the best surmise is that the disparity was caused by the incomplete evacuation of the city of New Orleans. Although approximately 90 percent of the population of Southeast Louisiana was successfully evacuated, an estimated 70,000 persons remained in New Orleans during the flood.[13]

The impression given by the media was that those who did not get out of New Orleans could not; either because they had no car or because they were disabled. This impression stuck even though the visuals that accompanied those media reports showed streets crowded with abandoned cars. *Failure of Initiative* confirms that the pictures were more reliable than the words by reporting that more than 250,000 cars remained in the city during the storm and that cars were found parked in the driveways of many of the dead.[14] The report chastises the Governor of Louisiana and the Mayor of New Orleans for being slow to issue mandatory evacuation orders. It even concedes that individuals "share the blame" for

incomplete evacuation.[15] Resort to the verb "share" shows just how reluctant the report writers are to concede that not all bad things that happen are the fault of the government. Those car owners who failed to evacuate in the face of mandatory evacuation orders that, however tardy, still left them plenty of time to leave, do not *share* in the blame, they *are* to blame.

If indeed a major, or perhaps even the major, cause of death in Southeast Louisiana was willful failure to obey an evacuation order this puts the whole Katrina problem in a different light. It shifts the blame from errors made by the various levels of government to the actions of the populace itself. Undoubtedly individuals who could have left had strong reasons not to obey the order. They feared looting. They assumed this evacuation order was just another case of the government crying wolf. Nonetheless the evacuation was mandatory. The presence of so many people in the flooded area was the reason so many people died. Also, because first priority had to be given to rescuing so many stranded people, other critical response tasks were not undertaken for many days.

In the New Orleans disaster, the deepest problem was not federal government initiative but rather a civic failure. Too many residents of New Orleans did not obey their mayor. Because so many were not evacuated the nature of the response had to shift from one centered on minimizing damage and restoring vital services, to one devoted to saving lives. The entire focus of the National Guard for the first two days after the flooding was on search and rescue. Helicopters boats and crews were diverted from other urgent tasks like restoring communications and other vital infrastructure, transporting food and delivering other vital equipment. In order to save more stranded people, the crews had to dump survivors and hasten back into the fray without providing those they had just rescued with food and water.[16]

SEEING THE PROBLEM DIFFERENTLY: OUTSIDE NEW ORLEANS

Outside of New Orleans, the problem should be defined differently. Given the magnitude of the storm and the number of people in the affected area, the Mississippi death toll of 219 does not seem inordinately high.[17] Here again, it is likely that at least some portion of the death toll is ascribable to a refusal to obey evacuation orders.

But, in any event, the problem cannot be defined as government inability to minimize death. Nor was it a failure of initiative at the local level. First responders were very alert and active in minimizing the impact of the storm. In Pascagoula, for example, the city government worked in close coordination with the local power company and electricity was restored in twelve days. The city had a pre-disaster contract in place which stipulated what services the contractor was required to provide in the event of a disaster and the prices to be paid for each service. Thus the city was spared having to negotiate to obtain services at a time when communications were difficult and when all the bargaining power belonged to the contractors.[18]

The complaint that one hears from residents and officials along the Mississippi Coast is not that the federal government lacked initiative but that it was unwilling or unable too respond to local initiative. They do not lament a lack of "push" but rather an inability of FEMA in particular to be pulled. The heart of the problem in Mississippi appears to be not a failure of federal government initiative but a failure of responsiveness, an over-abundance of federal "red tape."[19]

Red tape streamed from FEMA and HUD, the two agencies along with the Army Corps of Engineers most involved with the disaster. Neither was able to provide assistance without requiring myriad application forms, layers of application review and time consuming audits. This was not done capriciously. Red tape was used to cope with a real problem, corruption. Louisiana state government and New Orleans municipal government are notoriously corrupt. In the fall of 2004, less than a year before Katrina, three top administrators with the Louisiana Office of Homeland Security and Emergency Preparedness were indicted for the alleged misuse of up to $60 million in FEMA mitigation planning money.[20] Mississippi's reputation is not as bad, but a federal agency is hard put to devise one set of rules for giving money to one state and a more lax set of rules for another.

Sometimes the FEMA rules were downright humorous. According to Connie Rockco, a member of the Harrison County Board of Supervisors, her county was required by FEMA to prove that when using FEMA money to pay for removing tree branches obstructing streets and roads, it remove only "hangers" and "leaners." Hangers were defined as branches severed from a tree that were resting on other branches. Leaners were defined as branches that were leaning away from the tree at an angle of 30 degrees or more. FEMA conducted on the spot audits of the removal work to make sure that the "hangers and leaners" policy was being enforced.[21]

In Louisiana, the state government established a shuttle bus to enable New Orleanians who had relocated to Baton Rouge to travel daily back to New Orleans to work on their uninhabitable houses. FEMA cancelled its funding for the shuttle on the grounds that it did not meet the agency's definition of "emergency transportation."[22]

These extreme examples illustrate more than sheer stupidity, they exemplify the need for federal agencies to protect themselves from charges of enabling corruption by wrapping themselves in the protect cloak of rules literally applied.[23] If the federal government had sought to expedite response and recovery, it had merely to order FEMA and HUD to release funds despite insufficient proof of need and inadequate means of oversight. Of course, had it done so, the same Congressional committees hectoring it for acting too slowly would have cheerfully berated it for fraud waste and abuse.

POLICY DEFINITION

Only the White House report makes specific policy recommendations geared to respond to the problem of federal passivity it defined. The congressional report does not do so, but its critique of the federal government's failure of initiative suggests that its authors would probably go along with the explicitly centralizing recommendations of the White House report. Indeed, a year after these reports were issued Congress passed a defense appropriation bill granting the president clear authority to take control of the National Guard during a disaster without receiving any request to do so from the governor of the affected state.[24]

The model for the disaster response policy framework the White House proposes is that of national security. In that model the Secretary of Defense is the link between the President and the "combat commanders" in the field. With regard to disaster response, the Secretary of Homeland Security substitutes for the Defense Secretary but the same concept of a centralized national command structure controlling the forces in the field applies

> A useful model for our approach to homeland security is the Nation's approach to *national security*...Operationally organized, it stresses the importance of unity of

command from the President down to the commander in the field…[25]

Each department or agency with homeland security responsibilities needs operational capability—or the capacity to get things done—to translate executive management direction promptly into results on the ground.[26]

Thus, the national security analogy requires that the federal agencies that comprise the homeland security "army" acquire the capacity to engage in actual combat with hurricanes floods and tornadoes. It would need to be equipped with the appropriate artillery—bulldozers, backhoes, cherry pickers, speedboats, dump trucks—and the "soldiers" to run them. This then is the heart of the shift from a "pull" to a "push" role for the federal government. Its responsive role of providing assistance to stricken states and localities is to be supplanted by the active deployment of its own disaster fighting force.

This proposal is mistaken because the analogy upon which it is based is inapt. The threat posed by natural disasters is not really like the threat to national security posed by hostile, or even potentially hostile, nations. The latter is of such a far greater magnitude that it justifies maintaining large well equipped expensive forces, even in peacetime. The natural disaster threat does not make an equally powerful claim. Even a disaster of the magnitude of Katrina only affected a small fraction of the national population. Congress is most unlikely to fund a large "peacetime" disaster response force that would continue to eat up resources in the intervals between mega-disasters. For example, no such disasters occurred in 2006. The government saved millions by not investing in the immense capability the White House report seems to call for.

In war, the military goes it alone. But in Katrina, outside of New Orleans, local governments and private organizations demonstrated a great deal of operational capacity. There were of course serious communications and coordination problems. But to imagine that, in the midst of 90 mile an hour winds and bursting levees, those problems would have disappeared in the face of a centralized national command structure is wildly optimistic.

The White House report does what lawyers are taught not to do, argue on the basis of the extreme case. The "nuclear option" of abandoning the hallowed tradition of local and state primacy in coping with natural disasters is a response to the radical failure of one city in the face of one storm. New Orleans is among the very poorest and worst

administered places in the United States. Yet the report would rend the fabric of federalism on the basis of this atypical example. The other communities in Louisiana and Mississippi performed far better. Why not treat them as the paradigmatic example and gear federal policy to enabling good performance to become even better?

Among the many virtues the White House report claims for a centralized command structure by is that it will eliminate red tape.[27] And yet its own devotion to the national security analogy undermines that assertion. If the War in Iraq is any guide, the national security system has no genius for eliminating red tape without thereby incurring waste fraud and corruption As the storied examples of excessive spending, if not downright fraud, by Halliburton and other military contractors illustrate, the military has at least as much trouble as state and local agencies do in maintaining probity in emergency situations.[28] As its current heavy reliance on private contractors and suppliers in Iraq demonstrates, granting greater operational authority to a national government entity does not obviate the need to use private contractors. If it were to expand its natural disaster responsibilities, the national government would still need to devolve much of the actual work to local fire and police departments and to private firms.

The comparison to Iraq is also useful for understanding the deepest source of the Katrina's "red tape" problem. In neither case did the problems relating to the red tape/corruption tradeoff result mainly from poor planning, communications or management structures. In both cases, these difficulties were the result of executive decisions. And, since the president is the chief executive, the buck stops there. In Iraq, the red tape/corruption trade off was settled in favor of speed and decisiveness. In other words, the shenanigans of the likes of Halliburton were tolerated in order to more expeditiously prosecute the war. Regarding Katrina, the Executive Branch bent the other way. The chief executive and his top aides were unwilling to force agencies like FEMA to loosen their accountability requirements and to throw money at the problem.

Despite repeated pleadings from the governor of Louisiana and many local government officials, the Bush administration refused to waive the requirement that these governments provide a 10 percent match for the road, school, hospital and other forms of infrastructural assistance they received from the federal government. An exemption from the waiver requirement had been granted to New York in the wake of 9/11. For local governments whose entire tax basis had been obliterated by the storm, this matching requirement was especially onerous.[29] Unlike in Iraq, or in 9/11, the Bush administration chose to endure charges of tardiness, hard-heartedness and ineffectiveness in preference to getting pilloried as an enabler of waste and fraud.[30]

Those are the actual choices facing a government responding to disaster. Real time audits of debris removal waste time and personnel. But, if the audits are not done, what is to stop crews from deviating from their assignments to work as contractors removing debris from private property for a profit? If local governments bear none of the cost of cleanup efforts what is to keep them from spending the free money they receive from the federal government profligately?

In Louisiana, homeowners found themselves caught in a Catch 22. They could only receive grants to rebuild if they could produce documents proving that they owned the houses they claimed to own. But those very documents had been washed away in the flood. The government was blamed for demanding proof that was impossible to supply, and yet, who can doubt that if the standards were relaxed the government would have been bilked of huge sums by owners of non-existent houses?[31] As of May 2007, only 22,000 of the 140,000 applicants have received grants totaling 1.3 billion of the 7.5 billion dollars that the federal government has allocated for this purpose.[32]

POLICY ALTERNATIVES

The alternative problem definitions I have proposed require a very different policy framework than that contained in the White House report. In New Orleans the problem was civic failure. No national policy can "solve" a local civic failure. If, as in New Orleans, the residents of a city resist a mandatory evacuation order, it is not appropriate, indeed it is arguably unconstitutional, for the federal government to force them to leave. However, the federal government has many indirect means for prodding localities to avoid civic failure. It can threaten to withdraw federal disaster planning funds from them if they do not engage in satisfactory evacuation planning. It can use its "bully pulpit" to publicly embarrass public officials who are failing to make such preparations. But if those efforts fail, our federal form of government

requires that citizens suffer for their civic failure. Individuals, who ignore timely, mandatory [evacuation orders], have voluntarily withdrawn their claims upon government to provide for their security.

Outside of New Orleans, the problem was inadequate federal responsiveness to local initiative. Therefore, policy reform at the federal level should focus on ways to increase responsiveness. The first step is to acknowledge that a trade off between corruption and red tape is inevitable. In non-emergency situations there is no great harm in placing the primary burden of proof on the grantee to show that it is in full compliance. But in a genuine emergency, the burden of proof should shift. FEMA and other federal agencies should readily grant local requests for aid and ask questions later. For all the talk of the lack of "push" in both reports, neither one suggests a relaxation of the accountability requirements which are in fact the major source of the federal governments inability to push disaster relief resources in the direction of those who need them.

This is not to say that federal government abandons its responsibility to the taxpayers. Rather it is to accept an alternative, less exacting, form of accountability called into being after the fact, when federal agencies conduct[s] broad reviews of the overall response-recovery effort of the affected communities. No doubt this form of evaluation will fail to unearth many of the fraudulent and wasteful practices that took place. That is the point. If a community's overall response/recovery effort is satisfactory, then federal officials have more important things to do than to worry whether or not particular crews removed too much debris or some percentage of homeowner claims were fraudulent. If, when the emergency has passed, a local effort is shown to have been poor, then there is ample cause for the federal government to expend the time and effort needed to conduct exhaustive investigations.

This shift in the means for enforcing accountability might well prove less objectionable to the guardians of the federal treasury if it were coupled with a tightening of the definition of what constitutes a disaster. In the 1990's disaster expenditures soared. This was in part the result of the occurrence of some authentic mega disasters such as Hurricane Andrew. But i[t] was also the result of increased spending on minor disasters. Both presidents and congressmen delighted in having disaster emergencies declared so that they could take credit for handing out disaster relief checks.[33] The loosening of the eligibility for disaster relief that ensued was in its own way as great a threat to the taxpayers as the potential for fraud posed by a real disaster like Katrina. If the level of damage required to qualify for relief were raised, the funds saved could then be more liberally applied to truly serious natural disasters.

CONCLUSION

The gravest defect of these reports is an educational one. They convey the mistaken impression that federal government ought to acquire more power and control over disaster relief and response. Such a shift would not result in better response and recovery, and even more importantly, it would seriously mislead the public about how our federal republic works. The centralizing teaching of these reports facilitates civic failure. It conveys the idea that the government is the all-purpose redresser of misfortune. Principles of civic obligation and mutual assistance are excluded from the lesson plan. The citizenry comes to understand that even those who disobey their local authorities by ignoring mandatory evacuation orders are to be treated as "victims" whose safety and wellbeing the federal government is obligated to secure.

Katrina ought to teach a different lesson. The truth is that most citizens behaved responsibly, many generously, and some nobly. Outside of New Orleans, local governments did what the people elected them to do; they cleared roads, rescued stranded pets and farm animals, restored power and served as leaders and coordinators for community wide cooperative response and recovery efforts. The real lesson of Katrina is that the federal republic the founders established works well, even when put to a severe test. National disaster response policy should do nothing to undermine this remarkable resiliency and capacity.

Notes

1. United States. National Advisory Commission on Civil Disorders. *Report of the Commission on Civil Disorders.* New York: Dutton, 1969. The National Commission on Terrorist Attacks Upon the United States, July 22, 2004. http://www.9-11commission.gov.

2. *Failure of Initiative,* 10. Dan Pulliam, Democrats push for outside Katrina panel to investigate agency

response, GovernmentExecutive.com September 27, 2005 http://www.govexec.com/dailyfed/0905/092705p1.htm.

3. *Failure of Initiative,* vii.

4. *Failure of Initiative,* 2–5.

5. *Ibid.*

6. *Lessons Learned,* 52.

7. *Ibid.,* 73.

8. A pithy embodiment of this journalistic perspective is provided by an editorial in *The New Orleans Times Picayune* entitled "An Open Letter to the President" Sunday, September 4, 2005. Or, Tim Naftali, "Department of Homeland Screw-Up: What is the Bush administration Doing?" *SLATE,* September 6, 2005 http://slate.msn.com/id/2125494/

9. *Failure of Initiative,* 15.

10. *Lessons Learned,* 66.

11. I am grateful to Martin Wiseman, Director of the Stennis Insitute of Government, Mississippi State University, for giving me this insight. He is responsible for much of what I know about Katrina but is in no way responsible for the mistakes I have made or the opinions expressed herein.

12. "Death toll from Katrina Likely Higher Than 1,300," MSNBC.com, February 10, 2006. http://www.msnbc.msn.com/id/11281267

13. *Failure of [I]nitiative,* 115.

14. *Ibid.,* 116.

15. *Ibid.,* 114.

16. *Ibid.,* 117.

17. "Death toll from Katrina likely higher than 1,300." MSNBC.com, February 10, 2006.

18. Interview, Kay Johnson Kell, City Manager of Pascagoula MS., March 6, 2007.

19. This point of view was consistently expressed in the various interviews with local officials I conducted. In addition to Kay Johnson Kell, they were: Connie Moran, Mayor, Ocean Springs MS., March 6, 2007, Alan K. Sidduth, County Administrator, Jackson County MS, March 6, 2007 and Connie Rockco, County Supervisor, Harrison County MS, March 6, 2007.

20. "Louisiana Officials Indicted Before Katrina Hit," *Los Angeles Times,* September 17, 2005.

21. Rockco Interview, *op.cit.*

22. Interview, Andy Kopplin, Executive Director, Louisiana Recovery Authority, March 8, 2007.

23. The classic discussion of this problem is in Herbert Kaufman, *Red Tape: Its Origins, Uses and Abuses* (Washington DC: Brookings Institution, 1977).

24. "Congress Reconsiders Measure Expanding President's Authority over National Guard," *Austin American Statesman,* Tuesday, April 24, 2007 http://www.statesman.com/news/content/news/stories/nation/04/24/24bushtroops.html

25. *Lessons Learned,* 67.

26. *Ibid.,* 68.

27. *Ibid.,* 70.

28. See, for example, "Contractor Fraud Trial To Begin Tomorrow: Case Tests Reach Of False Claims Act," *Washington Post,* February 13, 2006; D1; "Halliburton Unit to Pay $8 Million for Overbilling," *Washington Post,* November 30, 2006; A9; "High Payments to Halliburton for Fuel in Iraq," New York Times, December 10, 2003.

29. The 10 percent matching requirement was finally lifted in May of 2007 as part of the overall compromise on the war spending bill. There is no reason to believe that the Bush administration would ever have been willing to lift the requirement if it were not forced to do so in order to conciliate the Democratic majority in Congress which had agreed to remove time limits on the Iraq War funds including in the spending bill. "Gulf Region Gains Help in New Law on War Funds." *New York Times,* May 26, 2007, A8.

30. This conclusion is mine. It does not come from any direct evidence but rather by a process of deduction. As is clear from my interviews, FEMA and HUD were persistently unwilling to deviate from their normal accountability requirements despite the tardiness this imposed. It is not possible that such a systematic approach could have imposed solely by career civil servants, especially in the face of the torrent of criticism directed at the federal agencies involved.

31. This policy was finally changed in the spring of 2007. "Title searchers warning of fraud; Road Home urged to retain safeguards" *New Orleans Times-Picayune,* May 17, 2007.

32. "Louisiana Sets Deadline For Storm Claim Damages," *New York Times,* May 31, 2007, A12.

33. Rutherford H. Platt, *Disasters and Democracy: The Politics of Extreme Natural Events* (Washington DC: Island Press, 1999, 24.) [S]ee also "Disaster Assistance: Information on Federal Costs and Approaches for Reducing Them," Statement of Judy A. England-Joseph, Director, Housing and Community Development Issues, Resources, Community, and Economic Development Division United States General Accounting Office (GAO), Before the Subcommittee on Water Resources and Environment, Committee on Transportation and Infrastructure, House of Representatives March 26, 1998.

4

When a Bridge Falls Down

Matt Sundeen

Everybody agrees that government should do more to help the nation's creaking transportation infrastructure, but state and federal governments disagree on who should pay.

From *State Legislatures,* October/November 2007.

The catastrophic collapse of the I-35 bridge over the Mississippi River in August sent shockwaves that reverberated well beyond the immediate vicinity of Minneapolis-St. Paul. The deteriorating condition of the country's network of highways, bridges and rail lines is a problem that has long concerned transportation experts. For most, the bridge collapse was a call-to-action to fund overdue improvements and fix the nation's aging transportation infrastructure. Although many federal, state and local lawmakers agree repairs are needed, what the appropriate response should be continues to be a matter for debate.

INCREASED DEMANDS

Rapid growth in population, personal travel and freight movement has put stress on the nation's roads and bridges and outpaced efforts to maintain and improve the system. Put simply, more people are traveling more miles than ever before. An estimated 300 million people now live in the United States, and since 1990, highway travel has increased 35 percent. Trade with Asia and South America has increased shipments across all transportation modes, and the Federal Highway Administration predicts that freight traffic will double by 2020.

Greater use has caused wear and tear on our roads and bridges. According to the Federal Highway Administration, 33 percent of America's roads are in poor or mediocre condition, and 26 percent of America's bridges are structurally deficient or functionally obsolete. Experts caution that major failures similar to the I-35 bridge collapse are, however, unlikely.

"It's a rare problem," says Federal Highway Administration Spokesman Doug Hecox. "It's undeniable that the infrastructure is aging. But if anything, bridge inspection programs over-scrutinize. It wasn't any shortcoming in the inspection process." States inspect every bridge at least once every two years, and some deteriorating bridges more frequently, according to FHWA officials.

The larger concern may be the everyday problems caused by poorly maintained infrastructure. Road conditions are a significant factor in approximately one-third of traffic deaths, killing approximately 14,000 people every year. Driving on bumpy roads and bridges, falling concrete, and potholes cost U.S. motorists an estimated $67 billion a year in extra vehicle repairs and operating costs—as much as $333 per motorist. Outdated facilities can handle fewer vehicles at slower speeds, creating traffic congestion and costly delays. Old roads or bridges might also be functionally obsolete—designed for smaller populations and unable to meet the current needs of an expanding community.

FUNDING RUNNING DRY

Considerable money is needed not only to maintain current conditions, but to make improvements to meet growing demands. But transportation funding resources are shrinking. A 2005 report by the National Chamber Foundation concluded that total annual transportation spending from all levels of government is now $42 billion short of the amount needed to maintain and $91 billion short of the amount needed to improve the transportation network. The report estimated a $1 trillion cumulative transportation funding shortfall from all levels of government by 2015.

Much of the problem in transportation funding can be traced to the declining value of the gas tax against inflation. Motor vehicle fuel taxes are the primary source of federal transportation revenue and a transportation funding staple in most states. But with gasoline prices hovering near $3 per gallon, few lawmakers have been willing to raise motor fuel tax rates. Over time, that's meant that gas tax revenues can't keep pace with the rising costs of construction, materials and labor.

During the last decade, the federal gas tax lost approximately 25 percent of its real value against inflation. Most experts agree that federal gas tax revenues deposited in the Federal Highway Trust Fund—the primary source of federal transportation funding sent to the states—will

Bridge Safety Facts
■ There are approximately 600,000 bridges in the United States, the District of Columbia and Puerto Rico.
■ The I-35 Bridge in Minnesota was 40 years old at the time of collapse. Nearly half (46 percent) of bridges in the United States are 40 years old or older. Approximately 29 percent of bridges are older than 50 years, and nearly 10,000 bridges are 100 years old or more.
■ The National Bridge Inspection Standards (NBIS) requires biennial safety inspections for bridges longer than 6.1 meters (approximately 20 feet) located on public roads.
■ Most bridges are inspected every two years. Those in excellent condition may receive exemptions from the NBIS standard. Bridges in poor condition may be inspected more frequently. Approximately 83 percent of bridges are inspected once every two years, 12 percent are inspected annually and 5 percent are inspected on a four-year cycle.

be insufficient to meet obligations in three years. Unless the problem is solved, much of the burden for fixing transportation problems may fall to the states.

"States have a justifiable concern about funding," says the Federal Highway Administration's Hecox. "We shouldn't bank on gasoline for the trust fund. New ideas are needed, and it's critical we nail down the funding issue now."

But states have their own funding challenges. Only a handful have raised gas tax rates sufficiently to keep pace with inflation. State general funds are increasingly consumed by big ticket items such as Medicaid, K-12 education and corrections, and little money is left for transportation needs. State lawmakers are exploring other traditional revenue sources such as tolls and transportation-related fees. But toll and fee changes often face the same political hurdles as gas tax increases and may not provide sufficient money to cover needs.

DEBATE ON SOLUTIONS

In Minnesota, legislators want to make sure that the I-35 bridge collapse doesn't divert them from finding solutions for long-term transportation funding. Lawmakers want to ensure the immediate safety of their constituents, but also worry that the tragedy will take attention away from broader transportation concerns. In the past two years, Governor Tim Pawlenty has vetoed legislation to raise the state's gas tax to pay for transportation needs. Recently, he's signaled that he may now be open to it.

> *"Highways aren't a sexy issue. But more oversight and watchfulness should be encouraged."*
>
> —Doug Hecox, FHWA

loss of gas tax revenues caused by hybrid and more fuel efficient vehicles. Critics worry that GPS technology used to track vehicle travel under the program could jeopardize privacy. They also charge that the new tax diminishes the incentive to use hybrids and other high mileage vehicles.

   "We've had a lot of negotiations, but we aren't getting anywhere," says Representative Bernard Lieder, chair of Minnesota's Transportation Committee. "The transportation issue is resonating because of the bridge collapse, but we can't divert all of our attention just to bridges. We've got to have a total transportation bill that includes highways and transit and involves local jurisdictions."

   Other states are also exploring solutions to specifically address bridge and road conditions. Missouri Governor Matt Blunt called a special session this summer during which legislators passed an ambitious plan to build or repair 802 bridges in five years. The new legislation allows construction groups to bid for the entire 802 bridge project[s] and then provide maintenance for 25 more years.

   Missouri House Transportation Chairman Neal St. Onge, the primary bill sponsor, says the Minnesota tragedy helped bring light on a long-standing problem in his state. "Missouri has some serious infrastructure problems," says St. Onge. "This bill will speed up repair and save money. But, it's important to also remember that it will vastly improve safety." Missouri has 1,000 bridges, according to St. Onge, that are structurally deficient or functionally obsolete. "You can't put a price on safety," he says.

   Other states that were already exploring comprehensive transportation plans and different funding alternatives will likely step up efforts in sessions next year. Many lawmakers are closely watching a pilot project in Oregon that is testing whether the state could replace the gas tax with a fee based on actual miles traveled. Proponents believe the "vehicle miles tax" more equitably charges motorists for highway use and helps compensate for the

   States are also considering initiatives like ones passed in Indiana and Chicago to sell leasing rights to operate transportation assets—such as toll roads and bridges—to private entities. "A lot of states wish they could do this," says Indiana Senator Tom Wyss who, in 2005, spearheaded legislation that authorized the sale of a 75-year lease to operate the Indiana Toll Road to a private entity for $3.8 billion. "This paid for our entire transportation program. It was a win for everyone."

   The concept is not without controversy, however. Critics worry that such leases cede too much responsibility for public assets to the private sector and could hamstring future transportation funding efforts. Similar privatization proposals have been at least temporarily rejected in New Jersey, Pennsylvania and a half dozen other jurisdictions.

BEYOND STATE FUNDING

In addition to appropriating state money, state legislators have other options for shaping transportation programs. "Personal legislative involvement is always good," says the Federal Highway Administration's Hecox. "Highways aren't a sexy issue. But more oversight and watchfulness should be encouraged."

   Minnesota's Department of Transportation is developing a list of best practices in response to the I-35 collapse. The document will likely include recommendations for inspections and proficiency standards for bridge and highway inspectors. Legislators worried about bridge conditions in their state can push their own DOT officials to standardize inspection practices or adopt more rigorous procedures.

   State lawmakers can also make their voices heard in Washington, D.C. In August and September congressional committees conducted hearings to examine the

U.S. Bridges in Poor Condition

More than a quarter of all highway bridges are in bad shape.

State	Percent of Bridges That Are "Structurally Deficient" or "Functionally Obsolete"	State	Percent of Bridges That Are "Structurally Deficient" or "Functionally Obsolete"
Alabama	26%	Nebraska	23%
Alaska	35%	Nevada	12%
Arizona	11%	New Hampshire	31%
Arkansas	23%	New Jersey	35%
California	29%	New Mexico	19%
Colorado	17%	New York	38%
Connecticut	34%	North Carolina	29%
Delaware	15%	North Dakota	23%
District of Columbia	62%	Ohio	24%
Florida	18%	Oklahoma	32%
Georgia	20%	Oregon	28%
Hawaii	45%	Pennsylvania	43%
Idaho	24%	Puerto Rico	49%
Illinois	17%	Rhode Island	53%
Indiana	22%	South Carolina	23%
Iowa	27%	South Dakota	25%
Kansas	21%	Tennessee	21%
Kentucky	31%	Texas	20%
Louisiana	29%	Utah	17%
Maine	35%	Vermont	35%
Maryland	27%	Virginia	26%
Massachusetts	52%	Washington	30%
Michigan	26%	West Virginia	37%
Minnesota	12%	Wisconsin	15%
Mississippi	26%	Wyoming	21%
Missouri	31%		
Montana	25%	**Average**	**26%**

Source: U.S. Department of Transportation, Bureau of Transportation Statistics: August 2007.

I-35 bridge collapse and consider proposals to fund bridge repairs across the country. In coming months, federal lawmakers will begin work on a new transportation funding bill. The most recent reauthorization legislation—the Safe Accountable Flexible Equity Act—A Legacy for Users (SAFETEA-LU)—passed in 2005 and will expire in 2009. It included a record number of congressional earmarks that supported projects such as the infamous "Bridge to Nowhere" in Ketchikan, Alaska. The new legislation will significantly shape future transportation policy and will likely address concerns about the viability of the federal Highway Trust Fund. State lawmakers concerned about deteriorating road and bridge infrastructure have an opportunity to work with their congressional delegations to ensure that reauthorization legislation addresses state concerns.

"Transportation is not just a state issue," says Minnesota's Representative Lieder. "We need to find solutions with the federal government and local governments that address a wide range of concerns."

5

Breathing Room

Katherine Barrett and Richard Greene

State governments are
giving local governments
more control and flexibility
over their revenue options.
Hopefully that flexibility
translates into more
economic competitiveness.

From *Governing*,
January 2008.

On January 29, Florida's voters will decide whether to approve a constitutional amendment—sent to them by the state legislature—that would set sharp limits on what the state's localities can collect in property taxes. While end-of-year polling data suggest that the amendment is not likely to pass, the specter of losing $2 billion for schools and yet more dollars for infrastructure, technology updates, public amenities and all the things that attract business, has been a constant worry for cities, counties and school districts.

Tax decisions are always a tradeoff. While the state's beleaguered homeowners would rejoice over any constraints on the much-loathed property tax, there's a downside to removing taxing power from localities: They come up short of money to invest in things that make an economy tick.

"Local governments are a key local economic actor— not just an extension of state government," says Michael Pagano, a dean at the University of Illinois at Chicago. "They need to be nimble in the face of economic circumstances—just like a company does."

Without flexibility, a locality is at the mercy of economic ups and downs and decisions made elsewhere. The locality can't even work with its local business community and taxpayers to craft a system that might best meet all their needs.

Flexibility also is key to global competitiveness, working to attract companies from all over the world and to keep a highly mobile labor force in place. "Any restriction on their ability to raise the money to invest," says Barry Bluestone, director of the Center for Urban and Regional Policy at Northeastern University, "can harm them"—and, by extension, the home state as well.

Yet a number of states hold local revenue streams hostage, even though most state and local tax experts agree that giving localities greater flexibility or breathing room —with appropriate controls by the state, of course—is solid fiscal policy. They also agree that it can lead, as Bluestone suggests, to more vibrant support for economic development.

CONTROL ROOM

When a locality has authority over its taxes, it can match its revenue-raising tools to the underlying economy. "If a state imposes a uniform revenue and tax structure on its localities," says Chris Hoene, head of research for the National League of Cities, "it ignores the variation of its localities' economic bases and their diverse spending needs." It is, [of] course, up to each locality to figure out whether a particular revenue-raising tool is worth levying on its constituents—whether the administrative or transaction costs outweigh the amount of revenue the tax would raise.

At the same time, localities with a great deal of flexibility need to be cognizant of how their taxes and rates fit in with those the state is already levying—and make sure that the sum total doesn't create an unsupportable tax burden. Or that different local variations on a single tax don't impose unfair strains on businesses in a state.

That said, flexibility is still key and one way states give cities or counties leeway is through a local option to control the tax rate and to use the revenues they raise as they see fit—that is, without state earmarks. Localities also can breathe better if they have a range of taxes to use. For a locality to weather economic ups and downs, it can't be overly reliant on any one source of revenue.

Most states limit localities to the property and sales tax as sources of revenue. A few keep their localities really short of breath, limiting them to one tax source. Cities, towns and counties in many New England states, for instance, have access only to a local property tax. "On its own, reliance on the property tax produces powerful inequities in development," Bluestone says. "Rich communities get rich because they can provide better schools and police protection than communities with stagnant and falling property values."

The intersection between local authority and revenue independence is what's known as "own-source capacity." That is, the extent to which fiscal policy decisions made by local government officials actually determine the fiscal direction of the locality. In addition to the tax revenue, there are fees and charges that localities set and that flow into the general revenue coffers. These add to the own-source capacity and enhance a locality's ability to pay for services it wants to provide. This is particularly important in localities that have the primary responsibility for their school funding.

There's another part of the equation, of course. Some states that allow for minimal own-source capacity help to make up for the shortfalls with state aid. While too much state aid can make localities too dependent on the state—and create state budget problems—generally speaking, state aid increases the overall capacity of a local government. In many instances, it provides a level of equalization and base support for localities that may lack other resources. State aid to school districts, for example, often relies on an equalization formula to ensure that the state meets its constitutional responsibility of providing adequate support to schoolchildren.

In Massachusetts, which keeps its localities dependent on one tax, state aid has been used to keep the local communities from diverging dramatically, making up in large measure for whatever inequities are produced by reliance on the property tax.

TEL TALK

Another way that local tax systems are constrained significantly is through tax and expenditure limitations—TELs. There are two main types of TELs: those that put restrictions on revenue raising and those that set limits for overall spending. Spending limits on localities are a good deal less common than tax limits.

Sometimes, TELs are imposed by voters. But state legislatures also do it or, as in Florida, ask voters to approve it. It can, however, be short-sighted. "There's an assumption at the state level," says Kevin O'Brien, former director of the Center for Public Management at Cleveland State University, "that every day is a sunny day and there are no extraordinary circumstances—that you won't need firefighters on the ridge."

For localities, the most common TELs have to do with property taxes. California's Proposition 13 and Massachusetts' Proposition 2.5 are the [ü]ber-TELs. They were imposed by voters, and they have made their mark. "Prop 13 turned California from a state that was

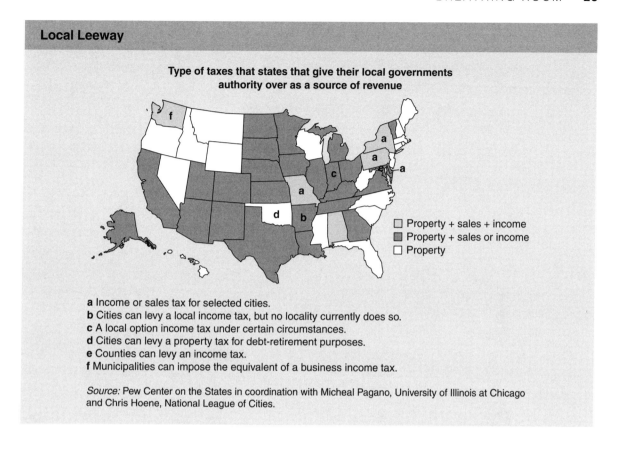

Local Leeway

Type of taxes that states that give their local governments authority over as a source of revenue

☐ Property + sales + income
■ Property + sales or income
☐ Property

a Income or sales tax for selected cities.
b Cities can levy a local income tax, but no locality currently does so.
c A local option income tax under certain circumstances.
d Cities can levy a property tax for debt-retirement purposes.
e Counties can levy an income tax.
f Municipalities can impose the equivalent of a business income tax.

Source: Pew Center on the States in coordination with Micheal Pagano, University of Illinois at Chicago and Chris Hoene, National League of Cities.

among the best in primary and secondary education to a ranking in spending that was near the bottom," says O'Brien, who is currently executive director of the Great Lakes Environmental Finance Center. "That is the legacy of their TEL."

The Massachusetts TEL limits towns and cities from increasing the total property tax levy to no more than 2.5 percent of the community's total assessed value (the levy limit) and from increasing the tax levy to no more than 2.5 percent of the prior year's levy limit. "Homeowners felt they were paying enormously high property taxes," says Bluestone. "And that was because the property tax was essentially the only real source of local revenue."

The bottom line, though, is that the TEL makes it much more difficult for cities and towns to raise the revenue they need. "That you can't raise revenue by more than 2.5 percent on existing property is a powerful constraint," Bluestone says. Towns and cities in Massachusetts often ask voters for an override but these are increasingly unsuccessful, leading to cutbacks in schools and social services—"just when," Bluestone says, "these communities are competing like never before for jobs and investment."

For state policy makers, there are obvious policy levers to pull to improve the fiscal and economic vitality of local governments. More local tax authority is perhaps most obvious. Maintaining or increasing state aid levels, particularly where state aid reduces inequities, is another—but one that is often pulled in the opposite direction, particularly in response to economic downturns. Doing so, however, can harm the ability of the state and its localities to recover from the downturn.

II

Elections and Political Environment

S tates and localities must like elections. After all, they hold an awful lot of them. Even in "off" or "odd" years—meaning no congressional or presidential races are being held—there are still plenty of state and local offices to fill and, like as not, ballot initiatives to be decided upon. In 2007, for example, there were governors to elect in Kentucky, Louisiana, and Mississippi; entire legislatures up for grabs in, among others, New Jersey and Virginia; and voters were asked to decide thirty-four statewide ballot initiatives ranging from big picture issues (proposed term limits in Maine) to the more mundane details of governance (a proposal to require the Texas legislature to publish its votes on the Internet). These elections can be useful indicators of the national mood and presage political futures at the national level as clearly as at the state and local levels. And if that is indeed the case, the political tea leaves offer a very mixed reading regardless of partisan, ideological, or policy preferences.

Recent state elections have provided much for Democrats and policy liberals (not necessarily the same thing) to cheer about. Democrats have made steady gains in state legislatures over the past couple of years, a trend that looks likely to continue.[1] In 2008, the party had majority control of twenty-three legislatures, one more than it controlled in 2007. These state legislative elections are particularly important to the future of national-level parties because the state legislatures shaped by elections in 2007, 2008, and 2009 will have considerable influence over the drawing of congressional election districts following the 2010 census. Thus Democratic gains in this arena may have implications for the partisan balance of power at the national level for years to come.

The trend in ballot initiative results seemed to continue being unkind to conservative causes. Flagship issues such as term limits, spending and tax cuts, and bans on gay marriage notched consistent wins during the 1990s and the first few years after the turn of the century. In the 2007 election cycle, however, term limit proposals failed in Maine, Utah rejected a school voucher bill, and voters in several states backed big spending proposals, including a $3 billion cancer research proposal in Texas. Still, there was plenty of evidence that voters remain fundamentally skeptical about taxing and spending. They turned down a proposed cigarette tax in Oregon and funding for stem-cell research in New Jersey.

So it has not been all doom and gloom for Republicans and conservatives. Although most political bean counters have the GOP losing ground at the state level during the most recent electoral cycles, there have been some successes. Former Louisiana governor Kathleen Blanco, a Democrat whose administration was tarred by its handling of the aftermath of Hurricane Katrina, left office in 2007 and was replaced by Republican Bobby Jindal, who was immediately tagged as a rising star within the party. Jindal seemed to have significant coattails, for although Republicans did not gain control of Louisiana's legislature, they cut the Democratic majorities to very thin margins.

Overall, however, what was seen in 2008 was a general continuation of the political environment signaled by the 2006 and 2007 elections. This political environment is generally more favorable to Democrats than Republicans, although Democrats tend to be winning close races and there are questions about whether the party's gains will be secure over the long term.

PARTICIPATION AND OUTCOMES: RECENT TRENDS

The essays in this section focus on elections and participation in states and localities. The piece by Tim Storey provides an overview of the 2007 off-year election and how it left the partisan balance in state legislatures and governor's mansions for 2008. The essay by Thad Beyle provides some eye-opening numbers on the cost of running for statewide office. Beyle focuses on gubernatorial elections and tracks how the price of being a serious candidate has steadily increased since the 1970s. In inflation adjusted terms, the price of running for governor has increased by more than 100 percent over the past thirty years, and there appears to be no upper limit for campaign spending on the horizon.

The other two essays in this section focus more on political participation than on the horserace or logistical aspects of elections. Mark Stencel's essay takes a look at the continuation of an old tradition in retail politics: the participation of political candidates in county fairs. Specifically, he visits the fairgrounds of Neshoba County, Mississippi, where large and demonstrative crowds still jostle to hear pols on the hustings. Alarkon Walker's piece takes a look at the revitalization of another old tradition, the poll party. Political parties once routinely encouraged turnout by offering beer to voters; now three political scientists, Donald Green, Elizabeth Addonizio, and James Glaser, are experimenting with an updated version of the partying hard for your party idea. Their version does not include the less savory elements of corruption, violence, and excess that went along with the original notion of a poll party, but it does incorporate creating a festive atmosphere around the idea of going to cast a ballot. Early results are encouraging. After throwing more than a dozen of these political parties, it appears injecting an element of community socializing into going to the polls does help boost turnout.

Note

1. Bridget Hunter, "2007 Elections Important Despite Low Voter Turnout," America.gov, www.america.gov/st/usg-english/2007/November/20071107121159abretnuh0.5257837.html.

6

Election Reflection

Tim Storey

Democrats take advantage of an off-year election to make gains in the South.

For voters in Louisiana, Mississippi, New Jersey and Virginia, 2007 was a big election year with all legislative seats up for elections. These "odd-year" elections often garner little attention and generate little suspense. But this year was different. Majority control was up for grabs in all four states.

Democrats fared well by gaining majority status in two of the eight chambers and retaining majorities in five of the others. They now control the Mississippi and Virginia Senates by narrow margins.

There was, however, a silver lining for Republicans. In addition to keeping their solid advantage in the Virginia House, the GOP made big gains in the Louisiana House, falling just short of control. Democrats have held the chamber since 1876.

For well over a decade now, southern legislatures have been fertile ground for the GOP as they steadily added seats and chambers. Before the 1994 elections, Republicans did not control a single legislative body in the South. By 2007, they were in charge of over half. In November, Democrats reversed the trend by winning back the Mississippi and Virginia Senates.

THE OVERALL PICTURE

With those gains, Democrats now control the legislature in 23 states—up one from before the election. Republicans control both chambers in 14 states, and 12 states have divided legislatures. Nebraska has a unicameral legislature that is not elected on a partisan basis.

There were a handful of governor races in 2007. Republicans gained one and lost one. In Louisiana, the open governor's race went to Republican Bobby Jindal while in Kentucky, incumbent

From *State Legislatures,* January 2008.

33

Republican Governor Ernie Fletcher lost to Democratic challenger Steve Beshear. As it was before the elections, 28 governors are Democrats and 22 are Republicans.

DEMS HOLD ON IN LOUISIANA

With all seats up, Louisiana Democrats managed to maintain a slim majority in the House: 53 D, 50 R and two independents. And they kept the majority in the Senate: 24 D to 15 R—unchanged from before the election. Term limits took effect in Louisiana this year creating 45 open seats in the House and helping Republicans edge closer to outright numerical control. Of the 15 states with legislative term limits, Louisiana is the next-to-last where they have taken effect. Term limits kick in for Nevada legislators in 2010. At press time, a fierce contest for the speaker's race in the House was taking shape between Democratic Representative Don Cazayoux and Republican Representative Jim Tucker. Both candidates were reaching out across party lines, so bipartisanship might be more prevalent when Louisiana convenes in 2008.

MISSISSIPPI SENATE BACK TO DEMS

Winning back control of the Mississippi Senate was definitely a big victory for Democrats after losing control earlier in the year due to a Democratic senator switching to the GOP. Democrats now have a 28 to 24 edge. With incumbent Republican governor Haley Barbour cruising to re-election, winning the Senate was even more important for Democrats.

In the House, there was no change in the partisan numbers. Democrats still control 75 to 47. However, like their neighbor to the west, the Mississippi House had a pitched battle for speaker going at press time between Republican Representative Jeff Smith and incumbent House Speaker Billy McCoy. Both claim they have the votes.

NOT MUCH CHANGE IN NEW JERSEY

Despite speculation of big change afoot before the election, afterwards the numbers looked very much the same. Republicans gained one seat, but Democrats still control both houses comfortably. In the Senate, it's 23 D to 17 R. Assembly numbers are 48 D, 32 R. The big story in New Jersey was turnover. Over a third of Garden State legislators will be new in 2008—term limits-like turnover in a non-term limited state.

SLIM VICTORY FOR DEMOCRATS IN VIRGINIA

The Old Dominion was the biggest battleground in November and Democrats emerged with a slim two-seat majority in the Senate at 21 D-19 R. Three GOP incumbent senators were defeated: Jeannemarie Devolites-Davis, J.K. "Jay" O'Brien Jr. and Nick Rerras. In the House, Democrats gained ground, but Republicans kept their majority 54 to 44 with two independents. The last time Democrats controlled either chamber in Virginia was before the 1999 election.

REDISTRICTING LOOMS

Virginia legislative candidates raised more than $60 million for the 2007 races, according to the Associated Press. That big spending is a hint of what is to come in many states. Legislative races garner more attention and campaign cash as redistricting looms closer. Barring mid-term party switches, the majorities elected in six of the chambers last November will control 2010 redistricting. New Jersey and Virginia have House races in 2009. Democrats now hold 3,988 of the legislative seats controlled by the two major parties, or 54.6 percent. That's their highest mark since they got walloped in 1994 by Republicans. 2008 is a year of opportunity for both major parties with almost 6,000 legislative seats scheduled for elections and many close legislative chambers with majority control in play.

Few Surprises in 2007 Ballot Measures

Voters in six states in November considered 34 statewide questions—a fairly typical total for an odd-year election.

Maine
Failed: A proposal to extend legislative term limits from 8 to 12 years.
Failed: A citizen initiative for a new tribal commercial harness racing track.

New Jersey
Failed: Public Question 1 that would have dedicated the second half of last year's 1 percent sales tax hike to property tax relief. Homeowners could have saved up to 20 percent.
Failed: A $450 million bond measure for state-funded stem cell research.

Oregon
Passed: A proposal to rollback controversial Measure 37 from 2004 that removed most land use regulation in the state and prompted measures on regulatory takings in Arizona, California, Idaho and Washington in 2006. (Only Arizona's passed.)
Failed: An 84.5-cents-a-pack tobacco tax hike for health care.

Texas
Passed: A proposal to deny bail in felony and family violence cases.
Passed: A measure to require that certain votes of the Legislature be recorded and publicized on the Internet.

Passed: A $3 billion bond issue for cancer research.
Passed: $6 billion in bonds for highway and construction projects.

Utah
Failed: A school voucher bill passed by the Legislature last February to provide scholarships between $500 and $3,000, depending on family size and income, for private school tuition.

Washington
Passed: A citizen initiative that requires a two-thirds vote for new or increased fees being considered by the Legislature. It takes away state agencies' authority to impose or increase fees and requires a detailed fiscal analysis, including a 10-year projection of costs to taxpayers. And, from now on, the people have to vote on any tax actions not already subject to a referendum.
Passed: A popular referenda that prohibits insurers from unreasonably denying a claim for coverage or benefits and allows claimants to sue for up to three times the amount of damages.
Passed: A legislative referenda to create a rainy day fund. One percent of general state revenue will be transferred to the account each fiscal year. Use of the funds will be limited to protecting life and safety in times of emergencies or job declines unless the account exceeds 10 percent of general state revenues. In that case, the Legislature can use the money with a three-fifths vote, or by majority vote, for education construction projects.

—Jennie Drage Bowser, NCSL

7

Race to Spend Money

Thad Beyle

Running for governor is an increasingly expensive proposition. Even losing costs a lot of money.

The cost of gubernatorial elections has continued to rise since the mid-1970s when campaign expenditures became available across the 50 states.

And there's no end in sight—signs point to continued increases in these costly campaigns.

Spending in governor's races increased 117 percent, from $467.6 million in the 1977–1980 election cycle to $1.02 billion in the 1999-2002 election cycle. These comparisons, which account for the gubernatorial elections in every state throughout a four-year cycle, are made by converting the earlier amounts into 2002 dollars.

Now we have another four years of elections to add to this analysis. The increases over that 30-year spread—from the 1977–1980 gubernatorial election cycle to the 2003–2006 election cycle—have also been astounding.

For instance, the costs jumped 416 percent from the 1999 election to 2003, when the same seats were open. Gubernatorial candidates across the country in 1999 spent $19.7 million in 2006 dollars; that jumped to $76.6 million in 2003, an increase of 389 percent. But that comparison does not include the 2003 California recall and special election, in which $23.4 million was spent.

The 11 races in 2000 cost $113.7 million; that increased 5.7 percent to $120.2 million when the same seats were open in 2004. Candidates spent 69.8 percent more for the two seats open in 2005 than candidates in those races spent in 2001. Expenditures jumped from $80.2 million in 2001 to $136.2 million in 2005, a nearly 70 percent increase.

But comparisons between the 2002 elections to the 2006 elections, when the same seats were open, paint a different picture.

From *State News,* January 2008.

The 319 candidates in the 36 gubernatorial races in 2002 spent $943.7 million, which averages out to more than $26.2 million per race. The 274 candidates running in the 36 governor's races in 2006 spent $727.6 million, an average of $20.2 million per race. These figures reveal a $216 million—or 22.8 percent—decline in total expenditures in these 36 races between 2002 and 2006, but there are several factors that explain the decrease in campaign spending.

First, 20 seats in the 2002 elections were open, compared to only nine races in 2006 where no incumbent was running. Open seats often attract more candidates who are willing to spend a lot of money because they believe this may be one of very few chances they could be elected governor.

Also, in 2002 four incumbent governors—Don Siegelman, D-Ala., Roy Barnes, D-Ga., Jim Hodges, D-S.C., and Scott McCallum, R-Wis.—lost their bids for another term. Three of the losses indicate the strength of the Republican Party in Southern states is gaining ground. In 2006, only two incumbent governors—Frank Murkowski, R-Alaska, and Robert Ehrlich, R-Md.— failed in their re-election bids. Elections in which an incumbent is defeated are usually expensive races.

Expenditures in seven of the 2006 state races exceeded $40 million. They were:

- **California:** Candidates spent $129 million, including $45.9 million spent by incumbent Republican Gov. Arnold Schwarzenegger, who defeated Democrats Steve Westly, who spent $43.95 million, and Phil Angelides, who spent $30 million.
- **Michigan:** Incumbent Jennifer Granholm, a Democrat, spent $11.2 million to defeat Republican Dick DeVos, who spent $41.6 million. This race shows money doesn't always win, but with Granholm term-limited, DeVos likely will run again in 2010, and is obviously ready to spend his way into the governor's mansion.
- **Illinois:** Incumbent Rod Blagojevich, a Democrat, won re-election in a race where $48.5 million was spent overall[.]
- **Pennsylvania:** Incumbent Ed Rendell, also a Democrat, won re-election in a race where candidates spent $41 million.
- **New York:** Democrat Eliot Spitzer won an open seat in a race where candidates spent $46.1 million[.]
- **Massachusetts:** Candidates spent $42.3 million in a race where Democrat Deval Patrick was elected to the open seat.
- **Florida:** Candidates spent $41 million in a race where Republican Charlie Crist won the open seat.

Four states in which the incumbent governor won re-election were at the lower end of the spending spectrum.

- Democrat John Lynch won in **New Hampshire** where campaigns cost $2.2 million;

The 36 Even-Off Year Gubernatorial Races, 1978–2006

Year	Open Seats	Incumbents Ran/Won/Lost			Where Lost Prim./Gen.El.		New Govs	$ Spen[t] Actual	$ Spent in 2006$
1978	13	23	16	7	2	5	20	98,537,610	299,506,413
1982	11	25	19	6	1	5	17	181,305,951	372,291,480
1986	18	18	15	3	1	2	21	270,383,448	488,939,327
1990	13	23	17	6	0	6	19	345,551,402	524,357,211
1994	13	23	17	6	2	4	19	417,872,658	559,401,149
1998	11	25	23	2	0	2	13	539,969,464	656,897,158
2002	20	16	12	4	0	4	24	841,416,833	927,692,208
2006	9	27	25	2	1	1	11	727,552,506	727,552,506
Totals	108	180	144	36	7	29	144	[3,422,589,872]	4,556,637,452

- Republican Jim Douglas was re-elected in **Vermont** after candidates spent $1.7 million;
- Democrat Dave Freudenthal won the $1.4 million campaign in **Wyoming;** and
- Republican Michael Rounds won in **South Dakota,** where candidates spent $1.3 million.

Except for Rounds, these successful incumbents were the big spenders in their races, while Rounds only spent 22.8 percent of the money in winning. In fact, Rounds' total spending of $295,846 was the least spent by any other successful or unsuccessful candidate in the 2006 gubernatorial races.

Looking ahead to 2010, the next year in which 36 governors' races will be on the ballots, we can see the potential for a great deal of spending. At least 17 seats will be open because the two-term limit will prohibit those who were elected in 2002, and re-elected in 2006 from seeking another term.

Some likely will also decide not to seek re-election and other incumbents will likely be defeated. That means more than 17 new governors could be selected in 2010. We could see the amount of money spent in the 2010 races resume that continual climb in money spent by people seeking the governors' offices that was missing in the 2006 races.

8

Bare-Knuckle Gentility

Mark Stencel

It's more than corndogs and horseracing. You can still get your politics up close and personal at a Southern county fair.

Every summer, but especially in off-year election seasons like this one, the Mississippi state capitol moves to a dusty fairground in Neshoba County. The unofficial seat of government is on the outskirts of Philadelphia, off a two-lane rural highway, behind a small Baptist church and cemetery. The livestock displays are just through the fair's main gate, next to the stables where horses with names like Gun for Hire and Battery Operated prepare for harness racing on a nearby red-dirt track.

The politicians come ready to run, too. Their arena is in the center of this temporary village, past spinning midway rides and fried-food vendors, where families and friends bunk up for the week in crammed cabins painted in bright blues, reds and yellows. Space and privacy are scarce, but political gossip is plentiful. Campaign signs hang from nearly every porch, utility pole and tree. And in the middle of it all, on a wide sawdust-covered square, is a tin-roof pavilion where a century's worth of lore lives in the raucous throngs who gather to eat up campaign speeches and roar at the tart-tongued exchanges between candidates.

At this year's fair, it was Governor Haley Barbour who delivered the zinger they'll be talking about in Neshoba for years. Barbour, a popular Republican who is heavily favored for reelection, came to the microphone just after his opponent had spoken to the hooting, stomping crowd. Supporters of Democrat John Arthur Eaves Jr. made a good showing for their candidate but were outnumbered by the governor's troops. This was Barbour country.

Eaves had laid into Barbour for his lobbying ties to "the money-changers of big oil, big insurance and big tobacco." The Democrat, perhaps aware that his divorce and recent re-marriage to an attrac-

From *Governing,*
October 2007.

tive advertising executive may not play well with conservative voters, also went out of his way to emphasize his anti-abortion beliefs and Christian values.

Barbour, seeming to sense his opponent's vulnerability, began his speech by introducing his wife of 35 years. He then veered from his prepared remarks with an acidic line aimed straight at Eaves' family-values credentials. "I got my trophy wife the first time around," Barbour said, setting off a minor firestorm that made headlines as far away as Washington.

The Neshoba County Fair has always been known for this kind of bare-knuckle gentility. Every Mississippi governor since 1896 has come to Neshoba to address the fairgoers, as has just about every other notable politician in the state. Occasionally, national figures show up, too. When Ronald Reagan launched his general election campaign in 1980, he came to Neshoba to do it. Reagan delivered now-legendary remarks about states' rights that rallied the crowd but rankled his opponents, who pointed out that it had been only 16 years since three civil rights workers were murdered in Neshoba County and found buried at a farm not far from the fairgrounds. History always seems close by, which is why the fair is not just a civic tradition but a reflection of Mississippi's own contentious past and the South's evolving politics.

Other states and communities have similar fairs and festivities, steeped in their own quirky politics. Few serious candidates for president bypass the butter sculptures and glad-handing of the Iowa state fair in advance of the critical party caucuses there. Likewise, any candidate counting on votes from the Florida panhandle would be foolish to ignore an invitation to the Wausau possum festival, where locals delight in watching ambitious pols wrangle marsupials while trying not to get bitten.

What distinguishes the Neshoba fair is the length and seriousness of its political agenda, which this year included nearly 80 speakers over three days. Almost every candidate for statewide and local office, from lieutenant governor to county tax collector, was scheduled to speak and schmooze. In an era of high-tech electioneering, with its automated calling centers, online fundraising, voter registration databases and targeted TV buys, the county fair is a reminder that turning the right phrase and shaking the right hands still matters an awful lot in state and local politics.

At the same time, the fair has had to evolve as technology—in particular, the way the media cover the event—has changed. The Neshoba County Fair isn't quite the same now as when it began in 1889. But one thing remains the same: In the steamy days of late July, there is no place this state's political class would rather be than the place they call "Mississippi's giant house party."

CABIN FEVER

As a teenager 46 years ago, Gloria Williamson was crowned with a tiara and named Miss Neshoba County. Now a state senator, Williamson has delivered nine speeches at the fair since she first ran and won office in 1999. If Williamson is a familiar face around the fair, she is also something of a rarity in this part of the state these days—she's an unapologetic Democrat. As she and her family prepared to host a lunch for other Democrats at their three-story yellow cabin overlooking the horse track, Williamson joked about her party's fortunes in the county where she grew up. "This is the only place they can eat," Williamson said, pointing to signs for Republican candidates on the surrounding cabins. "There are Democrats here. They're just too chicken to admit it."

Williamson is no chicken, nor is she sheepish about her party identification. That might be why Republicans have targeted her district this year in hopes of growing the GOP's narrow Senate majority. It also may be why she and her challenger drew a decent crowd when it was their turn to speak to fairgoers.

Republican Giles Ward spoke first, addressing the audience for his allotted 10 minutes while Williamson waited, fanning herself in a wooden seat along the wall behind the podium. She listened as Ward decried lawmakers who "haven't got a clue" about their constituents' beliefs and promised to "truly reflect your values" if elected. When a red light in the rafters signaled that Ward's time was up, the two candidates shook hands and Williamson approached the microphone.

The senator at the podium sounded like a classic Southern populist. She jabbed her finger in the air while trumpeting her support for local farmers and timber interests. She emphasized issues she was sure would appeal to her "kin folk," saying, "Do not let people tell you that just because I am a woman I'm against guns." But she also was unrepentant about other positions. "Call me a liberal," she proclaimed. "I've been called a lot of names....I'm used to it, so it doesn't bother me."

Back when Williamson was entering pageants, Democrats dominated the Neshoba fair. Its significance owed a great deal to the fair's timing, just ahead of the Democratic primary in early August. As in much of the old South, the winner of a Democratic primary was almost certain to carry the day in November. Now Neshoba is a solidly Republican county, and its fair is a microcosm of Mississippi's shift, and that of much of the South, from blue to red.

This year at the fair, the shift in Mississippi's allegiances showed in the lopsided number of signs for Barbour and other candidates from his party. It also showed in the size of the crowd at Pete Perry's cabin, a gathering point for top Republicans. Perry, a lobbyist from Jackson who grew up in Philadelphia, easily remembered a time when the fair was "a real Democratic institution" and "there were few other Republicans around"—even in his own family. Many in Perry's family are still Democrats. His mother, Lallah, made that clear enough in a conversation on the porch of her own nearby cabin. "I did my best," she said of her son's politics, sighing.

But as Pete's sister, Margaret, added, the fair's changing politics may not be quite as dramatic as it seems. "It's a change of title," she said. "It's the same point of view." And that point of view, expressed in campaign speech after campaign speech over three days, was conservative, with a heavy emphasis on abortion, gay rights, guns, illegal immigration and taxes—regardless of which party label the speaker wore.

While the fair is no longer a Democratic institution, it remains a predominantly white institution. Since cabins on the fairgrounds often pass from one generation to the next, the fair's complexion has changed little from the days when governors were cheered for proclaiming segregationist views. But dismissing the gathering simply as a holdover from a less tolerant time would ignore the progressive political candidates who also made bold stands for racial harmony in Neshoba County. One such politician was William F. Winter, a change-minded Democrat and frequent fair speaker. In one fair speech, a decade before his election as governor in 1980, Winter challenged state leaders to "raise the sights of people instead of playing to their fears and doubts."

POLITICAL HORSE RACES

Neshoba County may be the only place in the United States where one could schedule six dozen political speeches and still have a crowd that outnumbered the speakers. For the thousands of fairgoers who came to listen this election year, the hours and hours of oratory were an attraction—much like the musical acts, midway rides and harness racing that draw other attendees. As Jim Eastland, a U.S. Senator from Mississippi, put it half a century ago, "The Neshoba County Fair is the only place I know of where politicians and the horses are running at the same time, and it's hard to tell which ones are running the hardest."

Standing out in such a large crowd of speakers has always been a challenge. A dark-horse candidate once literally rode to the podium on a black horse. Another frequent speaker, former Governor Ross R. Barnett, often played guitar and sang folksy songs. Neither matched the fair antics of Dick Molpus in 1983, when the Democrat was one of nine candidates running for secretary of state. When it was his turn to address the crowd Molpus arranged for a group of majorettes to appear on stage with him, flipping up their skirts at the end of their routine to reveal letters on each of their rears spelling out the candidate's name. Conservative though the crowd was, Molpus knew his audience would eat it up. "I understood the culture," the Philadelphia native said.

Candidates rarely debate each other directly at the Neshoba fair, as Molpus and Governor Kirk Fordice did in 1995. But as a lengthy history of the fair compiled by Steven H. Stubbs makes clear, there has been no shortage of confrontations. In 1941, Governor Paul B. Johnson Sr. nearly got in a fistfight with the owner of a Gulfport newspaper. In an earlier showdown, U.S. Senator John Sharp Williams was challenged by a citizen, who asked if it was true that "during a recent debate in the Senate, you rose to speak and were so drunk you couldn't stand on your own two feet."

"It's a lie!" the senator answered. "If you want to know the truth, I was so drunk on that particular day that I never even got to the United States Senate."

In this light, Barbour's "trophy wife" dig fits a long tradition of verbal jousting at the fair. The butt of the governor's joke, Eaves' second wife, Angel, told reporters at the fair that she could not offer Barbour a lady-like response. But later in the afternoon, Eaves' aides confided that the snipe was probably good for their candidate—it was one of the first times the governor had paid much attention to his challenger.

When candidates finish speechifying, their attention turns to hobnobbing at the family cabins, where the house parties run well into the night. Sweaty politicians march from porch to porch, hands extended, introducing themselves and asking for votes. The impressions candidates make here are as critical as the ones they make at the podium. Several longtime fairgoers and politicos reminisced about a disastrous appearance by Charles L. Sullivan, who came to campaign in an immaculate white suit only to get caught in a summer deluge. "The man had to roll up his pants," Williamson remembered, laughing at the image more than three decades later.

IN WITH THE NEW

Whether any of the quips and slips at the fair matter as much as they once did is hard to say, now that so much of the politicking is carefully staged for the press. After the candidates in the highest-profile races finish their speeches, they exit the pavilion stage through a back door and step down five wooden steps into a mob of reporters, photographers and TV cameramen. A phalanx of supporters, armed with yard signs handed out by campaign aides, quickly form a backdrop, just to make sure that the candidate's name appears in any shot the television crews choose to use. Some candidates also wander to the far side of the pavilion, where Supertalk Mississippi, a statewide talk radio network, broadcasts live from the fair daily.

The 84-year-old man sitting on the porch behind the Supertalk booth, reading a newspaper, played a big role in bringing electronic media to the fair. William Howard Cole launched local radio station WHOC-AM in 1948 and quickly made plans to broadcast from the fairgrounds. "We strung eight miles of telephone line from here to Philadelphia," Cole said, marveling at the amount of media working the square in front of his family's cabin this year. When Reagan made his visit 27 years ago, power was in short supply for all the TV crews that traveled with him. "You had to get your name in the pot early," Cole said.

These days, the fair is far more connected. A temporary cell tower erected in the parking lot provided mobile phone coverage for pols, press and regular folk. Jim Prince, the editor and publisher of the *Neshoba Democrat,* sat in front of his cabin, logged in to his office with a laptop and a wireless modem, grumbling about signal strength. But plenty of newspaper editors and reporters were wired well enough to sustain continuous online blogs on the fair's festivities.

Can a fair-wide Wi-Fi computer network be far behind?

The technological and media revolution will no doubt make its mark on the Neshoba County Fair, just as electricity and running water did. But the fair itself will adjust. Some form of the quaint politics that has drawn so many politicians here for more than 100 summers will live on.

Just look at what the fair has been through already.

9

Poll Party

Walter Alarkon

In the old days, political parties boosted turnout by giving voters, well, a party. In New Haven, Connecticut, poll parties are being revived.

I n the 19th century, political parties plied voters with beer outside polls in exchange for their votes. Bribes (beer or otherwise) are illegal today, but researchers are now testing whether the less criminal aspect of 19th century turnout efforts—the festive atmosphere—increases voter participation.

Donald Green and Elizabeth Addonizio of Yale University and James Glaser of Tufts University held 14 festivals outside polls across the country in 2005. They offered cotton candy, soda and sandwiches and played family-friendly music in carnival tents.

At first, people were skeptical. Voters "would sometimes ask, 'Who was paying for this?' They had a lot of quizzical looks," said Green.

In Hooksett, N.H., local officials asked them to put signs up outside the festival proclaiming the event was paid for by Yale University.

But people gave in. Some started dancing and playing catch. One kid said that he wished every day was Election Day. In New Haven, Conn., a kids' boogie-down broke out, with the best dancer getting $14, donated by onlookers.

And the festivals did boost turnout a bit. In districts where about half of the electorate was expected to vote, turnout increased by about 6.5 percent. In places where few voters were expected—about 10 percent of the electorate—turnout increased by 2.6 percent.

In Hooksett, turnout went from 836 votes during the 2004 town elections to 1,494 votes in 2005, when the festival took place.

However, Leslie Nepveu, Hooksett's town clerk, was less than enthralled.

From *Campaigns and Elections,* November 2007.

"It's nice for the people who are working, but as far as for the voters, I think most people come and do their duty and leave," Nepveu said. She said she took only an ice water from the festival before leaving.

Still, at least some people were open to the idea: the festival Election Day saw Hooksett's highest turnout in its town-only races in recent years.

For fans of poll festivals, there's good reason to hark back to the way votes were cast 150 years ago. Between 65 and 80 percent of eligible voters went to the polls then, far greater than today's rates of 55 percent or less. Today, voting is a drab affair, and efforts to raise turnout, such as same-day and "motor-voter" registration drives, focus on making voting more convenient, instead of trying to make it more fun.

To be sure, the old-time festivities had major drawbacks, said Richard Bensel, author of "The American Ballot Box in the Mid-Nineteenth Century."

For starters, they were corrupt. Instead of casting secret ballots, voters used tickets, usually printed and handed out by political parties. A voter had to hand the ticket to an election judge, who was often hand-picked by party leaders and then surrounded by party loyalists on Election Day. If a voter was ambivalent, a party agent would give him alcohol, usually beer or whiskey, to weaken his resistance. In fact, many polling places were in saloons, turning Election Day into an all-day kegger.

The festivities were sometimes violent, Bensel said. One man was killed in Baltimore during the 1859 elections. Elsewhere in the city that year, an election judge considered his vote a success because roughhousing was kept to a minimum: only one man was arrested, for striking two other men.

Still, today's political [p]arties seeking more votes might want to try those old methods, Green said.

The festivals did a better (and cheaper) job of turning out the vote than door-to-door canvassing. It cost $3.25 for each new vote during a festival, compared to the $19-per-vote cost of canvassing.

"The test will be what will happen when really creative people who know something about entertainment—drawing crowds, public events—get into the act," Green said. "They'd do a better job of drawing crowds and raising turnouts than what we did."

III

Political Parties and Interest Groups

P eople tend to be skeptical about political parties and special interest groups. Mention either at a dinner party and grumbling about money and its corrosive influence on politics will surely follow. Truth be told, there are reasons for this skepticism. According to the Center for Public Integrity, a nonpartisan government watchdog organization, special interests spend more than a billion dollars a year lobbying state legislators.[1] That's a lot of money, and it is reasonable to wonder what the lobbyists and the special interests they represent are getting for it.

With all that money available, state political parties are not exactly slouches when it comes to going after it. And both Republicans and Democrats funnel tens of millions into state parties every year, each seeking to use those resources for electoral and partisan advantage with neither being overly fussy about where the money comes from. In the 2003–2004 electoral cycle (the most recent period available), contributions to state parties totaled about $735 million. Perhaps not surprisingly, a big chunk of that came from special interest groups and lobbying firms.[2]

While it is easy to let such numbers fuel cynicism about political parties and special interest groups, there is another side to this coin. Despite popular impressions political parties and special interest groups really are not organizations that exist to trade favors for cash. Both actually provide important services to democracy in the states.

POLITICAL PARTIES AND INTEREST GROUPS: DIFFERENCES AND SIMILARITIES

Political parties and special interest groups are alike in many ways. For example, both raise money, endorse candidates, and mobilize support or opposition for particular issues and causes. Yet there are also fundamental differences, the most important of which are that a political party runs its own candidates for office and helps organize the government. A special interest group might try to help get candidates elected, and it certainly tries to influence government, but it does not nominate candidates and people do not organize the government under its name. For example, the National Rifle Association (NRA) may contribute to a candidate's election campaign try to persuade that candidate to support a favored position on legislative proposals if elected to office. That candidate, however, will like as not be elected as a Democrat or a Republican, and will not be formally identified as an NRA representative. In addition, if the candidate is elected, his or her role in the legislature, such as committee assignments and relative power, will be determined by his or her party, not by the NRA.

Even in nominally nonpartisan governments, including most local governments and Nebraska's unicameral legislature, candidates often are not shy about declaring their partisan credentials and seeking party endorsements. In effect, informal party systems can exist even where they are formally prohibited. This is why political scientists view political parties as one of the natural byproducts of representative democracy: establish the latter, and the former will arrive sooner rather than later.

The same might be said for special interest groups. Give people a representative form of government that incorporates freedom of expression and assembly and the right to petition government for redress of grievances, and what you have is a gold-plated invitation to form a special interest group. It's an invitation enthusiastically accepted by citizens supporting every conceivable (and sometimes not so conceivable) political issue or position.

While natural outgrowths of representative democracy, political parties and special interest groups have never been particularly popular. What is often ignored in such judgments are the positive services these organizations provide to democracy. Both organizations play a critical role in aggregating interests and connecting them to government.

A single individual is unlikely to gain the attention of a legislature or a governor, whereas a well-organized interest group that can mobilize voters, gain prominent news coverage, and wage effective public opinion campaigns is much harder for a government to ignore. A team of candidates elected under the same label with a mandate to pursue particular policies or issues not only gains the attention of government, it *is* the government.

Yet for all of this, political parties and special interest groups continue to be viewed with suspicion, especially when it comes to their relations with each other. The scramble to win elections, control the key offices and institutions of government, and influence the decisions of policymakers tends to create a negative image of political parties and special interest groups. And the fact is (as we shall see in the readings that follow), political parties do try to tip the electoral scales in their favor, and lobbyists sometimes do cross the line from persuasion to less ethical—and less legal—means of trying to line up legislative support for their favored policies.

Historically, political parties and interest groups have been regulated with a relatively light hand. Most states view political parties as something akin to public utilities, that is, they are seen as organizations that provide a necessary public service. As such, what laws that do exist to regulate their behavior mostly try to ensure that certain people or groups do not unduly profit while providing these services. These same laws also try to ensure that individuals and groups are not unfairly excluded from the political process.[3]

Special interest groups, meanwhile, have been hard to regulate because of the constitutional issues involved in doing so. It is difficult to place constraints on special interest groups without also putting constraints on certain freedoms guaranteed to all by the Bill of Rights. Consequently, regulating interest groups has mostly been about registering and reporting, rather than placing limits on behavior.

THE GOOD, THE BAD, AND THE UGLY OF PARTIES AND SPECIAL INTEREST GROUPS

The readings in this section were chosen with two goals in mind. The first was simply to provide a contemporary look at how political parties and special interest groups shape each other at the state level. The second was to provide opposing perspectives on interest groups, because while there is plenty out there to be cynical about, what should not be lost is the fact that special interest can also play an important role in promoting the general good.

The first reading, by Charles Bullock and Karen Padgett, is an academic study of how changes in party fortunes lead to variation in how (and which) interest groups influence policy. Specifically, the study examines the relationship between lobbyists and legislators, and how these relationships were altered with shifts in party control of the legislature.

Alex Marshall's essay highlights the hypocrisy that sometimes accompanies interest group activity, and which no doubt fuels cynicism about politics. Marshall examines the contradictory policy aims of groups that call for less government intervention in public transit policies while strongly advocating publicly built highways. As Marshall points out *both* of these policies represent large and expensive government programs.

Lastly, Tom Arrandale provides an in-depth look at a form of interest group activity that by most perspectives is providing an important public good. Thousands of vigilant organizations are keeping watch over water quality and using the information they gather to effectively lobby government to crack down on polluters.

Notes

1. Center for Public Integrity. "Influence: A Booming Business," www.publicintegrity.org/hiredguns/report.aspx?aid=957.

2. Center for Public Integrity. "Contributions," www.publicintegrity.org/partylines/overview.aspx?act=maincon.

3. Malcom E. Jewll and Sarah M. Morehouse, Political Parties and Elections in American States, 4th ed. (Washington, D.C.: CQ Press, 2001), 76.

10

Partisan Change and Consequences for Lobbying: Two-Party Government Comes to the Georgia Legislature

Charles S. Bullock III and Karen L. Padgett

A shift in party control of the state legislature reshapes lobbying and interest group influence over policy outcomes.

The one thing that always follows divided government is the lobbyists always take control of the state of politics. Nothing contradicted that this session; lobbyists got more powerful daily. And I don't want to exaggerate my own importance, but I was more powerful.

anonymous environmental lobbyist

Critical to success for a lobbyist is access to political elites (Truman 1951; Milbrath 1963; Hansen 1991; Wright 1996; but see Browne 1985 for evidence that regular access is not sought by some state lobbyists). A precondition for effective access is for the legislator to trust the lobbyist. Thus, the universal mantra of lobbyists is "never mislead a legislator" (Dexter 1969; Zeigler and Baer 1969; Rosenthal 1993). Development of trust takes time and repeated contacts. Access may be established through activities ranging from purely social interactions to doing favors to sharing information (Dexter 1969; Schlozman and Tierney 1986; Nownes and Freeman 1998b). Increasing demands on members of Congress have reduced time for socializing, and ethics rules restrict opportunities for lobbyists to curry favor by providing goods or trips. Trust and access in Washington now largely derive from providing campaign funds or information relevant to a legislator's reelection (Ainsworth 1993; Hansen 1991), policy proposals under consideration (Wright 1990), or constituent preferences (Hansen 1991). Lobbyist-legislator relations at the state level vary: some states emphasize providing information to legislators while in others, socializing remains prevalent.

Lobbyists' relationships with legislators, once established, require periodic nurturing (Hansen 1991). In Georgia, the focus of this study, exchanges involve golf outings, campaign contributions, speaking fees,

From *State and Local Government Review*, 2007.

48

meals, receptions, tickets to sporting events, and access to research materials. One Georgia lobbyist who was interviewed for this study explained that access is gained through making deals and creating friends: "We try to give an information base, but we also recognize and appreciate [that there are] a lot of personal relationships involved." As long as lobbyists and legislators find relationships mutually rewarding, they are likely to be maintained. The longer the relationship exists, the greater the legislator's trust in the lobbyist.

Successful lobbyists identify key decision makers, establish access to them, and then concentrate on influencing them (Dexter 1969; Rosenthal 1993). For their friends in government relations, legislators may be willing to introduce legislation, hold hearings, or block or amend unwanted changes to proposals to render them insignificant. Business groups are especially likely to fight to maintain the status quo (Main, Epstein, and Elovitch 1992). Repeated interactions concerning shared policy objectives may prompt formalized lobbying efforts in which legislators ask colleagues to support policy positions. As Ainsworth (1997) explains, obtaining access and exerting influence are more easily accomplished when the overture is made by a legislator rather than a lobbyist. Under some circumstances, lobbyists, legislators, appropriate bureaucrats, and policy wonks may form a subsystem designed to shape a sphere of public policy (Cater 1964; Freeman 1965; Ripley and Franklin 1990) or become part of an issue network (Heclo 1978; Browne 1986; Walker 1991; Baumgartner and Jones 1993; Berry 1993).

Change threatens the continuation of mutually beneficial legislator-lobbyist relationships and creates uncertainty that lobbyists seek to eliminate (Salisbury 1990). Uncertainty about the locus of power and how to appeal to new legislative leaders increases the workload of lobbyists. Lobbyists must court those who have the newfound potential to affect policies critical to their clients, which demands cultivating new means of access. They must learn the leadership styles, interests, and constituency concerns of those who have gained control of the fate of their clients, with an emphasis on relevant committee chairs (Rosenthal 1993). Appeals are more likely to succeed when lobbyists show that the action sought by the interest group will promote a legislator's objectives. Demonstration of a linkage to the legislator's constituency confers a degree of legitimacy on interest group requests (Kingdon 1973; Wright

1989; Ainsworth 1997) and sensitizes representatives to the potential electoral consequences of their actions (Ainsworth 1995).

This study focuses on the dynamics of the relationships between legislators and lobbyists that result from change in partisan control. The 2002 election ended 130 years of one-party domination in the Georgia General Assembly, resulting in a Republican governor and senate majority and a Democratically controlled House. The shift in government forced lobbyists to forge new alliances. Interest group representatives who had occupied enviable positions in the *ancien regime* scrambled to establish influence with new leaders. In particular, they had to develop relationships with Republicans who were hesitant to rely on lobbyists who for years had been close to Democrats. Lobbyists had to become more involved in the legislative process, which meant that they had to spend more time selling the merits of their proposals rather than depending on a few key legislators' muscle.

The shift in party control allowed more legislators to participate, which paved the way for new entrants into the lobbying profession. In the altered environment, lobbyists with close ties to Democrats encountered obstacles when trying to access GOP leaders. More collaborative lobbying and changes in the distribution of campaign contributions resulted as lobbyists worked to reduce the uncertainty that they now faced.

To get a perspective on how lobbying in the Georgia General Assembly changed, telephone interviews were conducted with 44 lobbyists and 18 legislators.[1] Neither set is a random sample. The respondents included various legislators and lobbyists whose activities in the General Assembly took place before and after the 2002 election. Both chambers were represented among the 10 Republicans and 8 Democrats. Representing interest groups were 27 contract lobbyists, 11 agents of corporations and trade associations, and 6 representatives of public interest groups. Members of the largest lobbying operations were interviewed along with individuals who worked for a single client. Georgia's leading economic interests were represented, as were groups that have no economic clout. The study concentrated on the most active lobbyists and focused less on those who spent little time at the capitol. Lobbyists and legislators were asked a set of open-ended questions about how lobbying had changed as a result of divided government.

LOBBYING IN GEORGIA

Georgia's large legislature (180 representatives and 56 senators) remains relatively unprofessional (Fleischmann and Pierannunzi 1997). Its members earn $16,000 per year and meet for only 40 days per year. The legislature has little staff; most committees having a half-time secretary and an intern. Each chamber's research office has a small but permanent full-time staff. In most years, much of the controversy in the legislature involves the budget. Improving education, limiting health care costs, and maintaining low taxes are continuing items on the General Assembly's agenda.

With staff and private think tanks scarce, lobbyists are critical sources for technical advice on policy content and alternatives and their consequences. Lobbyists and organized groups also represent the interests of citizens before government. As Fleischmann and Pierannunzi (1997, 126) note, the state has a "hybrid political system with interest groups dominating policy at times and complementing (i.e., working with other institutions) on other occasions."

Democrats controlled all aspects of state politics from the 1870s until the 1990s and maintained majorities in both legislative chambers until 2003. Although the lieutenant governor, who presides over the senate, does not run on the same ticket with the governor, the two usually had a good working relationship. Democratic governors typically secured the support of the House speaker for their initiatives. Until 2005 the speaker appointed all House committee chairs and members (including members of the minority party); the lieutenant governor had comparable authority in the senate before 2003. Fleischmann and Pierannunzi (1997, 126–27) sum up the implications of the prolonged power centralization, concluding that "the historical lack of competition among political parties has helped nurture a network of influential interest groups."

During the era of Democratic Party dominance, leading lobbyists sometimes functioned almost as an arm of the party.[2] Powerful lobbyists met daily with the House speaker during the session. These regular meetings enhanced the perceptions of their power and attracted lucrative clients; in return the lobbyists shared information with the leadership while showering Democratic leaders with campaign funds, tickets and junkets. At times, lobbyists were pressed into promoting Democratic policy initiatives, as illustrated by one of the most controversial legislative actions in recent years. Gov. Roy Barnes enlisted the help of leading contract lobbyists to push through a change in the state flag so that the St. Andrew's cross of the Confederacy no longer dominated it.

Most observers expected the Democratic Party to retain the governorship and majorities in both legislative chambers in 2002. Lobbyists spent little time worrying that the ties they had forged with key legislators and the governor would suddenly be devalued. Few lobbyists had begun broadening their networks in anticipation of a new day. Instead, prudent group representatives invested in the future of the Democratic Party by contributing to the unprecedented campaign treasury aggressively amassed by Barnes. Only lobbyists who already had close personnel ties to the GOP contributed to challenger Sonny Perdue.

In 2002, Barnes, who had set the legislature's agenda and used his powers to secure most of his policy objectives (Associated Press 2000), lost reelection. Republicans, who emerged with 30 of 56 senate seats, stripped from the Democratic lieutenant governor control over committee assignments, scheduling, and appointment of conference committees. The 28-year incumbent House speaker lost reelection, although Democrats retained a majority. For the first time in generations, Georgia had divided partisan control.

CHANGING STRATEGIES

After the 2002 elections, the roles of lobbyists in Georgia became more complicated. With divided government came decentralization, and decentralization meant that lobbyists had to interact with more legislators. This study examines how lobbying used to be conducted up until 2003 compared with 2003–4.

Pre-2003

One of the most respected lobbyists interviewed for this study explained how his profession used to work before 2003. "In Georgia, lobbying [meant] meeting with one or two persons in leadership, [getting] their approval, and then…educating members that the leadership is behind this measure. And [the proposal would] pass or die depending on the movement of the leadership." A newspaper wrap-up after the second session of divided control made the same point. "Only two years ago, the General Assembly was the property of a small group of long-serving politicians with near-total control. Negotiations over budgets—and anything else—played out with the ease of a weekly poker game. It wasn't always fair, but it was predictable" (Galloway 2004). The belief that lobbying involved mobilizing no more than a handful of key leaders in the Democratic Party was echoed by nearly all lobbyists, several of whom referred to the approach as "one-stop shopping." "Lobbying is working the leadership because those elites in their respected chambers determined the flow of policy and legislation," said a public interest lobbyist. Some lobbyists referred to this approach as "securing the blessing" that could ward off defeat or modification[.]

When lining up sponsors to introduce proposals, lobbyists would ask a committee chair or a Democratic leader to sign on to a bill. The sponsor, after being educated about the bill's merits, potential opposition to it, and its consequences would speak in behalf of the legislation in committee and on the floor. Lobbyists would monitor the passage of their proposals through committee, trying to help members understand the legislation while discouraging detrimental amendments. Once the legislation passed out of committee, lobbyists usually would rely on the bill's sponsor and chamber leadership to ensure passage. "We stayed in the background, keeping the members pumped up," explained a contract lobbyist.

Many groups sought to maintain the status quo; these efforts had been centralized. If a "friendly" committee chair failed to keep a bill bottled up in committee, a lobbyist would ask the leadership to waylay the bill in the Rules Committee, kill it on the floor, or amend it to eliminate provisions that the client judged to be objectionable.

2003—4

Getting a bill through the General Assembly became more complicated in 2003. According to a contract lobbyist, lobbyists could "no longer depend on one or two people to shepherd their bills through. You've got to go in and work at the subcommittee level. You've got to talk to every member there. At the committee level [it is] the same. You've got to work every one of those members, just like they were the most important person there."

"In the past, people who you would go to just for a courtesy call are now helping us write the legislation," remarked a business lobbyist. According to a trade association representative, "more people have a voice now in the decision-making process. Freshman members are aggressive with their agendas, and as lobbyists, you can't ignore one because you may need his vote." "It takes longer and you have to talk to more people," lamented a senior lobbyist. "In the past all you had to do was talk to the leadership; now the leadership is not in control."

Divided control in the government enhanced the influence of the minority party in the House because senate Republicans could derail bills passed by the lower chamber if the concerns of House Republicans were ignored. Moreover, House Republicans exploited the dispersal of power among Democratic Party factions that resulted from leadership passing to a new speaker. When urban, liberal Democrats disagreed with their conservative, rural counterparts, Republican votes could determine floor outcomes. For example, a unified GOP joined by about half the Democrats passed a constitutional amendment banning gay marriages. Democrats declined to bring to the floor a bill to redraw House districts that had been invalidated by a federal court. Democrats allowed the court to take remedial action because they feared that if a bill came to the floor, Republicans would attract enough Democratic dissidents to hijack the pro-Democratic districting plan.

The need to touch base with more legislators forced lobbyists to spend more time walking the halls, interacting in the capitol and at social gatherings, and becoming familiar with the new leaders, junior members, and the administration. Lobbyists had to not only devote more attention to committee hearings but also draft bills that could stand on merit and that would have bipartisan appeal rather than rely on the reputation of the sponsor. The senate majority whip noted that lobbyists "spend more time coming before committees, educating [them] and showing the merit of bills."

With the chambers controlled by opposing parties, lobbyists worried about lining up sponsors for their bills. Prior to divided control, the identity of a bill's sponsor became a potential problem only when personal rivalries or an abrasive personality made an individual an unattractive sponsor. In the new environment, a legislator's history of partisan conflict became an issue and diminished the allure of some senior members who would have carried legislation in the past. One public interest group lobbyist commented, "We had to be careful who we got to sign on as sponsors so that the sponsor in one chamber [would] not be the kiss of death in the other chamber." "I'm careful not to show partisanship since our issues aren't partisan," a health care lobbyist explained. One Republican contract lobbyist noted that, "With divided control, it is sometimes better to find noncontroversial members in both chambers and start the bill simultaneously."

Furthermore, lobbyists sometimes preferred working with low-ranking committee members who had not been drawn into major partisan battles as opposed to high-profile actors. A new Republican senator concluded that lobbyists were not "using leaders, but asked rank-and-file members to carry bills. As a freshman, I was asked…to work with them on a local legislative matter." This statement contrasts with the more general finding that more experienced lobbyists tend to have the best relationships with legislators (Nownes and Freeman 1998a).

Once appropriate sponsors were identified, lobbyists had to push their bills through the legislature because they could no longer depend on respected Democrats to usher them through. According to one lobbyist, leadership remains important but "there's less assurance that even the most committed leader…is going to be able to help." "It used to be that you knew what would happen on the floor. If a bill came out of Rules [Committee], you knew that the Democrats had decided what they wanted and that they were in control. Now you don't know what will happen on the floor," said an agent for big business. "Nothing is easy. Even the tiniest piece of legislation is difficult to get passed." Moreover, the new leadership had a more transparent operating style and tried to fashion a consensus involving greater numbers of senators rather than rule by fiat.

Although lobbyists applauded certain consequences of the change in senate control, they also expressed frustration. A business representative who pointed to "a huge learning curve for the Republican leadership" said, "Republicans don't control their own caucus in the senate.… You will meet with the senate leadership, and they will make a commitment that they are going to have a vote on a particular issue or amendment the next day. You spend the afternoon polling the membership and lining up votes, but then you get a call at 8 o'clock the next morning and they say they are not going to bring the issue to the floor. They won't stand up for you. After making a commitment to have a vote, they don't go full steam ahead on it."

Increased uncertainty about the fate of legislation, decentralization of power, and the need to at least touch

base with a greater number of members prompted lobbyists to join forces more often than in the past. Approximately three-fourths of the lobbyists in the survey reported a higher incidence of coalition lobbying as Georgia moved in the direction of collaborative efforts that were already widespread in many states (Rosenthal 1993). "In the past," observed an attorney who had corporate clients, "a lobbyist gained access through the influence of money and contacts. Contacts with the speaker, the governor, or the leadership [were] what lobbyists cultivated. Now you have to build coalitions."

Divided control affected the distribution of campaign funds made by lobbyists and their clients. Campaign contributions may not buy favorable outcomes, but they do buy access (Rosenthal 1993; Herrnson 1998). Not surprisingly, most legislators reported that the greatest change in lobbying strategy involved the division of campaign contributions. Barnes and his party leaders had threatened to block access to lobbyists who gave to Republicans rather than Democrats. Now, said a junior Republican, "There is a better balance of campaign contributions. It is easier for Republicans to get money." According to a contract lobbyist, "Both sides are eager for money, and you can't ignore them." To illustrate how majority status helped the GOP, in 2001 only two Republican senators raised $100,000 in campaign funds; in 2003, nine Republican senators surpassed that amount (Salzer 2004).

THE RANKS OF LOBBYISTS

The challenges posed by divided government prompted an expansion in the ranks of those paid to influence public policy. Republican lobbyists hoped to exploit their party's new power and urged the governor and senate leaders to direct business their way. As a model, Republicans pointed to the K Street Project (named for the eponymous street in Washington, D.C.) that was launched after their party took control of Congress in 1994. The project allegedly was designed "to oust the Democrats from top lobbying jobs in Washington" by encouraging lobbying firms to hire Republican sympathizers, thereby granting lobbyists access to important GOP officials (VandeHei and Eilperin 2003). Several lobbyists who had good relationships with key decision makers in the past encountered a wall that prevented some interactions with Republican senate leaders and the new governor. A public interest lobbyist commented, "You could not get into the door. We felt we weren't allowed in the process." "Some Democrats [lobbyists] were scared and saw their careers in jeopardy," said a corporate spokesperson. "People remember who you supported in the past," said an agent for the health care industry. A lobbyist working out of a law firm concurred. "If you are recognized as in bed with one team then when you go to the other team, your plan may run into the wall. You get no traction with that other team."

Very few lobbyists thought Perdue could defeat Barnes in what Sabato (2003, 24) identified as "the GOP's most stunning upset" of 2002. No Georgia governor had been denied a second term, and polls always showed the incumbent running well ahead of the poorly financed challenger. Interest groups responded generously to Barnes's fundraising efforts, which generated more than $20 million—six times what Perdue spent. Few contributors hedged their bets, and many lobbyists refused even to return Perdue's calls. Once they got over their shock, well-heeled lobbyists quickly set out to make amends for their electoral miscalculations. A Democratic legislator spoke dismissively of how lobbyists "scurried to the [new] governor's door after the election with a check and a hand-shake of support." Lobbyists who had supported the Barnes reelection "started unloading money on Sonny and his enormous inauguration," observed a senior Democrat. Several lobbyists who had corporate clients acknowledged making "catch-up" contributions to underwrite the cost of the inauguration.

The impetus to get on Perdue's good side came from rumors that his receptionist maintained a list of those who had snubbed him, with instructions to deny them access. One lobbyist stated, "We were told lobbyists were not welcomed at the governor's office, only to be notified later by his chief of staff that this was a miscommunication." A GOP legislator confirmed lobbyists' perceptions. "Lobbyists had a tough time getting in to see the governor; they didn't know how to get him the information." Another Republican legislator saw the treatment of lobbyists as indicative of an administration that was less accessible than its predecessor: regarding the governor's attitude toward lobbyists, the governor "didn't ignore them or shut the door; he wasn't concerned with them." Explained a moderate Republican, "You don't forget those who supported the opposition, but you try to show them the other side and pull in more support for you if you can. You let them know now who is making decisions."

Some of the problems associated with access to the governor stemmed from the way in which he organized his office and his style of leadership. Even lobbyists who believed they had a close relationship with Perdue during his senate tenure had difficulty seeing the governor. "He had a bunch of new kids in there, and I don't think they really knew what they were doing, but tried to look like they did. Most of the time, responses or requests by a lobbyist were either ignored or they never got to the governor." The executive director of an organization of public officials fretted that Perdue and his staff did not want others to be involved in the decision-making. Several legislators believed Perdue shunned an open-door policy because he wanted to avoid appearing to be influenced by special interests.

Perdue's ideas about the governor's role also influenced his interactions with lobbyists. Perdue had a more restricted agenda than did his two predecessors. During the campaign, Perdue criticized Barnes's involvement in redistricting, education reform, and other items as indicative of a power-hungry tyrant. In other ways, "He is a hands-off governor," said a Democrat of Perdue. "He didn't come to committee meetings; his staff didn't interact with legislators. He gave us an issue to handle without an idea of his position." Perdue deferred to the legislature to the extent that he refused to veto a bill opposed by business interests, explaining to a lobbyist that if the General Assembly insisted on passing bad legislation, he would let some of it become law. Although partisanship played a role, Barnes's former chief of staff was not alone in criticizing Perdue for attending the NCAA Final Four and the Braves opening game and going home early as the legislature struggled with the budget, education funding, and other issues in the closing days of the 2004 session (Kahn 2004).

It would be inaccurate, however, to paint Perdue as a mere bystander. He actively courted Democrats by offering them inducements to change party and successfully wooed four senators and five representatives. When the legislature failed to follow his lead in arranging financing for a new indigent defense program, Perdue called members back into special session.

Increasingly lobbyists thought companies and organizations "need to have two lobbyists—one with Democratic partisanship and the other tied to the Republicans." A staunch Democrat employed by a large law firm explained that his employer met this need for balance, citing the example of a senior partner who was a leading figure in Republican circles. A contact lobbyist noted the need for three-person operations with a separate agent to work with the 50-member Georgia Legislative Black Caucus.

New firms led by Republican former legislators, campaign managers, and activists emerged to exploit divided government. "We've seen a little infusion of what I sometimes call 'wonder boys'—these new guys with this Republican administration and senate," said the leader of one of the premier contract lobbying firms. "Guys showing up that have never had much lobbying experience but do have some access with some of the leadership—they showed up, setting up shops."

The new Republican operatives solicited clients, claiming that lobbyists with close ties to the previous administration lacked credibility with its successor. "One of the biggest problems," according to a veteran lobbyist, "was all the pure, absolute, dedicated Republican young guys who thought they were going to run in and take everybody's clients." "Now some of these new 'wonder boys' and the shops they work for are inclined to try and take business away from people. That is something we have not seen before, because there's sort of a code amongst lobbyists that you don't solicit business from another lobbyist's client base unless someone is ready to make a move." Some of the new Republican-oriented firms have since flourished and succeeded in luring a share of the business away from established operators who prospered in the past.

Several Democrats reacted to the altered environment by criticizing what they saw as partisanship in the lobbying profession. In the monochromatic Democratic era, these lobbyists perceived little partisanship. Now, Democrats were unsettled by the discordant tones of Republicans. A senior urban Democrat characterized changes in the following manner, "Lobbyists try to be neutral, but this year we saw many firms hurrying to hire new Republican-leaning lobbyists or lobbyists with Republican access." An urban liberal remarked, "Some lobbyists just came out suddenly for the Republicans, which showed some officials that these participants weren't staying neutral anymore."

Objective measures indicate that the lobbying corps grew with divided government. According to an ethics commission official, from 2000 through 2002, Georgia had "approximately 1,000 registered lobbyists, but in 2003, [there were] 1,400 registered lobbyists" (Bonnie Reid, Georgia State Ethics Commission, telephone interview February 26, 2004). Although there is no evidence that the new practitioners were Republicans, the increased numbers jibe with claims that divided government created new opportunities, perhaps similar to those made available by the K Street Project initiated by the GOP in 1994.

INTEREST GROUP INFLUENCE

Scholars of lobbying note the difficulty in determining what role interest group representatives play in shaping legislation (Nownes 2001). Zeigler and Baer (1969) concluded that most legislators view lobbyists as "informants" who provide necessary technical information on policy. In contrast, lobbyists characterized themselves as "persuader[s]...trying to influence the legislators' decisions on policies" (1969, 107). Hansen (1991) noted that when groups acquire information and money, they achieve influence and rarely apply pressure (see also Wright 1996). Given these differing opinions, Georgia lobbyists who claimed more opportunities after 2002 might have perceived themselves as having more influence than they actually did. Half the lobbyists who felt they had gained power with divided government pointed to "the uncertainty in leadership decisions, no set agenda on the House side, and the ability to play a chamber against the other chamber."

Some lobbyists noted a leveling of the playing field. An agent whose firm prospered as a result of the shift in party control stressed that "in the past, the same people always won." Even a senior lobbyist with impeccable Democratic credentials was optimistic: "I always liked [former Speaker] Tom Murphy, but with him gone it makes it easier for me. I wasn't an ex-legislator so I wasn't one of his favorites." Thus, the evaluations of how lobbyists' influence changed under divided government did not simply parallel party lines. Some Democrats lacked clout in the era of Democratic hegemony, and they—along with the Republican upstarts—found the dispersal of power to their liking.

Whether a lobbyist felt more powerful may have depended on the client's objectives. Divided government helped interest groups who favored the status quo. Uncertainty created by new officeholders who were learning new roles and the increased number of legislators who could affect outcomes expanded the opportunities for those who wished to stall action. Heightened partisanship further abetted the agents of inaction. Legislators described Georgia's new political environment as "heated," "tense," and "more political and partisan-driven."

Groups seeking change confronted a system in which stasis was more likely. The General Assembly failed to deal with ethics reform, tort reform, increased funding for health care, more support for education, funding of a statewide system to provide indigent defense, and even court-mandated redistricting during the first biennium of divided government. The paralysis became so pronounced that in 2004, the legislature failed to enact a balanced budget—the one piece of legislation that must be passed each year—necessitating a special session.

CONCLUSION

As of 2003, the old system of Georgia state government in which a few powerful Democrats determined the fate of legislation ceased to exist. The two-party competitive system in Georgia allows greater numbers of interest groups and their representatives to affect state policy. Some groups pursued access by employing new agents while others retained firms that expanded their operations to include people with GOP connections. Many lobbyists embarked on a crash course in broadening contacts in a furious effort to obtain access as they recalibrated their efforts to devote more attention to Republicans or give more generously to the emerging party. Chances for new operatives and the entire lobbying community to act in different ways arose in response to the demise of an entrenched system with which many had been comfortable.

Lobbyists have had to be more vigilant in keeping up with bills throughout the enactment process and can no longer simply rely on endorsements by the governor, lieutenant governor, speaker, or committee chairs to guarantee outcomes. They have had to pursue access more aggressively and meet with the leaders of every legislative faction to educate them about the issues. Formerly, when power was centralized, interactions between legislators and lobbyists involved invitations to dinners, tickets to sporting events, golf outings, and visits to hospitality suites, but there has been a notable decline in such perks (Smith 2004). Instead, lobbyists must have more substantive knowledge and stress the merits of their proposals to the new generation of leaders.

To the extent that "what you know" supplants "who you know" as a criterion for successful lobbying, opportunities for new types of lobbyists have emerged. Repre-

sentatives of groups who heretofore lacked the resources to maintain a hospitality suite, host a reception, or take legislators to dinner may find legislators more receptive to lobbyists who are able to supply valuable information than to well-heeled operatives. The new atmosphere, in which the provision of information is emphasized, also may be conducive to the participation of women lobbyists, who formerly tended to be excluded when camaraderie served as the basis for successful interest group representation.

It is likely that a diffusion of power similar to what occurred in Georgia accompanied the end of one-party politics in other southern states, 10 of which already have seen divided control between the legislative and executive branches (Georgia was the last southern state to elect a Republican governor). Six southern states have experienced a period of divided control in their legislative chambers. This study captured the immediate consequences of partisan transition in Georgia. Should the opportunity arise, researchers may wish to study such transactions in the four states in which Democrats have maintained control of both legislative chambers since Reconstruction.

Notes

1. The survey instrument is available from the authors.
2. The ties between most successful Georgia lobbyists and the Democratic Party were stronger than those between the Farm Bureau and the GOP in the 1950s (Hansen 1991). Linking its fortune to one party caused problems for the Farm Bureau, as it did for many Georgia lobbyists when the Democrats lost their political edge.

References

Ainsworth, Scott H. 1993. Regulating lobbyists and interest group influence. *Journal of Politics* 55:41–56.

———. 1995. Lobbyists as interest group entrepreneurs and the mobilization of union veterans. *American Review of Politics* 16:107–29.

———. 1997. The role of legislators in the determination of interest group influence. *Legislative Studies Quarterly* 22:517–33.

Associated Press. 2000. Barnes still unbeaten halfway through a second year. *Athens Banner-Herald*, March 22, 6B.

Baumgartner, Frank R., and Bryan D. Jones. 1993. *Agendas and instability in American politics*. Chicago: University of Chicago Press.

———. 1993. Citizen groups and the changing nature of interest group politics in America. *Annals of the American Academy of Political and Social Sciences* 528:30–41.

Browne, William P. 1985. Variations in the behavior and style of state lobbyists and interest groups. *Journal of Politics* 47:450–68.

———. 1986. Policy and interests: Instability and change in a classic issue subsystem. In *Interest group politics.* 2nd ed., ed. Allan J. Cigler and Burdett A. Loomis. Washington, DC: Congressional Quarterly.

Cater, Douglass. 1964. *Power in Washington.* New York: Random House.

Dexter, Lewis Anthony. 1969. *How organizations are represented in Washington.* Indianapolis: Bobbs-Merrill.

Fleischmann, Arnold, and Carol Pierannunzi. 1997. *Politics in Georgia.* Athens: University of Georgia Press.

Freeman, J. Leiper. 1965. *The political process.* 2nd ed. New York: Random House.

Galloway, Jim. 2004. Partisan chaos the new normal for legislature. *Atlanta Journal-Constitution,* April 11, A1, A15.

Hansen, John M. 1991. *Gaining access.* Chicago: University of Chicago Press.

Heclo, Hugh. 1978. Issue networks and the executive establishment. In *The new American political system,* ed. Anthony King, 87–124. Washington, DC: American Enterprise Institute.

Herrnson, Paul S. 1998. Interest groups, PACs and campaigns. *The interest group connection,* ed. Paul S. Herrnson, Ronald G. Shaiko, and Clyde Wilcox. Chatham, NJ: Chatham House.

Kahn, Bobby. 2004. Perdue's power grab transparent. *Atlanta Journal-Constitution,* April 13, A11.

Kingdon, John. 1973. *Congressmen's voting decisions.* New York: Harper Row.

Main, Eleanor C., Lee Epstein, and Debra L. Elovitch. 1992. Georgia: Business as usual. In *Interest group politics in the southern states,* ed. Ronald Hrebner and Clive S. Thomas, 231–48. Tuscaloosa: University of Alabama Press.

Milbrath, Lester W. 1963. *The Washington lobbyist.* Chicago: Rand McNally.

Nownes, Anthony J. 2001. *Pressure and power.* Boston: Houghton Mifflin.

Nownes, Anthony J., and Patricia K. Freeman. 1998a. Female lobbyists: Women in the world of "good ol' boys." *Journal of Politics* 60:1181–1201.

———. 1998b. Interest group activity in the states. *Journal of Politics* 60:86–112.

Ripley, Randall B., and Grace A. Franklin. 1990. *Congress, the bureaucracy, and public policy.* 5th ed. Pacific Grove, CA: Brooks/Cole.

Rosenthal, Alan. 1993. *The third house.* Washington, DC: Congressional Quarterly Press.

Sabato, Larry J. 2003. *Midterm madness: The elections of 2002.* Lanham, MD: Rowman and Littlefield.

Salisbury, Robert H. 1990. The paradox of interests in Washington, DC: More groups and less clout. In *The new American political system.* 2nd ed., ed. Anthony S. King. Washington, DC: American Enterprise Institute.

Salzer, James. 2004. Lawmakers spread campaign wealth around. *Atlanta Journal-Constitution,* March 24, A1, A7.

Schlozman, Kay Lehman, and John T. Tierney. 1986. *Organized interests and American democracy.* New York: Harper and Row.

Smith, Ben. 2004. Assembly cleans up act, say legislators. *Atlanta Journal-Constitution,* April 4, C1, C7.

Truman, David. 1951. *The governmental process.* New York: Knopf.

VandeHei, Jim, and Juliet Eilperin. 2003. Targeting lobbyists has GOP payoff. *Washington Post,* June 26. www.washingtonpost.com.

Walker, Jack L. 1991. *Mobilizing interest groups in America: Patrons, professions, and social movements.* Ann Arbor: University of Michigan Press.

Wright, John R. 1989. PAC contributions, lobbying, and representation. *Journal of Politics* 51:713–19.

———. 1990. Contributions, lobbying, and committee voting in the U.S. House of Representatives. *American Political Science Review* 35:417–38.

———. 1996 *Interest groups and Congress: Lobbying, contributions and influence.* Boston: Allyn and Bacon.

Zeigler, Harmon, and Michael Baer. 1969. *Lobbying: Interaction and influence in American state legislatures.* Belmont, CA: Wadsworth.

11

King of the Road

Alex Marshall

Small government advocates oppose public transportation but favor big spending on public highways.

The ancient Romans had a saying: To make a road straight, you need to make someone's neck crooked. This chilling refrain is a vivid summing up of an obvious fact: Building a road is a manifestation of power, particularly state power. Carving a road across multiple jurisdictions and property lines—not to mention varying terrain—can be done only by an institution that can override the wishes of any one individual.

This was true in the days of the Roman Empire, when mighty roads were built so well that many of them still exist. And it's true today. In the exercise of that authority, local, state and federal governments spent more than $150 billion on roads in 2005, according to the most recent federal Highway Statistics report. That's comparable to what we spend annually on waging war in Iraq.

Given all this, I find it exceedingly strange that a group of conservative and libertarian-oriented think tanks—groups that argue for less government—have embraced highways and roads as a solution to traffic congestion and a general boon to living. In the same breath, they usually attack mass-transit spending, particularly on trains. They seem to see a highway as an expression of the free market and of American individualism, and a rail line as an example of government meddling and creeping socialism.

Among the most active of these groups is the Reason Foundation, a self-described libertarian nonprofit organization with a $7 million budget that has its own transportation wing. Some typical highway-oriented papers on Reason's Web site include "How to Build Our Way Out of Congestion" and "Private Tollways: How States Can Leverage Federal Highway Funds." Rail transit is taken on in papers with titles such as "Myths of Light Rail Transit,"

From *Governing*, April 2008.

and "Rethinking Transit 'Dollars & Sense': Unearthing the True Cost of Public Transit." I didn't see any papers about unearthing the true cost of our public highway network.

Many of the authors of these studies are a rotating cast of writers who pop up again and again, including Randal O'Toole and Wendell Cox. They "extol the autonomy made possible by automobiles" wrote fellow libertarian and New York Times columnist John Tierney in a 2004 article on the subject. Tierney calls them, including himself, "the autonomists." That is, libertarians who have embraced highway spending, although they focus more on the individually-bought car, not the government-built road it requires.

Reason Foundation's founder and former president, Robert Poole, leads the group's Transportation Studies wing, and it's clear he has a special love of the subject. He has authored many studies himself, and he puts out the Surface Transportation Innovations newsletter. In an interview, I ask him to square Reason Foundation's support for roads with its general dislike of government involvement.

"I'd never thought about it that way," he says. Poole insists Reason doesn't want to eliminate government from transportation. "We aren't going to have competing companies putting roads in where they like, and letting the chips fall where they may. We aren't anarchists."

But the organization does have a general premise, which, Poole says, "is that transportation infrastructure would work better if it were market-driven. Where it's possible, that infrastructure should be run in a business-like manner with users paying full cost."

All of this sounds good but is essentially incorrect. Transportation is like education: It works best through heavy general funding that pays off down the road in a community's or nation's overall prosperity. Our national road system would never have been built if every street were required to pay for itself.

Governments at every level have put in several trillion dollars' worth of roads over the past century. This system, open to all with a car, has created our automobile-based landscape of suburbs, single-family homes, office parks, mega churches and shopping malls. Love it or hate it, it is the product of massive government spending. As others have pointed out, the national road system is one of the most successful examples of pure socialism to be found: a comprehensive public system, well-used, almost entirely paid for with tax dollars.

Some of Reason's transportation ideas, such as truck-only toll lanes and congestion pricing, are worth considering. But the systematic bias in favor of roads and against mass transit makes the foundation's work suspect. City and state officials, who are frequently confronted with its studies, should view the work skeptically.

12

Confluence of Interest

Tom Arrandale

Grassroots interest groups help keep the nation's waterways clean, crossing political boundaries to protect the environment.

B ack in the summer of 1966, a rock group named the The Standells enjoyed their only major hit, "Dirty Water." The words were inspired by Massachusetts' befouled Charles River, a winding 80-mile-long stream that runs through Boston's high-tech suburbs, separates Boston and Cambridge and empties into Boston Harbor. The Red Sox still play the song to celebrate each home victory in Fenway Park. But the lyrics no longer fit the river itself: Most days, the Charles is safe enough for residents to swim and boat in its waters.

Of course, Cleveland's Cuyahoga River no longer catches on fire, either. All around the nation, water quality has improved since federal and state regulators began enforcing the Clean Water Act of 1972. But there's something more behind the Charles' remarkable comeback: Vigilant citizens, organized along the length and breadth of the watershed, are leading the charge to finish restoring their hometown river to its natural state.

Near Boston, those efforts have been orchestrated by the Charles River Watershed Association, a 40-year-old nonprofit group. Governance of the densely populated region, with some 900,000 residents, is divided among 35 cities and towns. But arguably no other institution, not even federal or the state government, has done more to clean up what had been one of the country's most polluted urban waterways.

CRWA's executive director, Robert Zimmerman Jr., seems an unlikely prospect to be leading revolutionary changes in protecting the environment. Nevertheless, for the past 16 years, the former prep-school headmaster has been recruiting some 1,200 volunteers to clean up the Charles' banks, organizing annual canoe and kayak

From *Governing,*
September 2007.

races, and training the association's 80 members to sample water quality at 37 sites.

Zimmerman also has bolstered the association staff to include eight engineers and scientists to analyze the results to pinpoint where untreated sewage and tainted stormwater runoff discharges into the Charles. Inside the watershed, "we know more—and we can prove what we know—than governments and their agencies," Zimmerman says. With trustworthy data and broad local support, "you get to sit at the table, and you get listened to."

The association put its research to use persuading federal and state regulators to crack down on pollution to make the river safe for swimming and boating. The group has also prodded Massachusetts officials to cap groundwater withdrawals by fast-growing towns that threaten to deplete the river's flow. CRWA's credibility demonstrates how citizen-led organizations are stepping up where the federal-state-local environmental partnership most often breaks down and leaves serious threats to fester beyond the effective reach of government control.

Around the country, federal and state officials concede that they'll never command enough money and manpower—or the uncontested political authority—to complete the job of cleaning up America's impaired waters. Nor can local officials be expected to force their constituents to take on the burden of cleaning up rivers or streams when communities many miles downstream will reap the clearest benefits. To make continued progress, "what you need to do is devise new ways to get local citizens engaged in solving the problem," says William D. Ruckelshaus, who served as the U.S. Environmental Protection Agency's first administrator in the early 1970s. "That's what watershed groups are doing."

LOCAL EYES AND EARS

Nearly four decades after EPA was established, federal and state regulators are still puzzling over how to deal with less visible "non-point" pollutants that run off with the rain from farms, ranches, logging operations, construction projects, streets, parking lots, yards, gardens and other sites. Standard top-down regulation by federal and state agencies is too cumbersome—and often too controversial—to effectively manage cumulative threats that literally come from people's backyards. As Ruckelshaus points out, "the same programs don't work for non-point sources; there's just too many of them."

So governments are turning to the grass roots for help. One approach, being tried all over the country, is to work directly with local citizens who organize themselves along natural watershed boundaries instead of by city, county or state lines. Instead of dictating solutions, government environmental officials now sit at the table with businessmen, farmers, ranchers, loggers, hunters, boaters, hikers and others to seek common ground on protecting the watersheds in which they live and work. Governments "have never had and never will have all the resources to do what the public expects and law clearly requires," says Don Elder, director of River Network, a clearinghouse in Portland, Oregon, that assists local groups around the country. "They need eyes and ears in the watersheds."

Carol M. Browner, Clinton's EPA chief, called that "place-based" environmental protection; similarly, the Bush administration's "collaborative conservation" initiative defers to local community efforts to deal with environmental issues as close to the ground as possible. Roughly 6,000 watershed groups are now at work to protect rivers that run through industrial neighborhoods in inner cities as well as blue-ribbon Rocky Mountain trout streams. Some gather once a year for trash pickup drives or a stream-bank restoration work day, but about 3,500 have established formal structures supported by private donations, foundation grants and government fiscal and technical assistance. The Oregon Legislature created and funds groups in all the state's watersheds; Washington State gives watershed-level organizations key roles in implementing growth management and salmon recovery programs.

Some groups operate like conventional environmental advocates, but many prefer to partner with other interests to build community consensus on balancing environmental and economic needs. Their focus goes beyond "not-in-my-backyard" resistance to a single landfill or sewage plant. At both the federal and state levels, environmental authority remains split between natural resource and wildlife conservation departments and pollution-control agencies with much different cultures and responsibilities. While government regulators are still bogged down writing pollution permits and fining violators, many watershed groups are working out common-sense local solutions to meet national environmental goals more effectively — then persuading governments to go along.

PUSHING THE ENVELOPE

After taking charge in 1991, Zimmerman built the Charles River Watershed Association into a $1.5 million-per-year operation that gets roughly one-third of its funding from EPA, as well as state grants for water quality monitoring and analysis. The association staff "brings strong technical skills, credible science and politically astute advocacy to their work," says John DeVillars, the Clinton administration's EPA regional director for New England who now sits on the CRWA board.

Twelve years ago, DeVillars approved the "Clean Charles 2005" initiative, which committed the feds to working with state and local agencies, the association and other stakeholders. Although the effort fell short of making the river fully safe for swimming within a decade, during that period EPA's scorecard grade climbed from D to B+. In addition to detecting illegal discharges, the association works with state regulators to devise a total maximum daily load (TMDL) limit for nutrients discharged to the river. It surveys the shoreline after heavy rains to target polluted storm water, and is collaborating with federal and state regulators to tighten controls on combined sewer overflows. CRWA "is willing to work with the agencies," says William Walsh-Rogalski, an EPA attorney. "There are times they give us a kick, but it's usually for a good purpose."

Once you look at an entire watershed, Zimmerman notes, you see connections that governments often miss. EPA focuses on water quality, for instance, while state agencies deal with water supplies. To clean up Boston Harbor, EPA and Massachusetts agreed to build the huge Deer Island sewage treatment plant that will collect and treat wastewater from 48 towns for discharge into the ocean. But the region relies primarily on groundwater for drinking, and it is losing 180 million gallons every day that seep through cracked pipes into the centralized sewage system. Zimmerman points out that cleaning up the river won't accomplish much if stormwater systems and leaky sewers keep diverting so much water from the river. In effect, he argues, "we're dewatering eastern Massachusetts with a solution to the Boston Harbor problem. The solution to a symptom is creating an environmental disaster of the first order."

To help stem groundwater losses, CRWA joined with the Boston-based Conservation Law Foundation in a lawsuit that has forced Massachusetts to prohibit town drinking-water systems from pumping more than 65 gallons per person from groundwater wells per day. That success now puts the association at odds with local governments looking to drill new wells to supply growing populations. Franklin, Massachusetts, town manager Jeff Nutting has lived his whole life within a half mile of the Charles, and he once was a CRWA member. He thinks the association went too far by singling out local water utilities in its efforts to restore the watershed. "They have a right to push the envelope, but they don't have to answer to the ratepayers, and we do," Nutting says. "Their goal is to have trout in the Charles, and that will take an act of God in my view."

The way EPA's Walsh-Rogalski sees it, "groundwater recharge is a state issue, and we don't think about it a lot. But Zimmerman is really good at pushing the envelope, in this case to bring recharge and water withdrawals together. It's a good example of how a local watershed group can bridge gaps." EPA New England officials are now encouraging groups along Boston's Mystic River and other heavily urbanized watersheds to emulate CRWA's monitoring and data-collecting model.

Meanwhile, citizen-led efforts in Houston; Portland, Oregon; and Washington, D.C., also are helping to restore degraded river systems. Baltimore and Philadelphia are promoting multi-jurisdictional watershed programs to protect drinking-water sources and manage storm water. Around Birmingham, Alabama, the Cahaba River Society has been working with local governments for 20 years to strengthen sewage treatment and stormwater measures for a watershed that hosts more wild species per mile than any other North American river. The society's board includes engineers, architects and business owners; and Beth Stewart, the director, says the group operates "very much in the consensus model of getting things done."

Two years ago, however, some Birmingham corporations and developers stepped in to stymie local counties' plans for stringent storm-water rules. Stephen Bradley, a public relations consultant there, dismisses the Cahaba River Society as "basically a no-growth group. We don't really trust them." Birmingham business leaders have turned down invitations to discuss their differences, and

Stewart says the society is reassessing its consensus-building strategies.

COFFEE AND CONSERVATION

With rancorous politics and numerous jurisdictions, urban watersheds can be difficult places in which to operate. Rural Western states are even tougher terrain, but in the past 15 years, collaborative groups have sprung up where anti-government sentiments hold sway in some of the region's remote ranching and logging communities.

Montana ranchers, for example, are leading a collaborative campaign to restore the Blackfoot River that Norman Maclean celebrated in his book *A River Runs Through It*. The Blackfoot drains 2,300 square miles in forested mountains just west of the Continental Divide in lightly populated parts of three Montana counties. By the early 1990s, ineffective federal and state laws left the Blackfoot ecosystem falling apart. Noxious weeds crowded native plants off the range; bull trout and cutthroat trout were disappearing; and Plum Creek Timber Co. was preparing to sell its huge forest holdings to subdivision developers. Ranchers owned crucial wildlife habitat along valley floors, and they were too suspicious of government bureaucracies to cooperate with either federal or state wildlife managers.

Alarmed by talk that Congress could declare the Blackfoot a federally protected Wild and Scenic River, landowners began meeting over pie and coffee at Trixi's Restaurant and Bar in Ovando (population 71). Then they invited government land managers and conservationists to sit in on the discussions. "At first, the government people were there to listen, but as our relationship grew, we started to play more of a role," says Greg Neudecker, a U.S. Fish and Wildlife Service biologist. Eventually, landowners, conservationists, and local federal and state agents formed a nonprofit group called the Blackfoot Challenge to forge mutual strategies for restoring the watershed.

Challenge participants follow what they term "the 80/20 rule," focusing discussions on problems where agreement is likely instead of getting bogged down in battles over a few emotionally charged issues. Now local landowners are working with Trout Unlimited, a national fishermen's group, to stabilize the Blackfoot's banks and restore its naturally flowing character. It's also teamed with Powell County officials to control invasive knapweed and leafy spurge.

With money from Congress and help from the Nature Conservancy, the Challenge also has brokered a precedent-setting purchase of 88,000 acres from Plum Creek Timber. Most will be turned over to the U.S. Forest Service and state agencies or sold to adjacent ranchers. But the group plans to hold on to 5,600 acres to create a community forest reserve as part of a 40,000-acre cooperative conservation area that will be managed for recreation as well as timber production.

In rural areas such as the Blackfoot, environmental agencies may accomplish more "by being good neighbors, versus telling people what to do," Neudecker says. "Native fish numbers in the Blackfoot have rebounded by 400 percent since the effort started. "You've got to have sound biology to do that, and that's strong evidence that collaborative conservation can work," he adds. "We haven't had a lot of hard-core environmental group action in the Blackfoot. That says something about our approach."

Last year, Harvard University's Kennedy School of Government gave the Blackfoot Challenge an award for innovations in government. The award came with a $100,000 grant that this summer funded workshops for similar groups from eight Western states. Montana alone now has 50 watershed organizations, and state regulators and county conservation districts fund efforts to come up with local approaches to complying with federal water-quality standards. On Montana's Big Hole River, ranchers and fly fishermen banded together to revise irrigation rules to keep enough water flowing during droughts to preserve an isolated Arctic grayling population. The group also persuaded conservative commissioners in three counties to enact setback ordinances that keep trophy homes from encroaching on the river's prized trout fishery.

The Bush administration is promoting collaborative community-level approaches to thinning fire-prone national forests. National environmental organizations, however, remain skeptical that collaborative groups are making much lasting progress. Oregon and California watershed groups faltered after their founders moved on to other challenges. Some academics contend that grassroots, watershed-level cooperation so far has produced more feel-good tales of homegrown cooperative spirit than measurable environmental improvement. Judith Layzer, an environmental policy professor at MIT, says: "You can't just abdicate to local groups and expect the environment to come out better."

PEER PRESSURE

William Ruckelshaus, though, is convinced that enlisting local communities in devising on-the-ground solutions will be crucial to further progress. A Seattle resident since 1975, Ruckelshaus is now leading a bold effort to restore Puget Sound's dwindling Chinook salmon runs that the federal government has listed as endangered.

Joined by former U.S. Senator and Washington Governor Dan Evans, King County Executive Ron Sims and other influential leaders, the former EPA director pulled together a nonprofit alliance called Shared Strategy for Puget Sound. The group then persuaded the National Marine Fisheries Service to let the region try drafting its own salmon-recovery plan instead of imposing federally prescribed habitat restoration measures. With Ruckelshaus actively involved, Shared Solutions spent five years working with the sound's 14 watersheds to draft separate plans for repairing salmon habitat in a 16,000-square-mile region. Some sessions got off to "stiff and accusatory" starts, Ruckelshaus recalls, "but then they started to listen to each other." In 2005, the 14 watersheds' separate proposals were wrapped into a 50-year strategy for bringing the Chinook populations back. NMFS approved the plan in January.

"That's huge, almost epic in scale, and it's amazing they pulled it off," says University of Washington professor Craig W. Thomas, who's studied collaborative conservation initiatives around the nation. Washington Governor Christine Gregoire tucked $50 million into the state's budget to begin implementing the salmon plan, and also named Ruckelshaus to head a state Puget Sound Partnership that will coordinate an $8 billion comprehensive cleanup program. Ruckelshaus acknowledges that monitoring plans for salmon recovery efforts remain "embryonic at this stage." Eight watersheds came up with solid plans, but others "need more work," he adds.

There are signs that county commissioners remain reluctant to follow through. But Ruckelshaus is confident that other watershed councils "will put peer pressure on the watersheds that drag their feet." Federal scientists—including Ruckelshaus' daughter Mary, the chief NMFS biologist for Puget Sound salmon recovery—may well have come up with stronger habitat protection in a federally dictated recovery plan. But William Ruckelshaus contends that "if you can't get the local citizens on your side, you're going to spend all your time in court or the state legislature or Congress fighting with them. That doesn't work for anybody."

The Puget Sound Partnership instead applies watershed collaboration on the largest scale ever attempted. "That makes it doubly difficult: It's complicated to think about what's necessary for an entire ecosystem, and you've got all the jurisdictional and social and economic complications to deal with at the same time," Ruckelshaus says. "It takes people who are willing to try new things from a governance standpoint to address this."

Legislatures

State legislatures are among the least loved government institutions. Approval ratings for these houses of citizen business tend to be on the less generous side of low, and majorities just about everywhere think they could be doing a better job. Ironically, though, legislatures *are* doing a better job. By most measures, they are more accountable, more effective, more diverse, and less corrupt than at any point in the country's history. That fact does little to sway public opinion, however. For example, back in the 1970s Alabama's legislature was judged to be one of the worst performing in the nation, yet it had a 65 percent approval rating. Fast forward to the present and the Alabama legislature has improved on virtually every possible performance measure, yet its approval rating has dropped to the mid-20s.[1] Talk about damning with faint praise.

WHAT LEGISLATURES (AND LEGISLATORS) DO

Perhaps part of the reason that legislatures (and legislators) are held in such low regard is that people do not really understand what they do. Legislatures do three basic things: they pass laws, they represent the people, and they oversee public agencies in other branches of government. Sounds fairly simple on paper, but in practice it is a phenomenally complex challenge. A typical state legislature deals with a thousand or more proposed laws in any given year.[2] These bills can cover everything from the death penalty to property taxes and from water regulation to welfare. Legislators, in short, tend to have an awful lot on their plates, and they are expected to be experts on, well, everything.

Representing people is no picnic either. Constituents outnumber state legislators by tens of thousands, even hundreds of thousands, to one. Ever try pleasing a hundred thousand people? Most state legislators would likely tell you not to bother, it can't be done. It does not matter what position you take on an issue or proposed law, chances are somebody in your district disagrees with you and is only too happy to point out your faults on the matter to their friends and neighbors. Keeping an eye on public agencies and employees is another mission impossible; there are, after all, only 24 hours in a day and 365 days in a year, and potentially hundreds of agencies and thousands of employees to oversee.

You might say that passing laws, representing constituents, and keeping an eye on public agencies is a full-time job, but you'd be wrong, at least in some states. Even some states with large populations, like Texas, still have only part-time legislatures. These legislators aren't expected to do any less than their full-time counterparts in other states. They're just expected to do it in less time and for less pay.

In thanks for all this hard work, legislators are generally viewed skeptically and cynically by the public. Evidence of this comes from the success of the term limits movement. In those states with the ballot initiatives, voters have enthusiastically supported limits on the amount of time legislators can spend in office, regardless of how popular they are with their constituents. Now there is an emerging consensus among observers of state government that term limits have hampered the ability of legislators to effectively pass laws, represent constituents, and maintain oversight of the bureaucracy.[3] Voters don't seem to mind, at least not yet. They still seem to view experienced, professional legislators as the greater problem.

RECENT TRENDS

The essays in this section reflect some of the key issues and challenges currently facing state legislatures. Alan Ehrenhalt writes on the difficulty of understanding what a legislature is and what it does, even for skilled observers like award-winning documentary directors. Mikel Chavers essay provides an update on diversity in state legislatures. It's a mixed picture, because while the proportion of female legislators is at a historical high, the numbers seem to have leveled off. As Chavers details, recruiting is key to promoting gender diversity in state capitols.

Tom Stuckey's "day-in-the-life" of a state legislator, in this case Speaker of the Maryland House of Delegates Mike Busch, includes twenty minutes for breakfast and a fifteen-minute break for lunch. In the final piece, Garry Boulard looks at one of the more regrettable, but probably necessary, changes in state legislatures. In a sign of the times, state capitols are becoming more security conscious, and law enforcement personnel are seeking to strike a delicate balance between safety and access.

Notes

1. Alan Ehrenhalt, "An Embattled Institution," *Governing,* January 30, 1997.

2. Kevin B. Smith, Alan Greenblatt, and John Buntin, *Governing States and Localities* (Washington, D.C.: CQ Press, 2005), 178.

3. Alan Greenblatt, "The Truth about Term Limits," *Governing,* January, 2006.

13

Clueless in Boise

Alan Ehrenhalt

A documentary on the
Idaho legislature captures
legislators debating, interest
groups arm-twisting in the
halls, and citizens sleeping
in the public galleries.

There are quite a few public institutions in this country that you can understand pretty well just by watching. Being a fly on the wall is a useful way to study a high school, a housing project or a public hospital. It works for a police department, a juvenile court or a county welfare office. Given enough time to observe people closely, listen to what they say and how they treat each other, one can come to a pretty sensitive understanding of who has the power, who makes the rules and how the rules are enforced.

The reason I'm quite sure of this is that over the past 40 years, every one of those institutions has been the subject of a documentary by the producer Frederick Wiseman, who simply turns on the cameras, watches and listens, edits the film, and provides his audience with genuine insights and remarkable dramatic moments.

From "Titicut Follies," his expose of a Massachusetts mental institution in 1967, through "Public Housing," his investigation of a Chicago housing project, Wiseman has created remarkable movies without the benefit of narrators or even interviews. There isn't much doubt that he is one of the greatest documentary film makers—and one of the more important social critics—of the past generation.

This makes it all the more interesting that Wiseman's newest film, "State Legislature," a close-up of one year's activity in the Idaho Senate and House, is an ambitious flop. When the film is over, you don't really know much more about the Idaho legislature than you did when you sat down to watch. This is true whether you are a state politics buff or an utter novice. You don't learn how power is exercised, who is being treated well or badly, or what the important players are like personally. It's essentially a black box going in and a black box coming out.

From *Governing*,
August 2007.

67

What's the reason? Well, one simple explanation would be that Wiseman has lost his touch. He's 77 years old now; maybe he doesn't possess the ability to create a powerful film the way he did when he was 37 and doing "Titicut Follies." But this is surely wrong: "State Legislature" skillfully uses every one of the standard Wiseman techniques—the revealing close-up photography, the emotional perorations from people who forget the camera is upon them, the trivial but poignant details, such as children singing in the Capitol rotunda or the bagpipe that closes it all out, 217 minutes from the opening scene.

A slightly different explanation might be that Wiseman is still a technical virtuoso, but he no longer has the critical edge that made "Titicut Follies" and "High School" and "Juvenile Court" acknowledged masterpieces. Those earlier films burned with indignation about the injustices inherent in large, impersonal institutions, and the quiet strength of those who did the best they could to survive in Kafkaesque circumstances. "State Legislature" doesn't have any of that: The Idaho House and Senate aren't overwhelmingly just or unjust; the characters are neither noble nor tawdry; without a cause to pursue, one might argue, Wiseman lacks the power to capture dramatic moments.

But I don't really buy that one, either. "State Legislature" has plenty of highly charged scenes: There's the impassioned debate on a gay marriage resolution; the argument in the hallway between a legislator and a pro-immigrant activist; the priceless moment when a senator drones on about how "government belongs to the people" while a citizen spectator snoozes away contentedly in the chair behind him. The parts of the movie aren't all that bad; it's the product as a whole that proves singularly unenlightening. And that's the truly challenging puzzle about "State Legislature."

But it's a puzzle that has a solution. The solution is that while a legislature is a public institution, it differs from a juvenile court or a high school or a mental hospital in a fundamentally important way.

As a fly on the wall in juvenile court, you can learn most of what you need to know from things the judge and the witnesses say, and the way they look and behave. A high school is a place virtually all of us attended and have clear memories of; you watch the students and the teachers and the principal, and you have a context to put them in. For better or worse, you are in a position to form judgments. A mental hospital is a little different; when you come face to face with a paranoid schizophrenic, you can't help wondering how he got that way. But the truth is that the people who work in the hospital don't really know, either. They're a little better informed now than they were in 1967 but not all that much. They're stuck watching the symptoms, just as any of us do when the place is on the screen in front of us.

A legislature isn't like any of these. The public events—the testimony, the floor debate, even the casual conversations in the hallway—bear only a tenuous connection to what is really going on. To understand the place, you need to know about all sorts of things that Wiseman's "direct cinema" technique can't possibly capture. You need to know which party is in control, and by how much. You need to know who the governor is, and how he gets along with the legislators. You need to know what sorts of people these legislators are: not just what they say but how long they have been there, where they come from, what they did before they ran for office and how they got elected.

You learn these things watching "State Legislature" only if they happen to come up in a conversation that made the final cut into the film. The governor of Idaho in 2004 was Dirk Kempthorne, a Republican. I listened to all 217 minutes pretty carefully, and I don't think his name was even mentioned. That year, Republicans controlled the state Senate 28 to 7 and the House 54 to 16. That's not covered, either. Nor was the clearly relevant fact that a term-limit law was passed in 1994 and repealed by the legislature eight years later. And most important, you know virtually nothing about the lives or backgrounds of any of the members, lobbyists or staff aides other than what you can glean from things they say in front of the camera.

Over the past few years, I've written in a couple of places about my fascination with and admiration for the ideas of Lewis Namier, the 20th-century English historian. I don't intend to revisit all the Namierite ideas at great length here, but I can't help thinking that a little bit of Namier would be a big advantage in trying to make sense of "State Legislature."

Namier devoted much of his long career to studying the legislative world. He didn't write a lot about America; his main subject was the British Parliament in the 18th century. But much of what Namier said applies to any democratic legislative body, at any time, anywhere in the world.

Namier's deceptively simple insight was that listening to what legislators or lobbyists or executives say in public is one of the worst ways to figure out what is going on. These people are always making speeches, but the speeches generally reflect what they feel they are expected to say— or what their colleagues or constituents want them to say. To understand a legislative body, Namier argued, one must use different methods. One must find out in detail who the members are: the communities that produced them, the families that raised them and the other families they were close to; where they went to school, what they did in private life before seeking public office.

Namier called this form of investigation "prosopography," a very unwieldy term that simply means "group biography." There have been skillful practitioners of it in Europe for the past half-century, but relatively few on this side of the ocean. Kevin Phillips and Garry Wills are probably the most important Namierites writing about politics today, whether they would accept the description or not. Michael Barone uses the technique effectively in his "Almanac of American Politics." By and large, though, there are few American journalists or scholars willing to take the time to do what Namier and his disciples did for Britain. They simply listen to the speeches and testimony, record them faithfully and pretend they know what is going on.

I first encountered Lewis Namier when I was covering Congress in the late 1970s. Reading a few pages of him made me realize exactly what I had been missing. Speeches on the House floor about farm subsidies or missile defense were window dressing; somebody had to give them to keep the place in session. What really mattered were the relationships: the big-city Democrats who sat together in a corner of the chamber and took their cues from the AFL-CIO; the southerners who rarely said anything on the floor but voted as a bloc on almost any important issue; the minority Republicans who spoke in impassioned terms about the importance of amending a bill but had no intention of supporting it no matter how it was amended.

Why did these people behave this way? The most important answer was that they behaved as they did because of where they came from. As Namier himself put it, "What matters most about political ideas is the underlying emotions, the music—to which the ideas are a mere libretto."

And this is why in the end, "State Legislature" not only doesn't work but couldn't work. Legislative bodies really are different. They're not like schools, or courts, or a welfare office. They're much more complicated places. Anybody who doesn't realize it will fail to understand them. That doesn't apply only to movie producers.

14

Making Their Mark

Mikel Chavers

Female legislators continue to make a difference, even as their numbers stagnate.

The spark started with a small group of women state legislators. They were interested in preventing cervical cancer and increasing screening for it.

But what that spark ignited was something much bigger—something that the women spread to state legislatures around the country.

Because of that interest, the Washington, D.C.-based nonprofit Women in Government began hosting conferences on preventing cervical cancer and exploring its link to human papillomavirus—known as HPV. In spring 2003, a task force met on the issue, dedicated to tackling it head on in state government.

Then in January 2004, the effort officially took off with the organization's Challenge to Eliminate Cervical Cancer Campaign. By the end of the year, women introduced or helped pass legislation on the issue in 15 states.

Most women didn't even know what HPV was, said Kathryn Guccione, associate director of public policy and public relations for Women in Government.

So in August 2004, the nonprofit established a policy resource center with a Web site, background information and access to sample pieces of legislation—all in the name of helping women in state government advance the cause of ending cervical cancer.

And the spark ignited a movement.

Today, all 50 states have introduced legislation or resolutions aimed at cervical cancer prevention, funding for screening, statewide task forces or study commissions, Guccione said.

From *State News,*
April 2008.

ISSUES COME NATURALLY

In fact, women state legislators naturally gravitate to health care and education issues, according to Women in Government. The nonprofit organization reaches an audience of roughly 1,700 women state legislators, and polls a smaller group of members yearly on top issues, according to Guccione. Health care and education are always big issues, she said.

"Women as natural caregivers and as mothers, in terms of caring for their families, are interested in health care," Guccione said. "Women are the primary caregivers—they're making the majority of the health care decisions in their households."

Women naturally were interested in the cervical cancer campaign because it's a women's health issue, said Sen. Connie Lawson of Indiana.

Back in 2002, Lawson attended her first meeting on the cervical cancer effort. The HPV vaccine wasn't even in existence at the time.

"We were concerned about the medical advice that doctors were giving," Lawson said of those days. "We were concerned about whether or not doctors were telling women that there was a new HPV test available."

Lawson formed a task force in Indiana on the issue without legislation in 2003. Then in January 2007, she filed legislation that would require girls entering the sixth grade to be vaccinated for HPV.

Although the attacks on the bill and vaccine requirement seemed to come from every direction, Lawson pushed Senate Bill 327 out of Indiana's Senate with the support of every female senator behind it.

The final version of the bill eventually passed without the vaccine requirement. It does require all public schools in the state to send home a pamphlet to parents prepared by the state hea[l]th department, using the latest scientific information about cervical cancer and HPV, Lawson said.

Rep. Karen Morgan of Utah followed a similar path. First, Morgan sponsored a cervical cancer and HPV awareness resolution in 2004. Then in 2007, she tried to get $1 million from the state to fund a public awareness campaign and also to aid in vaccinations for underinsured women. Although she didn't succeed in getting money from the state, her dream was funded by a private donor.

The $1 million private donation includes funds for HPV and cervical cancer awareness efforts as well as for vaccines for underinsured women.

"It's been a great success," Morgan said.

Sen. Julie Denton of Kentucky received an award from the American Advocates for Health in January for her work on health issues. The award recognized a diabetes bill, which passed nearly three years ago, mandating all public and private schools to have someone on site who can administer special shots to prevent children with diabetes from going into diabetic shock.

For the bill's success, Denton received the Legacy in Public Health Award from the Lexington, Ky.-based not-for-profit association formed to recognize health care contributions and achievements associated with chronic disease.

"I think women—and I think states have proven this-make most of the health care decisions in their families," Denton said. "It's a natural extension with public policy."

In fact, all the women in Kentucky's general assembly received the Health Achievement Award from the American Advocates for Health for their work in diabetes policymaking.

Education is also a natural public policy area for women. Of the eight female governors this year, five have major education priorities and initiatives.

In Arizona, one of Gov. Janet Napolitano's main priorities is education. Among her education achievements, Napolitano has secured raises in teacher pay and also created a new grade level by offering voluntary full-day kindergarten across the state, according to the Arizona governor's office.

In her State of the State speech earlier this year, Napolitano announced her intention to raise the high school dropout age from 16 to 18 years old. She also wants to give students—starting with this year's eighth graders—who agree to stay out of trouble and maintain a B average throughout high school free tuition at any of the state's universities or community colleges, according to the speech.

In Delaware, Gov. Ruth Ann Minner wants to expand one of her biggest education priorities by growing the state's Student Excellence Equals Degree—or SEED—scholarship program, which offers free college tuition to students maintaining at least a 2.5 grade point average and who stay out of trouble.

Minner calls it one of the most important accomplishments of her career in public service, according to the SEED program's Web site.

Women are Making their Mark Across the Country

Making History
North Carolina Lt. Gov. Beverly Perdue

If Beverly Perdue wins the North Carolina governor's race, she'll be the state's first female governor.

Perdue, currently the lieutenant governor, took a unique road to politics. She taught school for three years and, when her husband was serving in the military in Vietnam, she got into aging issues and caring for seniors. From there, she began a lifelong passion for gerontology.

When she moved to New Bern, N.C., in the 1970s, she ran a national program at a local hospital dealing with seniors' health care issues. Then she had an epiphany.

"Well why don't I run for office instead of sitting here complaining about it," she said of the moment of realization back then. "Nobody thought a woman could win then," she said. And when she did, "it was a big deal."

Prior to her election as lieutenant governor, Perdue served in the North Carolina House of Representatives for two terms and the North Carolina Senate for five terms.

But politics to her has never been about being in the minority—it's about hard work.

Today Perdue still focuses hard work on aging issues as well [as] other health care, education, environment and military issues.

"I've morphed over into energy and environment issues," she said. She was also involved in the fight to save her state's military bases during the military base realignment and has maintained an involvement in military issues.

In-Tune
Kentucky Sen. Julie Denton

Kentucky Sen. Julie Denton nearly had her third child at the Capitol.

Denton's water broke when she was in the Kentucky Senate. She was two weeks into the session and her third child was two and a half weeks early.

"I got into the car and drove straight to the hospital," she said. And she barely made it. The trip from the Capitol in Frankfort to the hospital in Louisville usually takes about an hour.

These days, Denton is very in-tune with health care and education issues—she's won an award for legislation on emergency diabetes treatment for children in school.

"For me, I think it's real natural because for the last 20 years, I've been a mom," she said. While at the Capitol,

she tries to make the best of her time so she can get back to her children—now ages 4, 10, 18 and 20.

"I'm not piddling around," she said. "I'm going to go home and cook dinner and do laundry and help with homework and get the clothes laid out for the next day."

Gathering Support
Indiana Sen. Connie Lawson

When Indiana Sen. Connie Lawson filed a bill in 2007 that sought to mandate the HPV vaccine for all girls entering sixth grade, she had no idea she'd find herself in the middle of a heated debate.

The 12-year legislator simply wanted to eliminate cervical cancer in her state.

With her passion, she was able to push the bill—Senate Bill 327—through Indiana's Senate with the support of every female state senator.

In the end, the bill was changed to require public schools to give out educational pamphlets on HPV and cervical cancer to parents, but did not require the vaccination.

"In the end we were successful," Lawson said.

And although Lawson is one of only 28 women state legislators in Indiana, she doesn't feel like a minority. "There's a minority of people who are interested in certain issues," she said. "Women have a better understanding and empathy for families and what families need to go through in order to get along in the world."

Answering the Call
Utah Rep. Karen Morgan

Before Rep. Karen Morgan served five terms in Utah's House, she was recruited to run for a seat in the state's House by a state senator and a state representative.

She answered that call and is now the chair of the board of directors of the national Washington, D.C.-based educational and policy organization Women in Government.

In 2007, Morgan answered another call, this time to eliminate cervical cancer. She went back to her state and tried to get $1 million in state funding for a cervical cancer and HPV educational awareness campaign as well as to fund HPV vaccines for underinsured women.

The state did not fund her bill, but a private donor provided the $1 million for the educational campaign and the vaccines.

The public awareness campaign began last August.

Women in State Government
By the Numbers

1975	Ella Grasso of Connecticut was the first woman elected governor of any state in her own right in 1975.
49	To date, women have been elected to statewide executive offices in 49 states. In Maine, the only statewide elected executive is the governor and a woman has never held the position.
37.8%	The highest percentage of women state legislators in the country is the 37.8 percent in Vermont. The top five states with the highest percentage of women state legislators this year (in order) are: Vermont, New Hampshire, Washington, Colorado and Minnesota.
10	There are 10 female lieutenant governors this year.
8.8%	The lowest percentage of women state legislators in the country is the 8.8 percent in South Carolina. The states with the lowest percentage of women state legislators this year (in order) are: South Carolina, Oklahoma, Alabama, Kentucky and West Virginia.
8	There are eight female governors this year.
2 to 1	Democrat women serving in state legislatures in 2008 outnumber their Republican counterparts by more than 2 to 1.

Source: The Center for American Women and Politics, Eagleton Institute of Politics, Rutgers University.

But beyond those top issues of health care and education, women state legislators are taking an interest in newer issues as well. Every year Women in Government surveys its members, and this year energy efficiency and environmentalism seems to be floating to the surface, Guccione said.

With new interest in topics like energy efficiency, sustainability and environmentalism, "we're going to see a shift in some of the trends," Guccione said.

WOMEN BY THE NUMBERS

And as far as trends, the number of women getting involved in state government speaks volumes. Though the percentage of women state legislators certainly hasn't decreased over the years—it hasn't really been increasing lately either. (Please see related graph.)

There are more women in state government than ever before, but since the late 1990s, the number of women state legislators has virtually stagnated—fluctuating only in miniscule increments of less than 1 percent, according to the Center for American Women [and] Politics at Rutgers University in New Jersey.

"This feels like we've been stuck since 1999," said Debbie Walsh, executive director of the center.

In fact, from 1999 to 2006 women state legislators made up 22 percent of all state legislators in the country, according to the center. That number barely changed during those years—increasing and decreasing by only tenths of a percent, the center reports.

Only last year did the percentage of women legislators in the country increase to more than 22 percent, growing to just 23.5 percent. This year, the percentage of women state legislators is virtually holding steady, according to the center.

Walsh offers several reasons for the stagnation in the percentage of female state legislators. First, term limits have hurt women, she said.

For example, when term limits kicked in during the 1990s in Michigan, the state lost more than half the women in office, according to Walsh.

Since 1993, state senators are limited to two terms of four years each, and state representatives are limited to three terms of two years each.

"If you look at states with term limits, we've lost women in those states. Women benefited in the past from incumbency," she said.

"There's not a bench of women coming in."

Behind the Numbers: Number of Women State Legislators Leveling

Back in the 1980s, the percentage of women state legislators in the country would increase by one or two points every election cycle. But a stagnation of growth started in 1999.

That's according to Debbie Walsh, executive director of the Center for American Women and Politics at Rutgers University in New Jersey.

There are various forces at work here. With term limits, lack of recruitment efforts for women and just the challenges of a tough job with often little pay, the percentage of female state legislators will continue to stagnate, Walsh said.

"All of those things combined make for not a rosy future," Walsh said.

In states like Michigan that have instituted term limits, women are not being replaced by other women, Walsh said. Women benefit from incumbency, she said. According to research from the center, women incumbents win about 95 percent of the time—"you could count on incumbents winning," Walsh said.

More than that, though, there's a problem of simple recruitment.

Walsh sums it up like this: "Women are much more likely than their male colleagues to need to be asked to be in office."

According to the Center for American Women and Politics, women are less likely than men to see themselves as qualified and less likely to be asked by their parties to run for office.

Some states are trying to address that problem. New Jersey, for example, began a program called Ready to Run, a one-day bipartisan training program designed to recruit women state legislators and help them get into office.

In 2004, with its low percentage of female legislators, New Jersey ranked among the lowest in the nation for the number of female legislators. But the 10-year-old program seemed to involve more and more women in state government over time. In 2005, New Jersey was 43rd in the nation for the percentage of women legislators—today the work has paid off and it's 15th in the nation.

Walsh attributes that improvement to the recruitment efforts of Ready to Run, where 70 percent of the graduates of the program have won office, she said.

"Women kind of need that push," she said.

The recruitment program—held at the center—is now branching out to other states, including Iowa and Oklahoma.

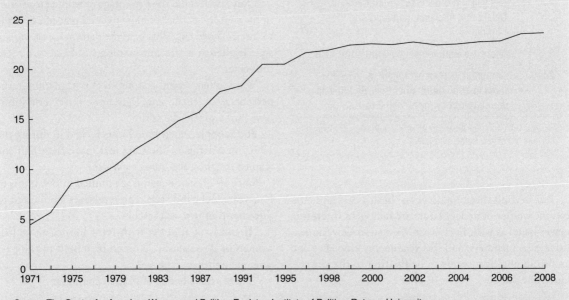

Source: The Center for American Women and Politics, Eagleton Institute of Politics, Rutgers University.

Behind the Numbers: Number of Women State Legislators Leveling (*Continued*)

For of the majority of state legislative seats, however, the job—and pay—is not often full-time, Walsh said. And women are more likely to be the full-time caregiver at home, making it a challenge to serve in state legislatures. Women tend to wait until their families are older, Walsh said, and that adds to the leveling off of women in state government.

And even at a time when Sen. Hillary Clinton is a viable Democratic candidate for president, although inspiring for many women, Walsh believes the media's treatment of her may be discouraging to a lot of women.

Citing the media's treatment of Clinton as an example, Walsh does not believe America is in a period of "post-gender, post-race politics," and "there really is this sort of resistance to it," she said.

But even in the current political climate, women can be seen as a welcome change, Walsh said. In New Jersey, four recent indictments of state legislators resulted in four open seats. All four were filled by women in the last cycle, she said.

"When there's corruption in government, it's interesting, women look like change," Walsh said.

15

Master of Consensus

Tom Stuckey

Mike Busch works for Maryland's Anne Arundel County Department of Recreation and Parks. He also heads the lower house of the state legislature. It makes for a busy day.

Michael Erin Busch was chairman of the House Economic Matters Committee in 2002 and looking forward to four more years when it became clear on Election Night that the incumbent speaker, Casper Taylor, would lose his race. Busch and his aides began making calls that night to line up support for his bid to succeed Taylor, who had been a friend and mentor. They moved so quickly that they had the commitments needed to win the speaker's post before anyone else could mount a serious challenge. Busch was chosen by House Democrats without opposition.

Busch, 60, was elected to the House of Delegates in 1986 to represent a district that includes the Capitol. A high school teacher and coach, Busch jokes that his victory was based on votes from people he had taught or coached, or their relatives.

Busch's job running the House is made easier by the fact that Democrats outnumber Republicans 104 to 37. He has, for the most part, maintained cordial relations with Republicans, although there are occasional dustups with some GOP members over issues such as taxes, gay rights and immigration. Busch and Democratic Senate President Thomas V. Mike Miller maintain a publicly cordial working relationship despite differences over a few hot button-issues such as slot machines, which Miller favors and Busch opposes.

Busch, a graduate of Temple University, works for the Anne Arundel County Department of Recreation and Parks when he is not involved in legislative duties. He and his wife, Cindy, have two daughters, Erin and Megan, and live in Annapolis not far from the Capitol.

From *State Legislatures,* July/August 2007.

MIKE BUSCH'S DAY

7:47 A.M.

Busch begins his day, as he usually does, driving daughter Erin to school. When he drops her off at her public middle school, she leans over, gives him a quick kiss on the cheek and says, "I love you," before jumping out of the car.

8:05 A.M.

Back at his modest shingled house, Busch waits a little impatiently as daughter Megan, a third grader, dashes out to the car. He drives a few blocks to her public elementary school and watches as she walks into the building. "This is the best part of the day," he remarks.

8:24 A.M.

Busch stops at a small deli for his usual morning sandwich—egg, cheese and tomato on a croissant. He settles in at a table inside with his sandwich, a cup of coffee and a newspaper. "Did you see him dip it in his coffee?" one of the regulars teases. Unfazed, Busch continues to dunk his sandwich as he chats with the owner and other customers. The breakfast break—19 minutes today—is a regular part of the speaker's morning routine during the nine months of the year that the legislature is not in session.

8:43 A.M.

Busch returns to the car, which he drives himself even though he has a state police officer at his disposal, and heads for his job, which he calls his real job, at the Department of Recreation and Parks. Like most members of Maryland's part-time legislature, Busch has a second job to help pay the bills.

9:02 A.M.

Busch joins a staff meeting at the agency where he has worked for 27 years; currently he is the assistant to the director.

9:42 A.M.

He slips out of the meeting for a short drive to the State House and the major item on his agenda for the day, a bill signing ceremony with two fellow Democrats—Governor Martin O'Malley and Senate President Miller at 10:00.

10:01 A.M.

Busch swings into his reserved parking place a minute late. (His staff, unable to contact him, is relieved that he has arrived.) As Busch walks into the State House, a reporter grabs him, asking about a Republican lawmaker's complaint about a new Spanish language service planned by Maryland Public Television. Busch is probably the most accessible major public figure in Maryland and rarely fails to answer a question at length.

10:05 A.M.

Busch reaches the ceremonial room on the second floor of the State House for a bill signing that won't start for several more minutes. He is collared by Delegate Curt Anderson, who is collecting money to take about 300 boys and girls to Cooperstown, N.Y., for Cal Ripken's induction into the Baseball Hall of Fame. When the bill signing ceremony starts, O'Malley offers Miller and Busch a chance to speak. Miller demurs. Busch talks briefly, praising the legislature for passing a state living wage law, the first of its kind in the nation. Busch, Miller and the governor spend more than an hour signing 203 bills passed by the 2007 General Assembly.

11:43 A.M.

When the ceremony finally ends, Busch walks down a flight of stairs on the way to his office but stops when he sees a group of elementary students peering through the door into the House of Delegates chamber. Busch invites them in, seats them in chairs normally used by members and gives an impromptu lecture on state government. "I always love to talk to the kids. I'm an old history teacher," he explains.

11:52 A.M.

Busch meets privately with Delegate Nancy King. After the meeting, Busch goes over his schedule, signs citations and letters, and talks to his staff about invitations to future events. Busch goes over emails that have been printed out by his staff. There is a notebook computer on his desk, but he doesn't even turn it on during the almost four hours he will be in the office. Asked why he doesn't make more use of electronic devices, he says: "I have good staff. I call people on the phone." He is also wary about the potential use of the public information law to access electronic records that would open up his family to public scrutiny.

12:35 P.M.

Busch gives an interview to a reporter for his local newspaper, then meets with Steve Carr, community liaison with the State Highway Administration. Carr has come to talk about community outreach, but he is a local political activist, and the two men spend most of their time chatting about Annapolis city politics.

1:20 P.M.

Busch takes a brief break for lunch—tuna salad on lettuce with crackers and a Pepsi. But he's a Coke drinker, and he kids his staff about running out of his favorite drink.

1:35 P.M.

Busch begins a light afternoon schedule with a meeting arranged by Nick Manis, a lobbyist who played high school basketball for Busch. Manis brings in representatives from a computer-learning company based in Texas who are talking to Maryland schools about using their products. They don't ask for any favors, but spend about 15 minutes talking to Busch about their learning programs and how they can help improve student performance.

3:05 P.M.

Busch meets with William Dabbs, his doctor, who has asked for an appointment to exchange ideas about problems facing health care providers. Health care is one of the speaker's favorite topics, and the two men spend about 20 minutes talking about what the state can do to improve the system and help doctors.

3:35 P.M.

Busch walks two blocks to a Senate office building where there is a small gym with exercise machines and treadmills. He spends more than half an hour lifting weights while watching a poker tournament on TV.

4:20 P.M.

Busch leaves the gym for the walk back to his car and then the short drive home, where a state trooper will drive him to the final event of the day, a speech on global warming by former Vice President Al Gore at the University of Maryland at Baltimore County. Before the speech, Busch and his wife, Cindy, attend a reception and dinner for Gore given by university officials.
From *State Legislatures,*

Provide Balance

"The legislature is like a school and the speaker is the principal. You are responsible for everything that takes place."

Speaker of the Maryland House of Delegates,
Michael Busch

On Achieving Consensus:

"Consensus is my goal. I can't force anybody to do anything. Everybody is elected. They can replace all of us in leadership at any time if they want to. My job is to provide the information and build consensus. My job as presiding officer, along with the governor and the Senate president, is to provide balance. You try to come to a consensus if you can."

On Accessibility to His Members:

"I hope they feel comfortable around me and that they believe I'm fair. They can walk into my office and talk to me at any time. No. 1, they deserve that. No. 2, that's how you achieve consensus."

On Dealing with Republicans:

"I appreciate the role the minority caucus plays. They have to question the majority. If they make logical arguments in opposing us, it makes the members question what we do. The important thing is that they feel included in the process and in the committee process. It's important to have dialogue from both political parties." Busch says that out of about 1,500 bills introduced each year in the house, "probably only 20 to 30 a year break down on party lines." Busch said Republican bills get the same treatment in committee as bills by Democratic lawmakers. "I never tell a committee chairman, 'Don't vote on so and so's bill.'"

On How He Persuaded House Democrats to Vote for a Major Tax Package:

"I began with meetings with core leadership, then expanded out from there to include vice chairs, whips, minor committee chairs, then to the entire Democratic

Provide Balance (*Continued*)

caucus." The tax program was Busch's alternative to slot machine legislation supported by Senate President Thomas V. Mike Miller and then-Gov. Robert L. Ehrlich as a way to pay for the school funding reform. Not only did Busch ask his caucus to support what would have been the largest tax increase in state history, he did it knowing that Senate leaders had already sent clear signals the bill would die if it was sent to them by the House. "To get 75 people to vote for that, I had to make them believe that was the only way to pay for reform. Everybody knew slots were not the answer," Busch said. House Majority Leader Kumar Barve said the tax bill exemplified Busch's leadership style. "He overwhelms his caucus with information and persuades them with intellectual brute force."

On His Mentors:

Busch considers Robert Pascal, a former Republican county executive, and former Democratic House Speaker Casper Taylor as the major influences on his career. Pascal encouraged him to enter politics, despite the difference in political parties. "I admired his accessibility and the way you always felt he identified with you. You could leave Bob Pascal's office when he told you 'No,' and you still felt he understood you. Cas Taylor was probably the most gracious person I've ever known in public life. He was very good to me."

16

Statehouse Security

Garry Boulard

Balancing access and security is becoming a tough call in legislatures across the country.

When Scott Renfroe visited the Colorado Capitol before his election as a state senator in 2006, a highpoint was always entering the ornate 1890s building through its grand front doors.

"Looking up high and seeing that gold dome with the flags flying around it was really very exciting," says Renfroe. "And then to walk up the front steps and go inside without anyone questioning you about why you were there made you feel that the government was accessible to anyone. That's the way it should be."

But that kind of open access may soon be over. In early September, Colorado Governor Bill Ritter announced a proposal that would require visitors to enter the building through only the side entrances where X-ray machines, magnetometers and a detail of security officers would be in full use.

Ritter also proposes beefing up the Colorado State Police security detail in the statehouse as well as installing an X-ray machine and magnetometer inside the Legislative Services Building, which is nearby the Capitol.

"The governor's recommendations are in response to ongoing security concerns," says Captain Mike Savage, a spokesman for the Colorado State Police. "It's an ongoing process designed to make the statehouse as safe as possible for both the people who work here as well as the many who visit."

Security concerns were exacerbated this summer when a 32-year-old man entered the Colorado Capitol and Ritter's office with a loaded .357-caliber pistol and a knife, declaring: "I am the emperor and I am here to take over state government." Aaron Snyder was in the process of being escorted by a state trooper out of Ritter's office

From *State Legislatures,* January 2008.

when he revealed the handgun beneath his coat and moved toward the officer. Ignoring two warnings to stop, Snyder was shot twice and killed.

In the aftermath of that incident, metal detectors, installed after 9/11 but dismantled within the year because lawmakers and visitors said they inhibited access to the Capitol, were re-installed.

SECURITY VS. ACCESS

Such decisions, says Tony Beard, chief sergeant-at-arms of the California Senate and a recognized authority on statehouse security, represent an ongoing debate among lawmakers across the country. What is the most efficient way to make public buildings safe? When is security, in a nation accustomed to government access, too much?

"It is obviously a delicate balance that each state has to maintain," says Beard. In his several decades handling security at the California Capitol he has seen everything from bomb threats, medical emergencies, a hostage-taking to a shoot-out in the basement.

"For us," Beard says, "the debate centers on how to convince lawmakers that equipment like magnetometers is not designed to inhibit or stop people from coming into the building. It is there to enhance the safety of the people who work in and visit the building."

Yet Beard admits that even in a building where magnetometers and X-ray machines are highly visible, and complemented by a security staff in excess of 60 people, the idea of the totally open-door statehouse remains powerful. "People just want to believe that they can walk into their capitol and talk to a lawmaker or any other official and not have to be stopped at any point and show their identification," says Beard. "That is a very powerful and honored tradition in our country and one that no one wants to see die."

And in states where the open town hall is among one of the most cherished principles of the local political culture, the challenge is even greater. "It is almost impossible to talk about enhancing security in our statehouse without people becoming extremely agitated," says Senator Susan Bartlett of Vermont.

"We have always taken great pride in having all the doors of our capitol open to anyone who wants to visit. It's an important part of our heritage," she says.

"So when you talk about maybe confining that access to just one door and having it manned by security, a lot of people here don't see that as a good thing designed to protect them," adds Bartlett, "but rather as a bad thing that is taking away one of their rights."

THE RIGHT TO BEAR ARMS

The question of rights also revolves around the issue of bearing arms and whether or not anyone besides security officers should be allowed to bring a weapon into a statehouse. "Other people in other states may not think this is a big deal," says Indiana Senator Thomas Wyss, who is a member of the Indiana Legislature's counter-terrorism and security council and has played a vital role devising new security rules for the Indiana Statehouse. "But this is a matter of tremendous importance for us here. We have had judges and lawmakers who for years have been legally licensed to carry their own weapons and have done so in the capitol."

Although a compromise was eventually reached allowing those legislators and judges to continue to bring their weapons into the Indiana statehouse, which is also the home of the state's supreme and appellate courts, Wyss says the lesson learned was a good one. "You don't want to launch any kind of new security program when you know that all it's going to do is get people angry. You have to be sensitive. In order for any program to really work it has to have the support of the people who are most affected by it."

The same principle may apply to the issue of access, thinks Bartlett. "The emphasis has to be on how to make the people coming into the capitol more safe and not on how some new procedure is going to make access more difficult. If people get the idea that you are doing anything that is somehow or other taking away one of their rights, it's going to be a disaster."

LITTLE OPPOSITION

So far, organized opposition to enhanced statehouse security from civil liberties advocates has been minimal. "I know that in different states our chapters have had questions, but in no state that I know of have we ever officially come out against any program to make state capitols more secure," says Liz Rose, a spokeswoman for the American Civil Liberties Union in New York. "The thinking is that these legislatures have really been trying to do a good job balancing questions of access with legitimate security needs.

"There is a feeling that putting up things like metal detectors, for example, does not prevent citizen access or really even make that access significantly more difficult," Rose says. "Essentially the measures we've seen at the statehouse level balance freedom and safety in a way that we have so far been willing to live with."

Similar balances regarding any number of security issues can also be found if lawmakers, when contemplating statehouse security upgrades, call in as many experts as possible to talk about the advantages and pitfalls of increased security manpower and equipment, according to Kansas Senator Jay Emler.

"This is an area where it pays to get a lot of advice," says Emler, who serves as the chairman for the Joint Committee on Kansas Security. His committee must review and make recommendations on the safety of the state's public facilities and buildings, including the Capitol. "We've had the experts come in and, in closed session, give us an honest review of what our issues and vulnerabilities are. Our thinking is that the more information we receive from as many different perspectives as possible, the more likely it is that we will do the right thing when we implement all of our new security measures."

WISDOM OF SECURITY GUARDS

Lawmakers can additionally benefit from the wisdom of those who end up doing the actual policing—security officers and guards. "The perspectives of the security officers cannot be underestimated," says James Carney, acting president of the United Government Security Officers of America.

"They are the ones who know the most about any given building. They are also the ones who, if treated well by their employers, will stay on the job year after year and will really get to know the people who work in that building," says Carney.

"The security officers know who the problem people are and who has been thrown out of a building in the past. They know which lawmaker, if he forgets his identification, will become testy by having to get in line and go through a metal detector, and which one won't," Carney says. "That is the kind of knowledge that is essential to the effective running of any statehouse security plan."

Beard in California agrees. "Because of term limits, the security officers can be the only people left in the statehouse who have an active memory of certain security

events," says Beard. "And that's important because it means that the officer will not only know how to respond in a way that a lawmaker or staff member might not, but that he might also know from past experience who is a security risk and how to best deal with him."

Security officers in the California Legislature regularly conduct training sessions for lawmakers. "The education process is extremely important," says Beard. "For example, a new member needs to know if the member they succeeded was the subject of any kind of threats or inappropriate behavior. There is always a chance that the person who made such threats might not have figured out yet that the old member is gone."

New lawmaker Renfroe said he regarded similar security education sessions in the Colorado Capitol as "extremely helpful, because in essence you learn about things to look for, the difference between a person who is angry and a person who may be on the verge of being a threat."

"So much of this business is about being proactive," says Beard. "It's about looking out for certain signs and empowering the staff. It's letting staff know that it is perfectly appropriate to report someone, if that someone is behaving in a strange manner."

In Vermont, being proactive has also meant adding an invisible layer of security to the statehouse in respect of the state's strongly independent constituents. "We have emergency buzzers in the committee rooms," says Bartlett. "These are less important when we are in session and there are a lot of people here. But out of session, when you may be all by yourself doing your work in one of these rooms, the buzzers are important if someone comes in who may be acting a little bit on the odd side."

SECURITY COSTS

When contemplating how to make a statehouse more safe, says Beard, lawmakers should also think not only about the layer of security that works for them, but how much each layer costs. "This is an expensive business," says Beard, "and it is getting more expensive all the time."

Indiana lawmakers who agreed to close off more than a dozen entrances to the statehouse in favor of two guarded sets of doors also signed off on a $610,000 contract that will provide technicians to staff those doors. California spent an initial $1.2 million on security equipment in 2001 and recently built two pavilions to house it at a cost of $2 million.

"We have between eight and 10 magnetometers that each cost $10,000 and eight X-ray machines that go for anywhere from $45,000 to $50,000," says Beard. "But keep in mind that in a building with a lot of use—and we have more than a million people a year coming through our statehouse—this kind of equipment wears out after a while and has to be replaced."

The plan to enhance security in the Colorado statehouse has an estimated cost from the governor's office of $1.6 million, which includes $735,000 for X-ray machines and magnetometers in the Capitol and $360,000 for the same equipment in the Legislative Services Building. The plan also includes $360,000 for more state troopers throughout the Capitol. But lawmakers on the Joint Budget Committee in October scaled back the governor's funding request to $621,835, saying they preferred to wait until the entire legislature is in session this month to make final decisions about the tougher security measures. The money approved is enough to install equipment at the public entrances of the Capitol, add quick-card building access equipment at the private entrances and increase the number of security guards and state troopers assigned to the building.

Carney of the United Government Security Officers of America says lawmakers should also think about the pay scales of security officers. "You can never underestimate morale and how that is tied into security," he says. "How you treat these security officers and compensate them has a direct bearing on the type of security you are going to get."

Carney says security officers should be treated well to avoid high turnover. "You can't expect to have the best quality of security for your buildings when you have high turnover."

In Indiana, says Wyss, "We decided to approach our security issues on an incremental basis. We looked at our vulnerabilities and options and made a point of trying to get as much support from both the administrative and legislative branches as possible. They are the ones who were going to be most affected by any new security procedures.

"We might as well face it—it's a different world today and we need to have a different approach to making our buildings safe," says Wyss.

Governors and Executives

"May you live in interesting times" is reputed to be an old Chinese curse. State governors can relate; times sure have been interesting, and some governors could be forgiven for cursing their luck to be living in them.

Those who sat in gubernatorial mansions in 2008 had little choice but to grapple with issues that most would rather not face. The economy slipped and with it went state revenues. Lean budgets meant downsizing prized gubernatorial agendas. The federal government continued to be occupied with foreign policy, meaning governors were expected to provide more leadership on difficult domestic issues like healthcare. Even some foreign policy issues, including illegal immigration, there seemed to be an expectation of action at the state rather than the federal level. Piled on top of lean budgets and tough policy issues were legislatures with deep partisan divides, just what an executive needs when trying to negotiate policy minefields with a slimmed down treasury. Yep, it was definitely an interesting time to be governor, and the faint of heart need not apply.

Governors used different strategies to meet the challenges presented by the economy and domestic and global affairs. As the readings in this section show, some applied pragmatic bipartisanship to get things done. Some stuck to their core political principles, even if doing so raised objections in their own party. Still others felt their way, learning some costly lessons along the way.

THE ORIGINS OF ELECTED EXECUTIVE OFFICE

States and localities are very different from the federal government both in the number and nature of their elected executives. There is no federal executive office elected by a nationwide popular ballot.

The U.S. presidency is decided in the Electoral College, which is not bound by the popular vote in making its decision. In 2000, for example, George W. Bush lost the popular vote to his opponent Al Gore, but won in the Electoral College.

If the federal government has a complete absence of popularly elected executives, state and local governments have a surplus of them. State and local governments do not just have elected chief executives such as governors and mayors, many other executive offices are also elected. Everyone from the insurance commissioner to the head of the education bureaucracy to the state attorney general may be elected rather than appointed, and this can create friction in the executive branch. The governor is technically the head of the executive branch, but key offices may be held by people with different partisan, ideological, and personal agendas, which can make governing hard. In many states, the executive branch more resembles a collection of independent electoral fiefdoms than a hierarchical organization with the governor at the top.

How did the states end up with such a different system from the federal government? The short answer is that their citizens wanted it that way. Specifically, they wanted limits set on the power that could be concentrated in the hands of a single executive. Early colonial governors were executives appointed by the British Crown rather than elected by the people, and they often wielded considerable influence that included the ability to veto bills or even dissolve colonial legislatures. Understandably, they were not always popular.

This suspicion of executives was reflected in how states organized their governments after the United States won its independence from Great Britain, and initially, governorships were fairly weak positions. In some states there were even plural executives, which meant the governor's job was essentially done by a committee rather than a single person. Most governors had no veto power, held office under stringent term limits, and possessed little in the way of appointment or budgetary powers.

In the 1800s power was further fragmented in the executive branch with the rise of the so-called long ballot and the Populist movement. The descriptively named long ballot was a reform that gave citizens the power to decide on a broad range of executive offices. This meant that everything from county sheriff to state treasurer became an elected rather than an appointed office in most states. Having so many elected executives further diluted the power of governors, who had little say over who ran key government agencies and how they ran them.[1]

This situation lasted until roughly the last half of the twentieth century. By then it had become clear that the drive to restrain and fragment the powers of the executive was interfering with effective governance as the responsibilities and expectations placed on states increased enormously. Public education, health and welfare, law enforcement, roads and utilities—the number of services taken more or less for granted these days would astonish a nineteenth-century governor.

And that was a key problem: the executive branch in the states and many localities was a nineteenth-century creation ill-suited for the full-service state governments of the late twentieth century. This led to the creation of a reform movement directed toward giving governors the tools to exercise true executive authority and make them in practice the real chief executive officers of state. Reforms included the provision of line-item veto power, expanded budgetary powers, and the authority to hire and fire people in key agency positions.[2] As governors began to exercise these powers in the 1970s, 1980s, and 1990s, they also emerged as increasingly important figures in the federal system. Today, governors not only hold considerable sway within their states, they collectively wield considerable influence at the national level through the National Governors Association.

RECENT TRENDS

Governors have come a long way in a hundred years. Rather than the weaker siblings of state legislatures, governors now often dominate state politics. This, however, is a double-edged sword. Having real power creates the expectation it will be used to effectively address the tough problems currently facing many states.

Mike Chavers's essay takes a look at some of those tough issues in a round-up of 2008 state of the state speeches. Governors are using their bully pulpits to spell out policy priorities and talk about grim economic forecasts and the potential fallout of all of this in key areas such as education and healthcare.

How governors go about addressing policy priorities can have a big impact on their success. And governors can have very different ideas about how to get things done. Three profiles by Alan Greenblatt show different gubernatorial styles in action. The first looks at Florida governor Charlie Crist, a Republican who takes bipartisanship seriously. Crist's reaching-across-the-aisle style contrasts sharply with that of his predecessor Jeb Bush, and Democrats and liberals seem to appreciate the approach. Republicans, however, are not so sure. The second profile details the sometimes rocky road taken by Indiana governor Mitch Daniels. Daniels came to office committed to privatization, which he continues to push even as it costs him politically. Greenblatt's final profile examines New Jersey governor Jon Corzine, a former U.S. senator and Wall Street CEO who took office at a delicate time in Garden State politics. His predecessor, Jim McGreevy, left office in disgrace as local news-

papers carried headlines of government corruption stings. Now the state financial outlook is less than rosy. Corzine is trying to make a difference, but the row's been a rough one to hoe.

Notes

1. Larry Sabato, *Goodbye to Good-Time Charlie: The American Governorship Transformed,* 2nd ed. (Washington, D.C.: CQ Press, 1983).
2. Nelson C. Demetrius, "Governors: Their Heritage and Future," in *American State and Local Politics,* ed. Ronald E. Weber and Paul Brace (New York: Chatham House, 1999).

17

Seeking Solutions

Mikel Chavers

Governors lay out their
policy priorities in state of
the state speeches.

Despite the onset of several key problems in many states, many governors vowed to tackle major issues such as budget and spending, health care, education and other priorities like mental health reform and cracking down on sex offenders with—or without—the federal government's help.

With slowing revenues and skimpier budgets, many states recognize the difficulty of addressing key priorities without the needed funds. Facing a budget crunch, several states are looking to the private sector—through public-private partnerships—to tap its wealth and efficiency.

"There isn't enough money in the public sector, we all know that. Can't do all of it," California Gov. Arnold Schwarzenegger said in his State of the State address. "We need to expand partnerships where government and the private sector work together to meet the needs of the people."

With that in mind, states are getting creative in solving issues new and old.

BUDGET AND SPENDING

State budgets are expected to tighten in 2008 as revenues nationwide are flattening out, according to a National Governors Association and National Association of State Budget Officers report released Dec. 5.

Newly elected Kentucky Gov. Steve Beshear described that economic climate—and it looks grim. "Because of the economic slowdown, the cooling of the housing market, oil prices and a gap between what we spend and what we earn, we are facing an unprecedented budgetary shortfall," Beshear said in his address.

From *State News,*
March 2008

88

Wisconsin Gov. Jim Doyle echoed those sentiments. "America's economy is in deep turmoil and this will be a year of great challenge for us," Doyle said. "In Wisconsin, steps have been taken to prepare for a national economic downturn."

In perhaps evidence of what's to come, Wisconsin was the only state forced to make a midyear budget cut for the fiscal year ending in June 2007, according to the December NGA/NASBO report, "The Fiscal Survey of the States."

And that predicted national economic downturn means even [in] states with a surplus from last year's budgets—such as New Hampshire's record $89 million rainy day fund—governors are still looking to rein in spending. "Barring an emergency, I will not support any bills that require additional spending this year," said New Hampshire Gov. John Lynch in his address.

South Dakota Gov. Mike Rounds said in his speech, "We cannot commit to expensive new programs or huge increases in existing programs, because we don't have the money to do so. We must live within our means."

In fact, governors in California, Delaware, Kentucky, Maine, Maryland, Massachusetts, Mississippi, New Hampshire, New Jersey, Rhode Island, South Carolina and Wisconsin said they were looking to cut government spending. With the exception of a few remarks, Rhode Island Gov. Donald Carcieri's address was entirely about cutting government spending with the state facing a nearly $600 million budget deficit—Rhode Island's largest since 1991.

In California, there's also a sizeable shortfall. California is spending $400 million to $600 million more per month than the state is taking in, according to Schwarzenegger. Put simply, he said, Sacramento is overspending. "The problem is that while revenues are flat, automatic formulas are increasing spending by 7.3 percent," Schwarzenegger said. "Now, even a booming economy can't meet that kind of increase. So the system itself is the problem."

To address next year's projected $14 billion deficit in California, the governor will submit a budget that cuts spending across the board. He also pledged to propose a constitutional amendment aimed at spending—modeled after a process in Arkansas—that would prohibit the government from spending the entire state surplus in good years. Instead, "we would set some of that good-year money aside for bad years," Schwarzenegger said in the speech.

New Jersey is $32 billion in the hole and Gov. Jon Corzine wants to freeze spending. "We are in a hole, and if we want to get out, we have to stop digging," Corzine said in his speech. "For nearly 20 years both parties bonded, begged and borrowed money from every pot we could find to fund a growing appetite for spending."

To pay off some of New Jersey's debt—and fund transportation projects at the same time—Corzine wants to capture the value in the state's toll roads. By raising tolls and forming a nonprofit entity to manage the toll roads—not leasing or selling state roads to the private sector—the governor plans to pay down 50 percent of the state's debt.

Other states are proposing creative ideas to pay off debt and increase revenue. To create a "reliable stream of revenue for cities, towns and the state," Massachusetts Gov. Deval Patrick urged legislators to pass a Resort Casinos Bill, which would license three proposed gambling venues.

Missouri has taken another creative approach, in this case, for transparency in government spending. Missouri's Accountability Portal is an Internet site that allows residents to monitor government expenditures in real time. Gov. Matt Blunt wants to make the Web site permanent.

EDUCATION

When it comes to the importance of educational priorities, perhaps New York Gov. Eliot Spitzer said it best: "Without world class education, we cannot have a world class economy," Spitzer said in his speech.

With that in mind, many states are focusing on education priorities. Alaska, Arizona, California, Delaware, Georgia, Hawaii, Idaho, Kansas, Massachusetts, Michigan, Mississippi, Nebraska, South Carolina, South Dakota, Tennessee, Utah, Vermont, West Virginia and Wisconsin are looking to improve K–12 education. Alaska, Arizona, Colorado, Delaware, Hawaii, Idaho, Kansas, Maine, Maryland, Massachusetts, Michigan, Nebraska, New York, South Carolina, Tennessee, Utah, West Virginia and Wisconsin are looking to improve higher education.

In K–12 issues, Arizona Gov. Janet Napolitano wants her state to raise the high school dropout age from 16 to 18. She also wants to create a special scholarship program allowing high-achieving high school students graduating in 2012 and beyond to attend any of the state's universities or community colleges for free. Delaware Gov. Ruth Ann Minner similarly wants to expand the state's SEED scholarship program to offer free tuition to four-year colleges to program participants.

In higher education, Napolitano laid out plans to double the number of bachelor's degrees awarded by Arizona colleges and universities by 2020. To help college students finance higher education Napolitano recommends a fixed rate tuition to span all four years of college beginning with next year's freshman class. Other states are also considering similar fixed-rate tuition policies.

To pay for educational priorities, some states are considering creative solutions such as leasing their lotteries. New York is one of them. Spitzer wants to unlock some of the value in the state's lottery either by "taking in private investment or looking at other financing alternatives."

In Vermont, Gov. Jim Douglas also wants to tap the state's lottery and proposes a long-term lease of the state lottery for an upfront payment of $50 million, plus a share of future revenues. Douglas proposed in his address to spend $25 million for school modernization projects. Georgia Gov. Sonny Perdue wants to pledge another $6.4 million in lottery funds to expand the state's pre-K program by nearly 80,000 slots.

Idaho Gov. Butch Otter proposes doubling the amount of funding allocated to community colleges from state liquor sales.

HEALTH CARE

Most states' governors mentioned health care as a major issue for 2008. Many of those governors want to expand access to health care, with strategies ranging from making health care more affordable to adopting universal health care. Thirteen of the 33 governors who gave State of the State addresses before Feb. 1 specifically mentioned expanding health care coverage in their state as a top priority. Countless others mentioned health care in general as a priority.

Governors aren't waiting for a national cure to health care reform, either. "In Colorado, we won't wait for reforms to come from Washington," said Colorado Gov. Bill Ritter Jr. "Instead, we will make smart changes to the system and do what we can afford as we work toward our long-term goals."

Maine isn't waiting either. "When the federal government passed a poorly designed Medicare drug benefit that actually hurt some senior citizens in our state, Maine stepped forward to ease the transition," said Maine Gov. John Baldacci in his speech. "When the federal government failed to deliver on affordable health care, Maine stepped forward. We will continue to step forward." The governor wants to expand the state's universal health care program known as Dirigo Health by finding more sustainable funding and by contracting with new health partners.

New Mexico Gov. Bill Richardson, who dropped out of the Democratic presidential primary in January, wants to expand health care coverage to all New Mexicans by 2010. He said 20 percent of New Mexicans do not have health insurance coverage. He proposed that 85 percent of premiums go directly to health care—not to overhead or profits—and advocates using technology to reduce medical costs and medical errors.

"A system that covers only those who can afford it leaves the most vulnerable behind, and values profits over patients," Richardson said.

In New Hampshire, the governor wants to expand health care insurance coverage by making it more affordable for small businesses to cover their workers. The plan, known as New Hampshire Health-First, will require insurance companies to offer a wellness insurance plan to small businesses—a more affordable choice for coverage, Lynch said in his speech.

A similar plan is in effect in Georgia and Perdue wants to invest another $17 million into the state's Health Insurance Partnership for small business employees. Several governors, including those in Wisconsin and South Carolina, unveiled similar plans aimed at making health care insurance more affordable for small businesses.

States are also jumping on board with strategies in preventive health care and are looking to reduce disparities in health care. In Delaware, Minner touted the successes of the state's Screenings for Life program, resulting in record rates of colorectal and breast cancer screenings. The state's cancer mortality rate is declining twice as fast as the national average, Minner said in her speech. That's in stark contrast to Delaware in 2001, when cancer incidence and death rates were among the worst in the nation. To combat gaps and inequalities in health care among minority and ethnic populations, Minner recommended the establishment of a health disparities registry, so the state can target its efforts.

In West Virginia, Gov. Joe Manchin III announced that every child entering kindergarten in the state will receive a wellness screening before they start school. After that, the program will conduct follow-up screenings when the children reach second, fifth and eighth grades. The program is funded through the State Children's Health Insurance Program.

Iowa Gov. Chet Culver has several wellness initiatives. Culver wants to provide additional funding for early detection dedicating resources to early screening for cancer. "After all, wellness and prevention are the key to reducing costs, reducing medical claims filed, and reducing the number of procedures performed, and most importantly, keeping people healthy," Culver said in his address.

OTHER PRIORITIES

Other priorities were brought to the surface by recent tragedies. In Virginia, Gov. Tim Kaine highlighted the need for mental health reform in the wake of the tragic shootings at Virginia Tech in April 2007. The gunman in the incident had been declared mentally ill by a Virginia special justice.

Kaine said 6 percent of Virginians have a serious mental illness and one in every four has a diagnosable mental illness of some kind. But in recent years chronic underfunding has plagued Virginia's mental health system. Kaine is calling for increased funding for more mental health clinicians and case managers as well as additional support for emergency care.

"We also need to do a better job of keeping people with mental illness from entering the criminal justice system and to provide better treatment to individuals when they are in jail," Kaine said.

He also wants to close a loophole in the law that allows individuals to purchase firearms at guns shows without a background check.

In Washington, after a 12-year-old Tacoma girl was killed last year, Gov. Chris Gregoire asked lawmakers to build on Operation Crackdown, a state program that targets the monitoring and tracking of sex offenders. In her speech, Gregoire proposed a new program that would automatically e-mail families if a sex offender moves into their neighborhood. She also wants to require DNA samples from every sex offender in the state.

18

Golden-Rule Charlie

Alan Greenblatt

Lots of governors talk about bipartisanship; some of them actually seem to mean it.

It's hard to imagine an entertainer anywhere in America more despised by the Republican right than pop singer Sheryl Crow. She's a boisterous supporter of abortion rights and other liberal causes, wants to ration toilet paper for environmental reasons, and pinched Karl Rove at a black-tie dinner. But when she visited Florida this spring to promote awareness of global warming, she drew a warm welcome from none other than Charlie Crist, the state's Republican governor. In return, she gave him a shout-out during one of her concerts. "It's awesome," she said. "We're just following him around worshipping him."

Crow is not the first liberal charmed by Charlie Crist, who has been perhaps the most surprising new governor anywhere in the country this year. In addition to making global warming a priority—he hosted a high-profile summit in Miami headlined by California's Arnold Schwarzenegger—Crist has promoted stem-cell research and endorsed civil unions for gay couples. He has changed state policy to increase teacher pay and restore voting rights for ex-felons. He has appointed a large number of Democrats to top administration positions.

It's not so much that Crist has turned into a liberal. It's that he has developed an almost religious belief in bipartisanship. Crist's penchant for reaching across the aisle extends beyond finding common ground with Democrats on occasional hot-button issues. On the bread-and-butter questions of governance, such as budget and regulatory policy, Crist has consulted regularly with Democratic leaders in the legislature, even though the GOP has plenty of votes to spare. His style marks a dramatic change from his predecessor, Jeb Bush, who was quick to stamp out dissent within his own party

From *Governing,* August 2007.

92

and almost never reached across the aisle. Dan Gelber, leader of Florida's House Democrats, says Crist treats them like "partners—junior partners, but not a nuisance."

Crist's bipartisan approach stands in sharp contrast not only to Bush but also to most recent American governors. It's natural for governors to seek out the political center as a means of building the broadest possible support for their legislative goals. But as a rule, they trouble themselves with the opposing party only as much as they have to. More often, state policy making is driven by concerns about the next campaign and the need to define differences between the parties. "Maybe 30 or 40 years ago, you had that hiatus before the next campaign season started, and during that hiatus you governed," says Morris Fiorina, a political scientist at Stanford. "Today, there is no interregnum, and you're running all the time."

Crist has consciously sought an end to that sense of standing on separate sidelines. "You get more done," he says, "and people have more fun." He might add that it's been spectacularly good politics as well. Even when he's taken unpopular stands—on re-enfranchising felons, for example—his positions have only mildly annoyed most voters, while making him a hero to a minority who otherwise would not be inclined to support him. Crist's constant populist rhetoric about being "the people's governor" who lives in "the people's mansion" can wear a bit thin, but his approach, so far at least, has been hugely successful. Steve Geller, the Senate Democratic leader, has taken to calling Crist "Mr. 77 Percent," in reference to the high water mark of the governor's approval ratings.

Among the 23 percent who don't seem too happy with Crist are many of his own party's legislators, who believe he has given Democrats more of a say in policy than they've earned through the electoral process. "It does concern me," says Dennis Baxley, who stepped down a few weeks ago as House speaker pro tempore. "If there's no distinction between us and it doesn't matter what party you belong to, why would people elect us?"

There is in fact a good deal of Republican grumbling that Crist is undoing the agenda successfully pushed by Bush, who was the first GOP governor to work with a Republican legislature in more than a century. It's true that Crist has started to roll back some of Bush's privatization efforts and is unimpressed by Bush's faith in standardized tests as the be-all of education policy. Crist rejected 283 of Bush's late board and commission appointees, and has not shied from putting some former Bush enemies in positions of power.

Yet most Republican leaders in Florida will concede, when pressed, that Crist has been politically good for them. Despite a favorable GOP redistricting map, the party showed serious weaknesses at the polls last year. With Crist leading the ticket—he was one of the few Republicans in the country able to hold on to an open governorship—his party managed to survive in relatively secure shape. "I don't know if I should call it fate," says Florida Senate President Ken Pruitt, "but when you have a Charlie Crist, he really is the right man for the moment."

POSTPARTISAN DILEMMA

Crist's conspicuous bipartisanship raises obvious comparisons to Schwarzenegger, who is successfully practicing his own brand of "post-partisanship" at the other end of the country. A Republican governor working closely with the Democrats in Sacramento, Schwarzenegger has presided over a long series of legislative victories, including a $42 billion bond package, a widely touted global-warming bill and major prison-building and prisoner-rehab programs. Much of Schwarzenegger's rhetoric sounds similar to the things Crist is saying right now in Tallahassee.

But there are crucial differences. Schwarzenegger became an apostle of bipartisan accommodation only after an initial two years as a strong partisan, during which he referred to the Democrats who dominate the California legislature as "girlie men" and proposed an unsuccessful series of ballot measures designed to weaken them through changes in redistricting procedure and union fundraising methods. Schwarzenegger began to work with the Democrats when it became clear he needed them. "What the governor has been able to do is strike deals with Democrats on Democratic issues," says Joe Canciamilla, a former Democratic state Assemblyman. "That's really not hard to do."

Crist, on the other hand, doesn't really have to work with Democrats at all. His own party controls almost two-thirds of the legislature. Every indication is that Crist has chosen the bipartisan path because he simply wants to. He describes himself as a golden-rule Republican, saying that if he were in the shoes of the minority, "I would want to be consulted and included."

Consultation goes a long way. For all his efforts to reach out, Crist clearly remains a conservative. He talks tough on crime—not quite the way he did in his legislative days, when the press nicknamed him "Chain-Gang Charlie" for proposing forced prison labor—but still tough. He insisted that an "anti-murder bill," which will make it tougher for violent criminals to stay out on probation, had to be the first bill he signed as governor, and it was.

He generally takes a hard line on taxes and spending and other issues that his own party cares most about. Crist broke Jeb Bush's single-year record for vetoing "turkeys"—Tallahassee talk for pork-barrel spending—and his first budget, coming at a time when Florida's long years of revenue growth finally stalled, was a budget conservatives found easy to accept. They were especially pleased when he called a special session in June on property taxes that led to the largest tax cut in state history. "He has proved to me that on the big-picture conservative issues, he is rock solid," says Senate Republican Whip Mike Haridopolos. "It's smart of the governor to take ideas from all sides, as long as it's not raising taxes."

Democrats ultimately balked at the property-tax bill, saying it would lead to deep cuts in fire and police protection, and in support for public schools. Here was a fundamental point of disagreement between the parties—cutting taxes vs. maintaining government services—and yet even on that issue, the argument's losers couldn't stay mad at the governor for long. Senator Steve Geller says the Democrats' honeymoon with Crist was merely "interrupted" by the tax controversy—not ended.

"You know that b.s. President Bush has said about being a uniter, not a divider?" says Geller. "Charlie Crist has honestly been a uniter. What Charlie has done is actually a model for the rest of the country."

LET'S MAKE A DEAL

Some governors will admit, privately, that they like having at least one chamber of their state's legislature controlled by the other party. There's a good reason for this. In a one-party state, governors often feel pushed to the far left or far right. Neither is a very good recipe for effective policy formation.

It's striking how many governors have stumbled this year in states where the legislature is controlled by their own party. Some, like Democrat Deval Patrick of Massachusetts and Republican Jim Gibbons of Nevada, have faltered through personal gaffes and public relations missteps. But others have simply found majority status to be tricky.

Democrat Bill Ritter of Colorado stunned his party's legislators when he vetoed a labor-organizing bill he had campaigned for. Republican Sonny Perdue of Georgia watched the GOP-controlled House vote 163 to 5 to override his veto of a budget bill, and both chambers are planning to hold override votes on a series of other Perdue vetoes that legislators believe were punitive and designed to undermine their authority. Illinois Democrat Rod Blagojevich, who has continually attacked the legislature his party dominates, suffered the most embarrassing repudiation of all when his plan to raise money to pay for universal health coverage was voted down in the House, 107 to 0.

In many cases it remains easier for a governor to promote an agenda when his or her party holds a majority of the seats. But governors can also get much of what they want out of the opposition as well. Ed Rendell, the Democratic governor of Pennsylvania, has been viewed by many as a partisan figure: He once served as national chairman of the Democratic Party. Yet throughout his first term, Rendell got most of what he wanted out of a legislature dominated by Republicans. He was, says Rendell spokesman Chuck Ardo, "more or less forced to accept reality and work with Republicans."

Rendell succeeded with plans to increase community and economic development funding through bonds, increase school funding to reduce class sizes and provide pre-primary education, expand the state's environmental efforts and expand gambling to pay for property-tax relief. Rendell pulled this off not just by sharing credit but by sharing appointment power and control of certain purse-strings with Republican legislative leaders. "He's not moored in a lot of fixed positions," says Terry Madonna, a political scientist at Franklin & Marshall College in Lancaster. "He's the consummate 'Let's Make a Deal' governor."

Ironically, things are more complicated for Rendell as a result of Democratic success at the polls last November. The governor's party took control of the House by a one-seat margin, but his working majority actually disappeared. His top Republican trading partners are out of office or out of power. A large class of new Republicans in both legislative chambers was elected on pledges not to cut deals with Rendell. They balked at several tax hikes Rendell had proposed, and their intransigence over part of his economic development strategy even led to a one-day government shutdown last month. In the end, said the deal-making governor, "We all blinked a little bit. Unless there is mutual blinking, there is no budget and no legislation that comes out of here."

NO FIXED COMPASS?

If there's any complaint about Charlie Crist that cuts across party lines, it's that he may be too willing to sacrifice principle in favor of cutting a deal that everyone can feel good about. "My concern all along," says Baxley, "has been, how does somebody that flexible keep us on the right course?"

More than either Schwarzenegger or Rendell, Crist came to the governor's office with bipartisanship in his background. He had used it during his term as attorney general, keeping in place many of the top officials who had served under his Democratic predecessor, Bob Butterworth. (As governor, Crist put Butterworth himself in charge of the state's troubled Department of Children and Families.) And while many were expecting Attorney General Crist to polish his reputation as Chain-Gang Charlie, Crist in fact spent more of his efforts on consumer issues. He crusaded against energy price-gouging and kept a telephone-rate increase tied up in court for two years.

Now, as governor, Crist likes to remain above the fray. Jeb Bush was a policy wonk who not only set the agenda but understood and insisted upon every detail of his proposals. Crist lays out the broad terms of what he wants to do and then leaves it to the legislature to work its will. At times, he can appear almost out of touch. When it looked like his property-tax proposal was in real trouble, with Republicans as well as Democrats raising objections, Crist took it in stride. "I'm not twisting arms," he told a gaggle of reporters. "If they want to support it, they should. If they don't, they shouldn't. The people will direct them to a good conclusion."

Even when he meets with legislators and interest groups, Crist sometimes acts as if he's more interested in being genial and sincere than in taking direct action. Talking with about a dozen representatives of the housing industry over lemonade on the sun porch of the governor's mansion one recent afternoon, Crist leaned forward and focused intently on each individual who spoke, furrowing his brow into an expression of concern and compassion. After each one finished, he echoed back the main

points or found some other way to convey sympathy—but didn't actually commit himself to anything. Throughout Crist's career in politics, some critics have found this style cloying and contrived. But it seems to work. "That friendly type of personality really serves him well," insists lobbyist Curt Kiser, who shared an office with Crist when both served in the state Senate, "not only around voters but in trying to make deals and trying to govern."

Kiser and others warn that the governor's frequent air of detachment should not be taken for fatalism. If Crist is willing to leave policy details to the legislature, he is still very much the driving force when it comes to budgets and tax cuts—and to his more liberal policies, such as a $68 million commitment to combat global warming. "He knows he has friends in the legislature who can get that fine print," says Haridopolos, "but he is the unquestioned head of the orchestra."

The big question Crist faces is not whether his approach can play well to the electorate. That's already clear. The question is whether his compromises will ultimately prove to be good policy. A homeowners insurance relief bill, passed in a special session early this year, has not led to the deep rate discounts that were initially promised. In the meantime, Citizens Property Insurance, a new state-run insurance pool, has almost instantly become the largest underwriter of wind-damage insurance for homes and condos. "Citizens is big in all the bad places," says Robert Hunter, director of insurance for the Consumer Federation of America. "If a hurricane hits, Citizens no doubt will get clobbered." Democrats had a great deal of input into the homeowners insurance law, so they will share some of the blame if the state's increased financial liability proves burdensome after a major storm.

On the other hand, Democrats weren't so happy with the property-tax cut, complaining that the $31.6 billion reduction, while enormous, will do little if anything to alleviate gross disparities in individual tax bills or problems for commercial landowners that were caused by an earlier tax-cap law. Voters will hear countless arguments about the law and its effects, including billions' worth of cuts to schools and other local government services, over the next six months, because their approval in an election next January will be required for much of the plan to take effect.

And that vote in January will serve as a reminder of a political reality that Crist fully understands: At some point, a rough collision between the parties is unavoidable in a state like Florida. Sustained bipartisanship is difficult even for a golden-rule governor with a 77 percent approval rating. Legislators who have to run every two years can't really escape a continuous campaign mind-set, no matter how much they may like a chief executive from the other party. Party leaders in the legislature play more of a role in controlling campaign strategy and cash than they used to, with competitive elections primarily funded out of legislative or caucus committees. That means the campaign is run very much from within the legislature itself, which serves to increase rather than defuse partisanship.

And so the reality that there's always another election looming weighs on Democratic minds even as they express their satisfaction with the way Crist has treated them. Although they are happy that he takes their pulse and has sided with them on some issues, Florida Democrats are already worrying that too much cooperation and agreement might seal their fate as the minority party for years to come. "Governor Crist says we're going to govern from the center in a bipartisan or nonpartisan manner, and we're going to do it with a different tone," says Gelber, the House Democratic leader. "If this catches on, I don't know what any of us are going to do for a living."

19

Private Instigator

Alan Greenblatt

Indiana governor Mitch Daniels pushes for privatization even when others push back.

Indiana likes to fashion itself as "the crossroads of America," with 14 interstate highways moving people into and through the state. As in so many other places, many of those roads could use some work, which is why Governor Mitch Daniels thought he could solve a lot of problems simply by leasing out the Indiana Toll Road, which runs across 157 miles of the state's northern tier. A Spanish-Australian consortium was eager to turn the road into a money-making enterprise—something the road had never been under five decades of state management—and the companies involved were willing to pay $3.85 billion for the privilege. That was enough money to leave Indiana's transportation and infrastructure funds flush for the next decade.

Full funding for transportation is something other states can only look on with envy as they continue counting up their infrastructure costs, particularly after the collapse of the bridge over the Mississippi River in Minneapolis. Daniels believed he got a great deal. What's more, he believed that the toll road lease would lead to more such ventures, notably a new set of privately run roads servicing the Indianapolis area.

But since the agreement was signed in 2006, things haven't gone as Daniels expected. Although out-of-state drivers would bear the brunt of the initial toll hike—70 percent for cars, 113 percent for trucks—public criticism has lingered in some quarters. In 2006, partly as a result of the controversy, Democrats narrowly gained control of the state House—turning a 52-48 Republican majority into their current 51-49 advantage. Two of their wins came in districts where the toll road deal was especially unpopular.

From *Governing,* January 2008.

With Democrats now sharing power, Daniels has had to shelve some of his other privatization plans. His idea for an "Indiana Commerce Connector" helping to move goods and people in and out of Indianapolis went nowhere, and his desire to privatize the lottery has also been put on hold.

But Daniels hasn't given up. His party is confident it can regain control of the Indiana House (the state Senate has been a GOP stronghold for years), because of the retirement of a number of conservative Democrats who represent districts that Republicans should be able to pick up. And Daniels, of course, is optimistic that he can win reelection this year. However, his current poll ratings against two potential Democratic opponents, who are not particularly well-known, suggest he is vulnerable.

PRIVATIZER IN CHIEF

Nevertheless, Daniels remains the most ambitious privatizer of any governor currently in office, turning over to outside entities not just control of a major cross-state highway but prisons, hospitals and welfare case management. Like most privatizers, Daniels doesn't like the term, but his pursuit of the idea led the New York Times last summer to dub him "Governor Privatize."

The toll road deal was the most striking illustration of Daniels' whole approach to government. The 58-year-old Daniels, who served as President George W. Bush's first budget director, is one of the most fervent believers in the familiar doctrine that government needs to operate more efficiently, in something resembling a competitive environment and with sets of incentives that bear some passing resemblance to the profit motive. Where government agencies or operations face no real competition, Daniels believes, you have to instill some. He has consistently challenged state workers and agencies to come up with ways of streamlining their shops and saving money. "The state government I see looking forward will be fewer people, better paid," Daniels says. "A lot of them will be overseeing contracts for compliance and results and therefore deserving of being very well compensated."

"He's not afraid to advocate and push for ideas that may be a little politically on the dangerous side," says Indiana House Speaker Patrick Bauer, a Democrat and perhaps the most persistent critic of Daniels' privatiza-tion efforts. He calls the toll road lease "a very, very bad deal," arguing that the state could have collected far greater returns by continuing to manage the road itself.

The strong political backlash Daniels experienced due to the lease has proved sobering not just to him but to other governors, who have grown more cautious about unveiling their own proposals. But with transportation needs continuing to grow at a time when budgets are getting tighter, more governors—not fewer—are looking to private leases as a means of financial salvation. In recent weeks, Charlie Crist of Florida has floated the idea of leasing major roadways in hopes of addressing his state's growing budget shortfall. "If you're totally flush and you'd rather have your money in the highway, you should leave it there," says John Schmidt, an attorney who worked on both the toll road deal and Mayor Richard M. Daley's earlier leasing of the Chicago Skyway to the same foreign consortium. "But if you have another use for that cash, why wouldn't you redeploy the capital from that infrastructure?"

HOW TO SELL A ROAD

Daniels still sounds flabbergasted when he recalls the opposition to the toll road lease, which he calls "a hell of a deal. At the beginning, I don't think anybody foresaw that it would be as controversial as it was. We took a toll road that was losing money and turned it into $4 billion of cold, hard cash." Daniels takes great pride in the fact that within months the upfront lease payment had earned more in interest than the road itself had cleared for the state in 50 years. As a result of the deal, Indiana is able to pay for some 200 projects that had previously been in limbo.

Although the Chicago Skyway deal served as a model for Indiana's approach, several things were different. For example, a lot of work had recently been completed on the Skyway, so there wasn't the same need for capital improvements that Daniels insisted on in his deal. Also, it wasn't practical to think about expanding Chicago's elevated roadway, but the Indiana Toll Road contract demands that the private operators expand lanes when congestion reaches a certain level.

Daniels attempted in the toll road negotiations to anticipate all manner of potential pitfalls and recognizes that the only way third-party contracts work is if they are monitored carefully. He created a toll road oversight board that includes local officials and citizens and reports quarterly on its new management. He used to carry with him a copy of his 285-page toll road contract to wave around while giving speeches, pointing out that it covered every conceivable contingency down to the amount of time road kill could stay on the highway (eight hours). More important, the contract addresses issues such as what happens to the road if the leasing consortium goes bankrupt (it reverts back to the state) and places limits on the size of toll increases.

Perhaps the fact that everything was tied up in a nice, neat bow created part of the problem. Daniels presented the deal to the legislature as a fait accompli, essentially saying here is this great deal—take it or leave it. Although successful in muscling the package through, he didn't do much of a job selling its benefits to a skeptical public. Politically, Daniels' approach—and this is characteristic—was quite the opposite. "The toll road thing was like a force-feeding," says University of Evansville political scientist Robert Dion. "It really did not sit well with people because it was jammed through."

DEAL OR NO DEAL?

Tolls had not been raised along the road for two decades, which made automobile drivers especially wary of the almost immediate increase from 3 cents to 5.1 cents per mile. (Truck tolls will increase incrementally from 9.3 cents to 20.3 cents per mile by 2010.) The sudden rise lent credence to the arguments of its opponents that the deal was a giveaway to private interests. "Clearly, the entities that leased the road were looking at it as a very lucrative deal," says Dave Menzer, of Citizens Action Coalition, which sued in an unsuccessful attempt to block the lease. "We felt that this deal was done behind closed doors, the public was not engaged and public opinion was ignored."

Part of what turned public opinion against the deal was the fact that the companies involved were foreign. Nobody seemed ready to argue that this was a happy example of "in-sourcing"—of foreign investment in construction that could never be taken back overseas. Instead, in the wake of the failed Dubai Ports World deal to lease U.S. ports, it was viewed as "a potential threat to our national security if foreign companies can monitor what is moving on our roads," Menzer says. Fears of Spain and Australia persuading private investors to turn over data

to their governments about the specifics of tonnage moving across the Midwest may sound overblown, but it was an argument that proved to have resonance.

There haven't been any fresh sources of controversy in the wake of the consortium actually running the road—no significant problems with maintenance or potholes, let alone security concerns. And construction already is underway along the road's western reaches, coming out of Gary, as the consortium spends a major portion of the $700 million it promised to devote to immediate improvements.

But Bauer and other leasing critics continue to register one complaint, namely, that Daniels gave away too much for too little. Sure, transportation funds are flush now, but if the lump-sum payment is spent during the next 10 years, the state could feel shortchanged for decades even as the private operators continue to raise tolls. "If they had gotten $2 billion to $2.5 billion upfront and then a share in the profits over 75 years," says Robert Poole, director of transportation studies at the Reason Foundation, "there would have been less political criticism."

The two toll road deals completed since Indiana's, involving Virginia's Pocahontas Parkway and the Northwest Parkway in Colorado, have both included revenue sharing. Because privatizing existing roads is a fairly new business, no one is really sure what they're really worth—how much money a state should see before it can be certain it's made a really good deal. Daniels was convinced that the size of his deal—$4 billion is a lot of money, relative to Indiana's $13 billion annual budget—would prove simply too lucrative to pass up.

The deal went through, of course, but because it was so politically costly, other governors have been more careful in their approach. Arguably, perhaps, too careful. New Jersey Governor Jon Corzine, for instance, floated the idea of "monetizing" the value of future tolls along the New Jersey Turnpike and the Garden State Parkway last February but has yet to release the specifics of his plan. He promises to do so in his State of the State address this month, but the fact is that opponents were able to tear into it throughout last year's legislative elections in New Jersey without his offering any specifics to counter their complaints, weakening his own hand.

Pennsylvania Governor Ed Rendell has sought a middle ground between Daniels' bluster and Corzine's caution, fully engaging the public and the legislature in his plans to lease the Pennsylvania Turnpike. The legislature has been skeptical and wants instead to impose tolls along Interstate 80. In addition to the political difficulties of collecting tolls on a highway that has always been free—almost an unprecedented act—it's doubtful that the legislature's plan will gain approval from the Federal Highway Administration, despite a congressional pilot program to allow states to collect tolls on interstates for road maintenance and improvement. Anticipating that the I-80 plans might not pass muster, Rendell has been openly soliciting bids for Turnpike leases, just in case. Since the numbers that are being bandied about reach as high as $18 billion, Rendell is betting, much as Daniels did, that a real deal laid out in actual, hard cash will be difficult for the legislature to turn down.

"The lessons from Indiana, which certainly Corzine and Rendell have taken to heart, are to brief your legislature early on so that you don't catch them by surprise, which is somewhat what happened in Indiana," says Ken Orski, editor and publisher of Innovation Briefs, a transportation newsletter, "and secondly, to explain the deal more clearly to the public."

CHANGING STRIPES

Daniels keeps a legal pad in his desk drawer on which he jots down a personal list of the errors of his administration. But that doesn't stop him from trying new ideas (and the toll road, by the way, isn't on his personal ledger). "To me, it is a fact of life that the more things you try, the more mistakes you make," he says. "There are folks, including some in my own party, who are still uncomfortable, who say it's been too much, too fast."

Daniels was not only the first Republican elected to govern Indiana in 16 years. He also represented a stylistic break with his predecessors, who tended to be conciliatory and generally sought consensus. That is in keeping with the character of the state, historians of which, Daniels notes, have described Indiana as "conservative," "cautious" and "risk-averse." That has not been Daniels' approach. He seems to believe that where there is consensus, there is little need for leadership from the top. And he combines a bold approach to leadership with a policy wonkishness that makes him the kind of governor who throws out a fair number of provocative ideas at any given time. During a typical State of the State address, he outlines so many brash notions that some

observers believe a few are just filler meant to give cover to legislative Republicans who are free to choose some things on which to oppose him.

Daniels worked as an aide to President Ronald Reagan and U.S. Senator Richard Lugar (while Lugar served as mayor of Indianapolis) before becoming a top executive at drug maker Eli Lilly. As director of the federal Office of Management and Budget during President Bush's first term, Daniels was known for his bite, suggesting that the congressional motto might as well be "Don't just stand there, spend something." In Indiana, he learned to tame his tongue after making a remark in 2005 about legislators "car bombing" his agenda, which drew widespread complaints. "He has had to adjust some," says Jack Colwell, a longtime columnist for the South Bend Tribune. "He's used to being an executive at Eli Lilly, where you give an order and people do what you say. In government, of course, it's a little different."

Daniels is fond of presenting charts demonstrating how much things are improving, sometimes through the simple act of being measured. But, as with the toll road, not everything has worked out well. He's been blamed for some major snafus, including a riot last April at a privately operated Indiana prison that involved inmates imported from Arizona. He's been criticized for the lack of governmental experience some of his hires have brought to their jobs, and he's also earned some criticism about how effectively contractors are handling the work of doling out social service money to indigent Hoosiers and the nonprofit groups that offer them aid. "It's a horrible disaster," Bauer says. "I know it's causing a lot of the help for the poor and sick not to get there in a timely fashion." In August, the state cancelled a chaplaincy program meant to help Family and Social Service Administration employees cope with the troubled privatization of some departmental functions, having determined that it was expensive but met few of its stated goals.

Perhaps no agency, though, demonstrates the ups and downs of Daniels' approach more clearly than the Bureau of Motor Vehicles. Such agencies are always politically sensitive as the place where the most citizens engage directly with the government. For Daniels, the BMV has been a public-relations disaster. A botched computer system changeover resulted in the system looking hapless. At the same time, Daniels' plan to close down license branches made for unhappy residents in affected areas of the state. Still, on Daniels' watch, the BMV has cut the average wait time from when a resident meets a greeter at the door—a Daniels innovation, although perhaps borrowed from Wal-Mart—to completing a transaction, from 40 minutes to 10 minutes.

UNPOPULAR BUT UNDAUNTED

The toll road lease controversy, and the surprisingly contentious reaction to his insistence on statewide adoption of daylight savings time, continue to alienate many Hoosiers. But Daniels' political fortunes may well rest on his hopes of overhauling the property-tax code. More than two-dozen Indiana mayors were ousted largely because of the issue last year, including Indianapolis Mayor Bart Peterson. Daniels has proposed a constitutional cap on rates, limiting residential rates to 1 percent of assessed value, rental properties to 2 percent and commercial property to 3 percent. He would pay for the package largely through a sales-tax hike.

But Daniels hopes to save money as well through efficiencies. His property-tax plan would eliminate 1,008 elected township and county assessors, replacing them with 10 regional administrators. He appointed Joe Kernan, the man he beat to win office in 2004, and Randall Shepherd, the chief justice of the state Supreme Court, to head a commission that recently unveiled a plan to modernize and streamline local government, which has largely been unchanged in structure since the 1850s.

Consolidation of local government has been the doomed hope of many a governor in recent years. But Daniels enjoys setting his sights on big targets. So far, he has more often than not delivered on what he has promised to do. If some of his ideas, notably his efforts in the area of privatization, have proven to be unpopular, Daniels has simply moved forward with his agenda, undaunted. "This is a governor who is not concerned with the political implications of anything that he does," says Ed Feigenbaum, editor of Indiana Legislative Insight, "and he views that as a positive."

20

Tougher Work Than Wall St.

Alan Greenblatt

Running a state can be a lot harder than running with the bulls on Wall Street.

Jon Corzine's political success has been based to a remarkable extent on one attribute: his enormous wealth. Part of it has been his willingness to spend his own money on elections—roughly $100 million so far—but that may not even be the most important part. Another crucial element in Corzine's victories for the U.S. Senate and the New Jersey governorship has been the confidence of voters that a man worth as much as he is—several hundred million—is simply beyond the reach of material temptation. In a state with a history of political corruption that never seems to end—11 public officials were arrested by the FBI on bribery charges in September in one sting alone—Corzine's riches constitute a form of reassurance.

This is something he understands as well as anybody. "The public at some level believes if you don't need to take money, maybe you'll stay more focused on their business," Corzine said in an interview. "It gives me a sense of freedom that I'm not checking the contribution list when we're trying to make a decision."

When he became governor at the end of 2005, following the departure of fellow-Democrat Jim McGreevey in a sex-and-patronage scandal, significant numbers of people believed he might be not only incorruptible but invincible: able to solve long-standing state problems that none of his predecessors had dared to tackle.

And, in fact, Corzine has shown a consistent inclination to do this, to address not only the state's ethical climate but also its exorbitant property-tax rates and school funding problems, among other dilemmas. Most important, he has broken with his predecessors by ending old habits of borrowing against the state's future needs to prop up current-year budgets. "The governor certainly arrived on

From *Governing,*
December 2007.

the statehouse scene with the right attitude and with an action platform," says William Dressel, head of the New Jersey League of Municipalities. "We've built a monument of problems here, and now we're looking for one man to ride his white horse down State Street saying, 'I've got the Rolaids bill that's going to spell relief.'"

But it is turning out to be a very difficult ride. Although Corzine's party controls the legislature—Democrats reaffirmed their majority status in both chambers during last month's elections—the governor has encountered resistance at nearly every turn. New Jersey's political culture is highly fragmented, dominated by legislators fixated on controlling their own turf, by public employee unions, by party chairmen in the counties and by myriad other interest groups intolerant of big changes in the way business is done. "He's working with the legislature and the bureaucracy that helped create the problems he's trying to solve," says Christian Bollwage, the mayor of Elizabeth. "That paradox alone makes it difficult in looking for a solution."

Corzine inherited a tough hand and a lot of problems, but there's one other factor that has puzzled many of his earlier supporters: his reluctance to insist on his own way. Corzine has spent much of his two years in office waiting rather than acting, promising to release bold plans to untangle perennial problems but arguing that a given issue requires more deliberation. "It takes a while," he says, for "people in an organization to buy into things."

Few would quarrel with the idea of formulating policy carefully and deliberately. But in several cases, Corzine has let the preparation period go on so long that his solutions have become targets and gathered opposition before he even released them. In other cases, he has made the bold announcement but backed down after presenting it, essentially yielding to New Jersey's deeply entrenched coalition for the status quo.

CONFLICTING ROLES

In many ways, Corzine's career offers a case study in the disparities between a governor's two roles—as a manager who formulates workable ideas and policies and as a politician who has to sell those ideas to other players in the political process and the public at large. "He's an honest public servant and took the governor's job with an agenda for making New Jersey a better place," says Ingrid Reed, of Rutgers University's Eagleton Institute of

Politics, "and ran into political issues that he hadn't counted on. So far, there has not been any kind of real rigor that says, 'Look, this is what we're up against, and these are the hard choices we have to make.'"

Such criticism may be a little strong. Corzine has made some important changes. He's helped to reform the long-neglected agency that takes care of abused children. He devoted $1 billion to a pension fund that had been ignored for a decade. He negotiated an agreement with the major state workers' union that called on public employees to contribute to their own health care premiums for the first time. And he showed courage during his first year in office when he forced a brief government shutdown in order to ensure passage of a sales-tax increase he deemed necessary to put the state on firmer financial footing.

But even then, he traded away a substantial portion of the revenue increase in order to win passage of the tax. Corzine proved willing to accept half a loaf in the ethics package the legislature passed in response to the latest series of scandals, refusing to issue a provisional veto, as some suggested he should, to reshape it in the way he wanted. He backed off from a threat to call a constitutional convention if the legislature failed to produce "real reform" on the property-tax issue—even though all the legislature produced were temporary rebates and another commission to study it.

For months, Corzine has claimed to be on the verge of announcing innovative policies to address the state's finances, sentencing laws, energy consumption and school funding. But he held off on any such announcements or even broad outlines until after this fall's election—letting his opponents define the possible effects of his proposals in whatever way they chose. Some of the delay was due to Corzine's near-fatal car accident last April, but he had recovered remarkably well within a couple of months and soon enough faced complaints that it was time to let voters know what he had in store for them. "These are critical issues confronting the state," says Leonard Lance, leader of the Senate Republicans, "and yet the administration has refused to release any of the details of the proposals."

Corzine's intentions on many of these issues are bound to become clearer as the legislature meets this month in a lame-duck session, in which more than one-third of state lawmakers will be on their way out of office and thus will be facing fewer immediate political pressures. New Jersey has a long history of tackling big bills in these sorts of post-election sessions. Next year, the governor will welcome many new faces to the legislative ranks, a source of encouragement that any reform momentum that builds in the lame-duck session may continue.

Close associates say that Corzine's brush with mortality in his car accident has strengthened his resolve to make the right decisions and push the right policies for his adopted home state. And, as the 60-year-old governor seeks to regain the initiative heading into the second half of his term, he faces a problem that may, perversely, turn out to be an advantage. Things are becoming so difficult that big steps will have to be taken.

Corzine has already said that the state will face a $3 billion shortfall as it prepares next year's budget, and he's ordered agency heads to plan for major reductions. One thing he is certain not to suggest is more borrowing: The state is already highly leveraged and devotes nearly 10 percent of its annual budget to debt service. Throw in pension and retiree health costs, and pretty soon you're talking about real money—well more than $100 billion in unfunded liabilities. The state's tax rates on property, income and sales are all among the nation's highest, making further increases unpalatable—especially at a time when job growth has been sluggish and more people are moving out of New Jersey to other states than are moving in, as a well-publicized Rutgers study pointed out in October. The study found that those who had left—a net departure last year of 72,000 residents—took $680 million in potential sales- and income-tax revenues with them.

For Corzine to fulfill his potential as a reformist governor hoping to overcome the hesitations of an entrenched political culture, a crisis environment offers the best possible opportunity to push through major changes. "The problems are big, and the budget is going to be a Herculean task," says Hal Bozarth, a lobbyist for the state's chemical industry. "This may be the year when we see what the character of Jon Corzine really is, because it's not going to be pretty."

GOLDMAN TOUCH

Jon Stevens Corzine had something close to a Midas touch during his long career on Wall Street. A product of central Illinois farm country, he went to work as a bond trader for Goldman Sachs in 1975, quickly rising to positions of real influence. Within a few years of his taking over bond-trading, which had been marginally profitable, he'd made it into the firm's first billion-dollar division. When he became CEO, Goldman Sachs was experiencing its worst quarter in decades, but two years later it was the most profitable privately held company in America. Soon after that, Corzine took the company public, earning vast sums for his partners and himself. Going public was sufficiently controversial within the firm, however, that Corzine was eased out of the top spot in favor of Henry Paulson, who is now the U.S. Treasury secretary. Corzine decided to enter politics and began a new life in the U.S. Senate before running for governor five years into his term.

In Trenton, Corzine has surrounded himself with several Goldman Sachs veterans—people who are, like him, universally praised for being smart, well-intentioned and diligent. Perhaps too diligent. Goldman Sachs was nearly unique on Wall Street in maintaining a partnership structure that discouraged rapid changes of course and fostered decades-long relationships with clients based on an in-house culture of concentration on the longer term. As Lisa Endlich notes in her history of the firm, it was a place where, when it came time for a major decision, "discussion had just begun [and] further study was needed."

It's this quality of prolonged deliberation and study that has proved most frustrating to many of Corzine's allies. Given the state's structural deficits, for example, Corzine has expressed interest in converting the long-term value of the New Jersey Turnpike and Garden State Parkway into ready cash. He began talking about the idea this past February, claiming that he would issue a proposal that was more sophisticated and advantageous than highway leasing plans adopted elsewhere. (Goldman Sachs has been a leading financier in the highway privatization field.)

But as the year dragged on, nothing specific was ever forthcoming, not even a more politically palatable name for the idea than "asset monetization." Opponents, whose ranks grew as the election season approached, didn't have to wait for specifics. They could point out, with likely justification, that any plan would translate into higher tolls. Public opposition to the privatization idea continued to grow and became a central campaign issue this fall.

Corzine might still get his way on this. The state is going to need the money. But the long months of delay—whether out of deference to the election season or the need to continue pondering a complex issue—are in keeping with his administration's overall means of operating. There always seem to be months of internal deliberation, whether the issue is highways, school funding or crime prevention. Meanwhile, opponents siphon all the air they can from the various trial balloons. "It's a combination of letting the perfect be the enemy of the good," says Dan Pringle, an environmental activist, "and not having a good enough understanding or willingness to use the powers at the disposal of the governor."

A FINE BALANCE

In fairness to Corzine, the challenges he faces are enormous and complex. Massive income-tax cuts in the early 1990s propelled Republican Governor Christine Todd Whitman into the national spotlight but have left the state short of money ever since. Subsequent leadership has made matters worse, short-changing both the pension fund and the operating budget, borrowing money to fill the gaps. And straightforward financial mismanagement has been exacerbated by waste and fraud. Several billion dollars were misspent over the past five years by a state agency meant to satisfy a court order on school construction; the agency was abolished this summer.

McGreevey, Corzine's immediate predecessor, presided over an ethically compromised administration even before he startled the state by resigning, admitting that he was "a gay American" and had placed the object of his affection in a sensitive state job. McGreevey's regime had freely practiced "pay-to-play" with state contractors, treating campaign contributions as all but necessary to obtain major state business. That practice has not been fully eliminated from New Jersey government. Companies that received $5.4 billion in state and local contracts last year paid $11.6 million to candidates and fundraising committees, according to recently released disclosures required under a 2005 campaign finance law. The law bans campaign contributions from most state contractors to candidates for governor and other executive offices, as well as to the state parties. But contractors are still able to give to state legislators, legislative leadership PACs and local officials who can exert an indirect influence over contracts.

Since taking office, Corzine has talked often of the need for further measures to abolish conflicts of interest, but the ethics package enacted this fall fell far short of what reformers, and the governor himself, said they wanted. The main piece of legislation was a ban on dual officeholders—state legislators who simultaneously serve as mayors or hold other local posts. But the ban exempted existing legislators, as well as those first elected last month. And it didn't address the nearly 700 elected officials throughout the state who also hold non-elected public-sector positions. Legislators managed to pull off a classic run-around on the ethics question.

LOCAL CONTROL

On item after item, Corzine has run into resistance not only from legislators but also from the local party bosses who stand behind them. New Jersey still is made up of a multitude of political fiefdoms, and legislators tend to feel more allegiance to the people who put them in office than to the nominal head of their party sitting in the governor's chair. The legislature is a part-time body, and, even when it's in session, the chambers meet only on Mondays and Thursdays, with most legislators driving home each night. This contributes to the inclination of members to remain beholden to local interests while short-changing the needs of the state as a whole.

And for a geographically small state, the number of local interests is staggering. New Jersey is home to 566 municipalities and more than 600 school districts. Many of the state's major problems—including property taxes, school funding and pay-to-play shakedowns—can be traced to this prevailing parochial culture. "State and local politics is often tainted," Corzine says. "When you have lots of local politicians like we do, you're more susceptible. We have to raise the bar."

Even a political opponent such as Lance gives Corzine credit for engaging in more honest budgeting than his predecessors. But the new batch of GOP senators elected in November has been talking about replacing Lance with someone who will take a more aggressive stance against the governor.

Corzine's instincts clearly are decent. He wants to govern as a chief executive without any commitment to the way things traditionally have been done. The question remains, however, how much credit Corzine deserves for trying—versus how much he can actually accomplish while the state faces a serious financial crisis.

Like so many other businessmen who have become politicians, Corzine has found that it's harder to impose ideas within the public sector because there are so many more players to be persuaded than in private industry. Still, Corzine has not consistently challenged legislators, the way neighboring governors Eliot Spitzer of New York and Ed Rendell of Pennsylvania have done, or shown much appetite for butting heads with local bosses and county chairmen. There are only so many fights a governor can pick before he's on a kamikaze mission, but Corzine generally has erred on the side of caution and bowed to the expectation that he would need their help more on some other fight.

During the recent election season, voters clearly considered Democrats to be responsible for the state's most recent corruption scandals. One poll found that 88 percent of registered voters viewed government corruption as a "very serious" or "somewhat serious" problem. Yet the same poll found that a majority of voters were no more likely to vote for Republicans as a result of the arrests of a disproportionate number of Democrats.

Nothing Corzine has done so far has dented the profound political skepticism of the electorate. The hopes that many voters may have harbored about this fabulously wealthy governor who would be free to generate real change have, so far, been unfulfilled. But Corzine is by no means out of time. He can do both the state and his own governorship enormous good if he's able to force such change during the coming budgetary battles. And in all likelihood, he can win a second term if he chooses to seek one in 2009.

Still, Corzine has to do a better job than he's managed thus far of convincing people not only that his diagnosis of the state problems is correct but also that his solutions will work. "People who observe politics closely felt that since he's not beholden to the political leaders, he might have the ability to shake things up in Trenton," says Patrick Murray, a Monmouth University pollster. But among the general public, Murray adds, there was an underlying fear that, in the end, a governor of enormous intelligence and promise might still accomplish little more than less impressive ones. Those fears are, as yet, nowhere near being put to rest.

Courts

Judges are typically viewed as powerful people. Courts, after all, make decisions that can end up taking peoples' property, liberty, and even their lives. Given this, it is only natural to view judges as having enormous influence over the lives of those who stand before the bench.

Yet there are limits to the power of judges and the courts, and we are not just talking constitutional limits or the shackles of precedent. Judges depend on the good graces of executive branch agencies to enforce many of their rulings. A court order to make, say, child care payments is not worth much without a means of insuring compliance with that order. And when it comes to influence, there are some pretty unsavory characters who can wield their share in a courtroom through bullying and intimidation.

The readings in this section focus on this theme of power and influence in the judicial branch of state government. As the readings will show, judges are not all powerful, much less infallible. Turns out that making decisions and enforcing decisions is a complicated business for the courts, and reforming the process is a challenge many states are struggling with.

THE STRUCTURE OF STATE COURTS AND THE SELECTION OF JUDGES

The United States is unusual in that it has a dual judicial system. This parallel, two-track system is a byproduct of federalism. The federal system, at least in theory, makes state governments and the federal government co-equal partners. Just as a governor is not subordinate to the president, neither are state courts subordinate to federal courts.

Broadly speaking, the federal courts deal with issues of federal law and the U.S. Constitution. State courts deal with state law and state constitutions. The only real point of overlap between federal and state court systems is at the very top. Sitting at the head of both systems is the U.S. Supreme Court, which has final say on what both levels of government are empowered to do under the U.S. Constitution.

State courts thus constitute an independent system with their own jurisdictions. State criminal justice systems are structured by state constitutions and state law. The latter covers most criminal law and a good deal of civil law. State courts handle everything from traffic tickets to murder, gay marriage to divorce. That all adds up to a lot of work: There are roughly one hundred million cases filed in state courts every year.[1]

Most state court systems are organized into a basic three-level hierarchy. At the bottom are trial courts, or courts of first instance. This is where a case is initially heard, where the parties involved make arguments, present evidence to a judge (and often to a jury). The judge and jury decide what the facts of the case are, and which side the law favors. These are the most numerous type of state court. Roughly thirty thousand people work for state trial courts nationwide, a figure which includes judges, magistrates and other court officers.[2]

Above trial courts are courts of appeal. The basic job of an appeals court is to examine whether the law and proper procedures were followed by trial courts. Appeals courts do not provide "do overs" for the losing party in a trial court; they exist to hear claims that some legal or procedural error at a lower court damaged the loser's chances of winning the case.

At the top of most state court systems is a state supreme court. This constitutes the highest legal authority within a state. The only place to appeal the decision of a state supreme court is the U.S. Supreme Court. To do so requires making a federal case of a dispute through a credible argument that some element of the state court process or state law violates the U.S. Constitution. This is usually a tough argument to prove, and relatively few cases jump from state supreme courts to the U.S. Supreme Court.

Though this basic three-level system serves as a generic example of state court systems, there is a lot of variation. Some states have courts specializing in criminal or civil cases, others have specialized courts for juvenile offend-

ers or for drug cases. Some states have no trial courts at all. If you're interested in how a particular state organizes its courts you can go to the web site for the National Center for State Courts, which includes an interactive page on the organization of state courts:

http://www.ncsconline.org/D_Research/Ct_Struct/
Index.html.

Just as the structure and organization of courts vary from state to state, so do methods of selecting judges to preside over these courts. The process of selecting judges is important because it must reconcile two conflicting values. Most people want an independent judiciary, judges who make decisions based on an honest reading of the facts and free from any partisan or political interests. It is generally reckoned that judges are less likely to respond to such partisan and political interests if they can make decisions without worrying whether their choices will cost them during the next election or prompt the legislature to remove them from the bench. Judicial independence, then, argues for insulating judges from the ballot box and from the other branches of government. This is what is done in the federal courts; a federal judge is appointed for life and does not worry about winning elections or staying in the good graces of an executive or a legislature.

Yet this approach, some argue, raises a problem of accountability. Paradoxically, we want judges to make independent decisions free of outside influence, but also want them held accountable to outside forces for the choices they do make. Thus some argue judges should be elected, and if they make unpopular decisions voters have the opportunity to remove them from the bench. While electing judges makes them accountable to the voters, it obviously makes them less independent. Remember, we wanted judges making decisions based on the law, not on what will get them the most votes.

There's no objective way to decide whether independence or accountability should take precedence when it comes to selecting judges. While independence wins out at the federal level with judges appointed for life, at the state level accountability is given more of a role. Some states elect rather than appoint judges. Roughly half the states use some form of popular election to select at least some judges. Many of these are non-partisan elections, but a few states still use partisan ballots for judges. Most of the remaining states use some form of appointment system, although only a handful use a pure appointment system where the governor or the legislature has the sole power to select judicial nominees. Many states use a hybrid system called "merit selection" where a nominating committee, typically a nonpartisan group that includes representatives from the court system and the legal profession, draws up a list of candidates highly qualified to serve as judges. The governor (usually) or the legislature (more rarely) picks judges from this list.[3]

Even judges in appointive or merit systems may still have to face voters. Judges, regardless of how they are selected to serve on the bench, often have to run in retention elections. In such elections they run uncontested; voters are simply asked to vote whether they want to retain a judge in office.

COURT ORDERS

The readings in this section take a look at the complicated business of making and enforcing court rulings. The first essay by Susan Robison takes a look at how judges address child welfare in their courtrooms. Judges can wield enormous power over the lives of families involved in child welfare cases, especially in cases involving abuse. Yet children are often poorly represented in court.

The second essay by Danielle Langone takes a look at the enforcement of court decisions. For a variety of reasons, court ordered payments for child support and victim restitution are never made. A special report by the Council of State Governments offers guidance on how to improve that record.

Finally Anya Sostek's piece examines how some criminal cases are being influenced by the brutal expedient of witness intimidation. The result is witnesses who recant, or who fail to show up to testify.

Notes

1. National Center for State Courts, *Examining the Work of State Courts 2005.* Http://www.ncsconline. org/D_Research/csp/2005_files/1-EWFront% 20Matter_final_1.pdf

2. Ibid.

3. David Rottman et al., "Courts and Judges," in *State Court Organization 1998* (Washington D.C.: Bureau of Justice Statistics, 2000).

21

Kids, Not Cases

Susan Robison

The courts hear increasing calls for accountability. Better representation for kids in child welfare cases seems a good place to start.

I never went to court. I have been in and out of foster care since I was a baby, and I really resent that I never got the chance to speak on my behalf or even be present when my future was being discussed." This South Dakota foster youth's experience is all too common. In addition to being excluded from the courts that make life-altering decisions, many children in foster care do not receive the legal representation that the rest of us expect as a fundamental, democratic right.

In Colorado, during 12 years in foster care, 19-year-old Andrew has been in 42 placements. And not once was he present for the numerous court hearings about his case. Despite state statutes requiring that all children with dependency cases have an appointed advocate, an "attorney guardian *ad litem*" who acts in the child's best interest, Andrew has met with his only a couple of times, and they have never had what he considers a meaningful, private conversation.

Access to court and legal representation for children who have been abused or neglected can vary from case to case and even from proceeding to proceeding. Both the decision-making process and the results for children can stray far from legislative intent, often without legislators even knowing it. The courts, the ultimate decision makers in these cases, are far removed from legislative scrutiny.

Instead of playing the blame game that seems to dominate child welfare discussions, a growing number of legislators are determined to forge a new, more informed and productive dialogue with the courts. And that includes shining a light on court performance.

From *State Legislatures,*
December 2007.

KIDS IN COURT

Although executive branch child welfare agencies are more often in the public and legislative limelight, the courts have a powerful role in the lives of children who have been abused or neglected.

"Once you are in the system, your life is in their hands, not yours," says a former foster child from California. Courts decide whether children are removed from their homes and families, how long they remain in the system, and what education and health care services they receive. Only the courts sanction foster care, terminate parental rights and grant adoptions.

Historically, children have been barred from the courtroom because of the belief that it was inappropriate and unhealthy for the young to hear bad things about their parents. Many young people in foster care see it differently. They want a choice. These youths report that by the time they enter foster care, they've already experienced trauma. Court participation helps them gain a realistic view of their family and a sense of control—both important for getting on with their lives.

In a 2006 California survey, youths in foster care who attended court reported real benefits. Some were able to take an active role in decisions about their lives, while others found it helpful to simply be present and see how the decisions were made. Young people and their legal advocates believe that better decisions result when the judge can interact with children face-to-face instead of only reading a case file. The judge can observe the child's appearance and interaction with others, hear firsthand the child's hopes and opinions, and see that the child is getting older and needs a permanent family. One lonely child in foster care was unable to convince her case worker, foster parents or guardian *ad litem* that she desperately needed to see her sister at least once a week—despite busy schedules and conflicting demands on the adults' time. When she presented her case directly to the judge, a visitation arrangement that met her needs was accomplished.

A KINDER, GENTLER COURT

In some states, legislators have required courts to notify young people about hearings and to consider whether their presence is appropriate. Minnesota and California lawmakers make participation in court proceedings a

right. Recent federal legislation supports this approach. It makes court and agency consultation with children a requirement for states to receive Title IV-E foster care funding.

At the same time, foster youths and their advocates are not saying that it should be business as usual in the courtroom. Los Angeles County, home to 36,000 children in foster care, allows all children over 4 years of age to attend court. According to Leslie Heimov of the Children's Law Center of Los Angeles, children need support from a caring adult before, during and after the proceeding. They also need special kid-friendly waiting areas, opportunity for private discussions with the judges, and plain talk instead of legal jargon.

Many lawmakers are surprised when they learn that vulnerable children in their state do not receive adequate legal representation and are not given the opportunity to speak directly to judges. After all, every state has enacted statutes requiring appointment of an advocate to obtain firsthand understanding of the child's situation and to make recommendations to the court. Thirty-five states require an attorney to represent the child. But rarely do either statutes or court rules define the attorney's role, specify duties and responsibilities, or describe the necessary training. And there are few mechanisms for legislators to monitor the workings of the judicial and legal aspects of the child welfare system.

LAWYERS AND COURTS

All too often, capable lawyers find little incentive to represent abused and neglected children or their parents. Attorneys object that they are not appointed in time to prepare a case or allocated the necessary time, resources and compensation to perform even the most basic legal services. In New York City, poor compensation accompanied by higher caseloads and court backlogs led to an exodus of attorneys. In turn, families were disrupted, and children remained longer in foster care.

In addition to numerous caseloads and low pay, lack of specialized training and performance standards for both attorneys and judges plague the judicial process. Not only are procedures for handling dependency cases unique, but they require skilled professionals who understand the complex dynamics of troubled families and the maze of resources and rules for responding to them. Only half of the 2,000 judges participating in a 2004 survey had received child welfare training before hearing child abuse and neglect cases.

LEGISLATIVE OVERSIGHT

Ensuring that children's voices are heard in court is but one example of the need for greater oversight over courts and the critical decisions they make. Federal and state statutes make courts responsible for overseeing the actions of child welfare agencies in individual cases, but who oversees the courts? Although legislation and investment in the judicial system are necessary, some legislators are beginning to think they are not enough. With the public's eyes and ears on state government, legislators feel a responsibility to monitor court performance and its impact on children and parents.

This summer, NCSL took the unusual step of convening a group of lawmakers, judicial leaders and child welfare agency executives to examine how legislators can help strengthen the courts on behalf of vulnerable children. These leaders quickly cut to the heart of their dilemma: the risk that vulnerable children are caught in the middle of the constitutional separation of powers among the three branches of government.

To ensure an independent judiciary, courts traditionally resist legislative oversight. A Minnesota judge worried that legislators would attempt to manage the judiciary. Privately, judges admit their fear that legislators will try to influence the cases of individual constituents.

"We hold the public purse strings and are responsible for some oversight of how it's spent," says Washington Representative Ruth Kagi, chair of the House Early Learning and Children's Services Committee and member of the Appropriations Committee. Fellow Washington Representative and Human Services Committee Chair Mary Lou Dickerson agrees: "The Legislature funds state agencies and expects them to be accountable. The courts need to be accountable for taxpayers' money, too."

SITTING DOWN TOGETHER

Consensus among legislators was that it's up to them to improve communication and understanding as well as accountability. According to Fernando Macias, a former New Mexico legislator who now serves as a district Children's Court judge, "It isn't one branch of government ignoring another, but there is no transition." Texas Rep-

Representing Parents

Parents also face serious court obstacles that ultimately delay safe and permanent homes for their children—barriers that lawmakers often assume legislation has eliminated. Although 39 states require counsel for parents at some point during a child abuse and neglect case, representation is often too little and too late.

One parent described an experience that is not unusual: "When I arrived at court that morning, I was told this is my lawyer. My lawyer sat down with me for five minutes, asked me a couple of things, and told me to admit to drug addiction. I wasn't told the procedure of court. I didn't have any idea what was happening, and I was very much afraid, because the most important thing in my life had just been lost."

Many parents—especially absent fathers—aren't engaged until parental rights are being terminated. Parents' absence robs the court of the opportunity to correct case information that is all too often inaccurate, to give instructions and explain orders, and to have a direct impact on parents' behavior. In Washington, a cost study requested by the Legislature showed that family reunification rates improved after appropriations for legal representation of parents increased.

resentative Harold Dutton, chair of the House Juvenile Justice and Family Issues Committee, agrees: "Judges don't feel included in the development of legislation, but legislators don't hear from judges upfront."

To receive new federal Court Improvement Grants authorized in 2005, state courts have developed multidisciplinary commissions, and they are ready-made vehicles for legislators to hear the judicial perspective. In some states, legislators themselves have created court commissions or other workgroups, and they serve on these bodies in Arkansas, California, New York, North Dakota, Utah, Vermont and Washington.

"It's a continuing process of court-legislative education—not just during session," says Arkansas Judge Joyce Williams Warren.

LIVES BEHIND THE NUMBERS

Legislators now have better tools for monitoring court performance. National judicial and legal organizations have joined together to develop performance standards for courts that handle child dependency cases. State courts are taking advantage of federal court improvement grants to ramp up data collection and analysis, so more courts are able to provide statistics about the cases they hear, how they are handled, and how they progress.

But legislators worry that courts will game their numbers, and Judge Macias, the former New Mexico legislator, says that caution is justified. "Everybody—the court, child welfare agencies, even the legislature—paints the most positive picture possible," he says. Instead of disregarding data, judicial expert Mark Hardin of the National Child Welfare Resource Center on Legal and Judicial Issues warns legislators, "Be careful when using statistics in connection with requests for funding or for the expansion or termination of programs." Hardin advises policymakers to ask impartial resource people to help them interpret court numbers.

New Mexico Representative Jim Trujillo speaks for other legislators who want to see beyond the numbers to ensure that individual children and families are getting fair treatment, "I'm worried about the quality, not just numbers." Experts suggest a method called quality service reviews to scrutinize performance of the child welfare system—agencies and courts alike. Independent reviewers randomly select a few cases to examine in depth, dig beyond case files to interview key parties (children, parents, teachers or others who know the family, case workers, attorneys, foster parents, court appointed special advocates and others), and carefully analyze actions. Findings can help identify and correct problems that affect both individuals' lives and child welfare system performance.

HOLDING COURTS ACCOUNTABLE

Some legislatures have gone beyond shining a public light on the courts to make them more accountable. The Oregon legislature has directly imposed court performance measures and requires the judiciary to report on them. In both Idaho and Oregon, the legislature refuses to approve the judicial budget unless courts meet statutory guidelines.

Judge Nancy Sidote Salyers retired from the Cook County, Ill., bench where she was presiding judge of the Child Protection Division. At a time when foster care caseloads were growing unchecked, she worked with the state child welfare agency to reduce the court's dependency caseload from more than 58,000 to 19,000 and to quadruple the number of permanent homes secured for children.

She says the key to better performance for kids is getting beyond separation of power. "Incentives and outcome-based legislation can be tied to a shared vision when the powers come together."

Judge Salyers invokes the words of Andy Warhol—words that many youth in foster would no doubt find true: "They say that time changes things, but you actually have to change them yourself."

22

Payment Due

Danielle Langone

Policymakers grapple with the problem of enforcing court-ordered payments.

The Council of State Governments Justice Center recently released *Repaying Debts*, a first-of-its-kind comprehensive guide, supported by the U.S. Justice Department's Bureau of Justice Assistance. The report details how policymakers can increase financial accountability among people leaving correctional facilities, improve rates of child support collection and victim restitution, and make individuals' transition from prisons and jails to the community safe and successful.

Victims and children of individuals released from prisons and jails often don't get the restitution and support they are owed, according to *Repaying Debts,* a report recently released by the CSG Justice Center.

Former inmates typically must make payments to a host of agencies, including probation departments, courts, attorneys general's offices and child support enforcement offices. While coordinated collections efforts among these agencies could increase rates of repayment to victims, families and criminal justice agencies, there is rarely a single agency tracking all of an individual's court-ordered debts and facilitating payment.

Exacerbating the problem, state and local governments often have conflicting policies governing collection of fines, fees and restitution. For example, some agencies prioritize the collection of fines, fees or surcharges, while others prioritize victim restitution. These agencies often lack coordinated collection efforts.

LEAVING PRISON OR JAIL IN DEBT

Many people leave prison or jail with a substantial amount of debt, including supervision fees, victim restitution and child support. For

From *State News,* November/December 2007.

114

example, 58 percent of men released from prisons in Ohio and 39 percent of men released from prisons and jails in Texas report owing monthly probation or parole supervision fees, according to a policy associate with the Urban Institute.

Even further evidence from the report: An analysis of restitution debt in Maricopa County, Ariz., Probation Department, found that the 15 percent of people on probation with restitution orders owed an average of $3,500.

A 2001 study by the Center for Policy Research in Denver found that people released on parole owed an average $16,600 in child support.

The financial obligations of people released from prisons and jails often go unfulfilled, according to an examination of court-ordered obligations in 11 states by the National Center for State Courts. That organization found an average of $178 million per state in uncollected court costs, fines, fees and/or restitution.

Typically, people released from prisons and jails have insufficient resources to pay these debts—leaving victims, families and criminal justice agencies to compete for a share of the small payments that can be made. Nationally, two-thirds of people detained in jails report annual incomes under $12,000 prior to arrest, according to a 2002 Department of Justice report. In one 2004 Urban Institute study, three-fourths of people released from prison owing child support, restitution and supervision fees reported difficulty paying off these debts.

Federal law provides that a child support enforcement officer can garnish up to 65 percent of an individual's wages for child support. But at the same time, probation officers in most states can require that an individual dedicate a percentage (without a cap) of his or her income toward the combined payment of fines, fees, surcharges and restitution.

The inability of people released from prisons and jails to meet their financial obligations can contribute to their reincarceration. A national study from the U.S. Bureau of Justice Statistics found that 12 percent of probation revocations were due at least in part to a failure to meet the financial portion of probation requirements.

STATES MAKE HEADWAY

While no state has addressed this issue comprehensively, several have made headway, including consolidating the debt collection process; prioritizing the collection of victim restitution over other payments to the state; and modifying child support orders for parents who are incarcerated, when appropriate to improve long-term compliance.

In New Jersey, the Adult Probation Department consolidates the debts of people under supervision, and the department's staff is charged with helping people under intensive probation supervision with all their repayment requirements. Staff collects information about all debts an individual has been ordered to pay by various courts and directs payments toward restitution and other financial obligations. Then, judges determine how payments are proportioned, prioritizing child support, a victim compensation program and restitution.

Texas took another approach. In 2005 the Texas legislature reviewed the collections practices of courts statewide and found the courts were unable to provide information about what percentage of the total assessed court fines and fees were actually collected. A legislative review body was directed to study the purpose, collection, and use of court fines and fees. The review found that a Collections Improvement Program implemented in a handful of courts was effective in increasing compliance with financial obligations. The legislature approved legislation requiring cities and counties with population levels above a certain threshold to implement the program and to provide annual reports about their collections practices.

Arizona prioritizes the collection of victim restitution before other obligations. As part of the Financial Compliance Program of the Maricopa County Adult Probation Department, 14 full-time probation officers are dedicated to collecting probation supervision fees and victim restitution. They review individuals' assets and obligations at the first probation contact, set up payment plans and advise individuals of the sanctions associated with nonpayment. As a result, administrators of the Arizona program report a high collection rate.

Arizona's Department of Corrections is also piloting victim impact classes in six of its 10 prisons. The 10-week

Repaying Debts, a comprehensive guide that details how policymakers can address issues regarding financial obligations of former inmates, can be downloaded for free on the Justice Center's Reentry Policy Council Web site, *www.reentrypolicy.org*.

program is designed to help prisoners realize the consequences of their actions. As part of the program, victims make presentations to prisoners about how crimes such as robbery, substance abuse, drunken driving and violence can affect victims.

Yet another approach is a North Carolina statute that provides for the suspension of child support orders during any period when the supporting party is incarcerated, is not on work release, and has no resources with which to make payments. The provision is meant to minimize the accrual of child support arrears during periods of incarceration. It's also meant to provide an opportunity for the individual to find legitimate employment upon release from prison or jail that can provide steady child support and other debt payments.

To address the issue in Massachusetts, the Corrections Department each month sends a list of people who are incarcerated to the Department of Revenue, which is responsible for child support enforcement statewide. The Department of Revenue, in turn, performs a data match to identify which people have outstanding child support orders and sends this list back to the Corrections Department. A Revenue worker helps incarcerated parents submit a modification request to the court, and also informs court personnel of a parent's release date, so child support modification orders can be reversed when the parent returns to the community and resumes making regular support payments.

Though a handful of state and smaller jurisdictions have had great success, the failure of people returning from prisons and jails to meet their financial obligations is a growing concern as the number of people in the nation's prisons and jails continues to increase. To learn more about this issue and the CSG Justice Center's report, *Repaying Debts,* visit the Justice Center's Reentry Policy Council Web site at *www.reentrypolicy.org.*

State Officials Can Address Debts Owed

For state officials who want to address the debts owed by individuals leaving prisons or jails, the CSG Justice Center report includes six broad recommendations and guidance for implementing them. Here is a look at those recommendations:

1. Identify all state and local laws that can affect the financial obligations of people released from prisons or jails.

Laws and policies that govern what financial obligations may be imposed on a person sentenced to prison or jail vary significantly from one state to another, and even possibly across the cities and counties within a state. The report recommends that states compile relevant information and data from various agencies involved in this process, and use the information to inform the collaborative development of a strategic plan.

2. Coordinate the collection systems of the different agencies involved in collecting debts held by people sentenced to prison or jail.

Policies governing the collection of fines, fees, restitution and child support are often at odds within different units of government, making it difficult for people released from prisons and jails to meet their financial obligations.

The report encourages policymakers to pursue a number of strategies for improving and coordinating collections practices, including determining financial sanctions in one lump sum and setting priorities for disbursement, consolidating collection efforts, providing resources to pursue unmet obligations, keeping individuals apprised of the status of their payment efforts, capping collections at a set rate, and calculating realistic payment plans.

3. Enact child support laws and related policies that encourage parents released from prisons or jails to maintain legitimate employment, which will help enable them to provide long-term support to their children.

While a child's needs for financial support do not diminish when a parent is in jail or prison, most incarcerated parents have little or no ability to meet their child support obligations, according to a 2003 article in Corrections Today.

Research highlights the importance of programs that support employment and stable lifestyles, and in appropriate situations, facilitate and strengthen family connections during incarceration. Parents who make regular child support payments are likely to have improved familial ties that

(continues)

State Officials Can Address Debts Owed (*Continued*)

can help reduce recidivism and restore stability, according to a 2005 study. Realistic payment amounts can also help to ensure longterm payment compliance.

To this end, the report recommends child support policies that increase compliance by people who are incarcerated or returning from prisons and jails. This includes working with custodial parents to determine appropriate child support during incarceration, including modifying child support orders of people who are incarcerated and have no means to pay child support, and using enforcement mechanisms other than reincarceration when warranted by the circumstances to encourage payment.

4. Ensure victims receive the restitution they are owed by ordering restitution when appropriate; enforcing restitution orders; and educating crime victims, criminal justice personnel and people who owe restitution about its importance.

Despite the value and emphasis lawmakers have placed on restitution, it is not always ordered or enforced, according to a 2004 U.S. Sentencing Commission report. This happens for several reasons: the victim may not know his or her rights; law enforcement personnel may not collect information about a victim's financial losses; the prosecutor may not seek restitution; the judge may not order restitution; or the agency responsible for collections may not pursue restitution. The report recommends several methods for ensuring victims receive the compensation to which they are entitled. This includes educating criminal justice staff, victims and people who owe restitution about the restitution process and importance of restitution; pursuing civil remedies for outstanding payments; and withholding state tax returns and garnishing wages.

5. Make certain new fines, fees and surcharges do not reduce the ability of people returning from prison or jail to pay child support and restitution.

Court-ordered fines, fees and surcharges, unlike child support and restitution, are financial obligations to the city, county or state—not to individuals. With a growing percentage of criminal justice agencies' budgets dependent on these fees, tensions arise surrounding the priorities of these agencies and the needs of victims and families who rely on individuals released from prisons and jails for compensation and support, according to the report.

The report recommends policymakers take steps such as preparing re-entry impact statements when introducing legislation that contemplates new or increased fines, fees and surcharges, and limiting the reliance of criminal justice agencies on fee collection to support operational costs.

6. Establish sanctions and incentives to more effectively encourage people released from prisons or jails to meet their court-ordered financial obligations.

When people released from prisons and jails fail to meet their financial obligations, it's often either because they are unwilling, but able, to do so, or because they lack the necessary means to pay their debts despite their best efforts. The report's recommendations address both cases, suggesting sanctions and incentives or rewards (e.g., waivers of interest on accumulated debts). These recommendations also suggest strategies to increase the earning capacity of people with limited education or marketable job skills. They also consider the possibility of nonmonetary payment options, such as community service, for people who are indigent or disabled.

23

Terrified to Testify

Anya Sostek

Witness intimidation slows the prosecution of criminals.

In November 2004, when Baltimore City State's Attorney Patricia Jessamy obtained a copy of a profanity-laden street video that advocated murdering "snitches" who cooperate with police, her first reaction was disgust. Her second reaction was to make hundreds of copies and get the tape into the hands of every legislator in the state of Maryland.

The previous year, Jessamy had tried—and failed—to get the legislature to strengthen its witness-intimidation law. She felt that while she hadn't been able to convince legislators of the severity of the problem, the video contained the necessary shock value to effectively make her case. "It's like someone hands you lemons and then you make lemonade," she says. "The video was a horrendous thing but we were not going to allow the opportunity to use it for good escape."

In 2005, Jessamy's volley of videos paid off: Lawmakers passed a bill that elevated witness intimidation to a felony, quadrupled the maximum jail term and allowed limited testimony from intimidated or absent witnesses. Maryland's measure is just one of many either enacted or debated in the past few years seeking to address witness intimidation—a problem that big-city prosecutors insist is happening in up to 90 percent of their homicide prosecutions. But questions remain as to whether legislation or other conventional tactics can actually make a dent in a problem that has become ingrained in inner-city culture.

HEARSAY EXCEPTIONS

Witness intimidation, of course, is nothing new. Examples of jailhouse snitches date back centuries in England, while the concept of omerta, or a "code of silence," has also existed for hundreds of

From *Governing,*
November 2007.

years in Mafia communities. The difference between those concepts and what is going on today is that the "stop snitching" mantra has become a cultural phenomenon affecting law-abiding citizens and even children.

"People on the outside can't even conceive of what is happening here," says David Kennedy, director of the Center for Crime Prevention and Control at the John Jay College of Criminal Justice. "It's gotten just unbelievably bad. Even if you're afraid, even if you're a good citizen, good citizens don't deal with the cops."

Blatant examples of witness intimidation are unfortunately abundant. Six members of the Dawson family were killed in East Baltimore in 2002 when their house was firebombed in apparent retaliation for their repeated calls to police to complain about drug dealing. In 2004, Newark police attributed the murder of four people in a vacant lot to the fact that one was a murder witness; a witness to the quadruple murders was later killed as well. Last year, at least eight witnesses to the murder of a 10-year-old boy in Philadelphia went silent when called to the witness stand.

Jessamy says that she started to notice the growing incidence of witness intimidation about five years ago, in the course of looking at statistics charting why certain cases hadn't moved forward. Increasingly, cases were being stalled because witnesses either weren't showing up or were recanting their testimony.

In 2004, she promoted a bill in the legislature that would have both increased penalties for witness intimidation and enabled lawyers to introduce previous statements from a witness into evidence if a witness was unable or unwilling to testify because of wrongdoing from the defendant. That piece of the legislation, known as a "hearsay exception," drew ire from defense attorneys concerned that their clients would lose their right to confront their accusers. The federal government codified such an exception in 1997, and at least 13 other states have done so since.

The concerns over hearsay doomed the bill in 2004, and when it was passed in 2005 after the "Stop Snitchin'" video, compromises left parties on both sides unhappy. The hearsay exception was included in the bill, but only for statements that were made under oath, written and signed, or videotaped. In other words, if witnesses disappear before they are called to testify at a trial, a prior statement that they made to a police officer could be introduced into evidence, if it could be proven that their

disappearance was a result of wrongdoing by the defendant. A prior statement that a witness made to a friend, however, could not be admitted in Maryland.

"You have to work with the rules of evidence," says Lynn McLain, a University of Baltimore law school professor who supports a hearsay exception. "You want to give a fair trial to the defendant but you also don't want to give a payoff for witness intimidation."

The two sides in the witness-intimidation debate also clashed over the crimes for which the law should apply. Jessamy complains that the bill is a "toothless tiger"—in part because it does not apply to domestic violence and some child-abuse crimes. And many defense attorneys still consider the bill overkill. "The position of the defense bar was that the changes were unnecessary," says Maureen Essex, president of the Maryland Criminal Defense Attorneys' Association. "There was already a witness-intimidation statute in place, and I think that that was sufficient."

Since the passage of the bill, about 35 people have been charged in Baltimore under the new law, and the hearsay exception has been used a handful of times—including when a defendant's sister refused to testify against him.

CHANGING STORIES

Other states and localities have also seen a flurry of activity on witness intimidation. Massachusetts passed a bill last year to create a statewide witness-protection program and increase witness- intimidation penalties. This year, another bill was introduced there that would sentence juveniles charged with witness intimidation as adults. California saw a bill to lengthen the maximum time that witnesses could receive state protection. In Newark, county prosecutors this year started redacting witness information from documents given to defense lawyers before an indictment.

But states also are finding that the problem runs deeper than just the intimidators, and are developing strategies to deal with reluctant witnesses. About 15 states have witness-protection programs, although many have extremely limited budgets—New Jersey exhausted its initial $100,000 budget last year before coming up with more funds—and others have protections limited to six months or one year. In Congress, Representative Elijah Cummings of Maryland has repeatedly, and unsuccessfully, introduced a bill authorizing $90 million for state witness-protection programs.

But even when protection is available, many witnesses do not want to leave behind their families and their jobs. In contrast to the exotic locales and new identities popularly associated with the federal witness-protection program, state and local witness protection generally involves moving witnesses across town or to the suburbs.

And some witnesses—often after being intimidated—just stop showing up or cooperating in any way. It is against those witnesses that prosecutors are taking an increasingly hard line. In Newark earlier this year, prosecutors charged a murder witness with making false statements to police after he changed his story about witnessing a gang killing. Since 2001, Baltimore has been arresting and jailing witnesses who do not show up when they are supposed to testify. Jessamy argues that the practice, which she calls a "body attachment" and used 179 times in 2006, is a necessary step when there's no other way to get a witness into court. "That's the last resort, but we do everything to deal with this witness-intimidation issue," she says.

DISCONNECTED FROM POLICE

There's also the fact that witness-protection laws and tough witness tactics reach only the witnesses who cooperate in the first place—not the many witnesses who never identify themselves or refuse to talk with the police. That problem was dramatized in an April "60 Minutes" television segment in which the rapper Cam'ron explained that not only did he not cooperate with police when seven shots were fired into his vehicle in an attempted carjacking but also that he wouldn't call the police even if he found out that a serial killer were living next door. (He later apologized for the statements.) The show also featured several children saying that they wouldn't cooperate with police because it was against their "code" of behavior.

The real issue, says John Jay's Kennedy, is that witness intimidation is just one symptom of a larger problem: the distrust of African Americans toward police. While prominent rappers might have helped make "Stop Snitchin'" a catchphrase, he says, the problem of non-cooperation stems as much from anger as from fear of retribution. "It's not intimidation—it's racial schism," he says. "The community is by free choice withdrawing from any contact with law enforcement. People are handling their business themselves rather than going to police."

Kennedy says that many in inner-city communities believe that the roots of the problem date back to slavery, and that the distrust—and the prevalence of witness intimidation—has ratcheted up over the past few years because of heavy-handed police tactics used in drug enforcement. Laws to strengthen witness-intimidation penalties, he says, will have "no traction whatsoever" because the black community is already so disconnected from police authority. Kennedy argues that the only hope in reconnecting a neighborhood with law enforcement are major changes in policing, such as involving drug dealers in an effort to eliminate overt drug markets.

For her part, Jessamy agrees that legislation is just a small part of the solution. Her office, for example, produced a "Keep Talking" video to counter the "Stop Snitchin'" video and is making sure that every witness-intimidation conviction is trumpeted in the press in order to deter future intimidators. Still, witness intimidation shows few signs of abating: So far this year, her office has charged about a dozen people with the crime. "It has to be a comprehensive strategy," she says. "Legislation alone is not going to cut it."

VII

Bureaucracy

Americans are not exactly known for demanding more bureaucracy from their government. Bureaucracy has never been popular with the populace, who tend to equate government agencies with red tape and inefficiency. Here's the thing though: state and local governments simply cannot operate without bureaucracy.

Collectively, state and local public agencies employ roughly 18 million people. And despite the popular image, most professional students of the bureaucracy agree that most of the time they do a pretty good job.[1] Actually, so do most citizens. Ask them if they like government bureaucracy and the answer is likely to be a firm negative. Ask them about teachers in the local schools, the local librarian, the cop on the beat, or the crew down at the firehouse and you're likely to get a much more positive evaluation.

The funny thing is that public agencies such as schools, libraries, and police and fire departments *are* bureaucracies. Those who work for them, technically speaking, are bureaucrats. Governments rely on public agencies—what generically are called "the bureaucracy"—to get things done. It's not legislators or executives that enforce the law or actually implement and manage the programs they pass. The job of translating the intent expressed in budgets, bills and executive mandates into action is turned over to the bureaucracy. A reading program might be required by a state legislature, for example, but somewhere along the line it's a teacher who actually has to make that program a reality. We seem to like teachers and what they're doing, even if we do not like the idea of "bureaucracy."

Bureaucracy does a whole lot more than teach kids, catch crooks and put out fires. It insures that water is drinkable, that doctors, drivers and barbers are properly qualified and licensed, and that a record is kept of government actions so if a bureaucracy does screw up someone can prove it.

The readings in this section highlight bureaucracy as the institution that does "dirty work" of government, the detail oriented labor that makes the expressed wishes of representative institutions reality. They also highlight the people who run and staff bureaucracy and the challenges public agencies face in carrying out the specific wishes of state and federal legislatures.

WHAT BUREAUCRACY IS, AND WHAT BUREAUCRACY DOES

Broadly speaking, bureaucracy can be thought of as all public agencies and the programs and services they implement and manage. Most of these agencies are housed in the executive branches of state and local governments and run the gamut from police departments to schools, state health and welfare departments to public universities.

These agencies exist to implement and manage public programs and policies. In effect, bureaucracy is the "doer" of government. When a legislature passes a law to, say, set maximum speed limits on state highways, it expresses the will of the state. The law, however, does not catch speeders zipping down the highway. A traffic cop does. To translate the will of the state into concrete action requires some mechanism to enforce that will, such as the state highway patrol in the case of speeders on state highways. Virtually every purposive course of action that state and local governments decide to pursue requires a similar enforcement or management mechanism. Collectively these are public agencies and the people who work for them—the police, fire, and parks departments, schools, welfare agencies, libraries, and road crews. In short the bureaucracy.

The bureaucracy is not just an agent of policy. In many cases bureaucracies and bureaucrats make policy. Public universities, for example, have broad leeway to set the required courses for their degree programs. Such policies affect the day-to-day lives of millions of college students, determining where they will be on certain days of the week and what they will be doing (maybe even studying state and local politics!).

Public agencies do not just shape the lives of college undergraduates—they have an effect on everyone who lives within the jurisdiction of state and local govern-

ments. Consider, for example, the role of state regulatory agencies, which, among other things, are responsible for licensing a broad variety of professional occupations. If you intend to be a doctor or a lawyer, or a barber or a bartender, you may require a state license. To get that license means at some point—and probably on an ongoing basis—you have to take the steps required and monitored by the relevant agency as a prerequisite to licensure.

Bureaucracies are thus heavily involved in rules and regulations; it's just the nature of what they do. And this goes a long way to explaining why bureaucracy has such a negative reputation. Few people relish filling out forms at the Department of Motor Vehicles, dealing with building inspectors or getting a speeding ticket. Yet bureaucracies do not have much choice. Laws and public programs require rules, and the job of bureaucracy is to make sure they are enforced. This does not always make them popular, and there is a constant search to find a better way for the bureaucracy to do its job.

RECENT TRENDS

This section's readings look at bureaucracy from two different perspectives. The first is from the perspective of rules and regulations, both those bureaucracy has to enforce and those it has to abide by. The essay by Ellen Perlman looks at one of the least loved state-level bureaucracies – departments of motor vehicles – and their role in the REAL ID Act. The latter is a federal law passed in 2005 mandating tighter security requirements on state-issued driving licenses. DMVs are the lucky agencies charged with carrying out the federal law, which as it turns out is pretty much every bureaucracy's nightmare; they are being forced to take actions their clients will hate and being asked to pay for the privilege.

Penelope Lemov takes a look at a set of rules that few people have heard of, but have a tremendous impact on the way state and local agencies do business. The Government Accounting Standards Board set the rules for how state and local governments keep their books. A shift in those rules has set off a storm of controversy; in effect state and local governments are facing bills in the millions to comply with these rules.

The other two essays take a look at people rather than regulations. Specifically, they look at the looming problems state and local government agencies face in staffing the public sector. Chris Taylor takes a look at the looming exodus from state and local agencies and the debate over what, if anything, to do about it. Zach Patton looks at how the younger generation can be recruited into public sector jobs.

Note

1. Kenneth J. Meier. Politics and the Bureaucracy: Policymaking in the Fourth Branch of Government. 3rd ed. (Pacific Grove, Calif: Brooks/Cole 1993).

24

REAL Nightmare

Ellen Perlman

For state DMVs the REAL ID Act is turning out to be a real problem.

For the past five years, clerks at the Colorado Department of Motor Vehicles have been enforcing new rules for getting a driver's license. It hasn't been pleasant. As the new system has been put in place—a new requirement here, followed by another one there—DMV employees have been dressed down, yelled at, spat on and cursed by those in line.

This is not the usual situation at today's DMVs, because states have gone to great efforts in the past decade to make license renewal a friendlier, more convenient experience—letting drivers renew online or by mail; putting small DMV offices in local shopping malls. But there's a reason why Colorado clerks are under fire: The new rules, which have to do with creating a more secure license, have brought back long lines and frustrating misunderstandings about just exactly what documents drivers need to bring in and how long it will take the DMV to verify those papers. That's why Colorado, which established its own rules for securing licenses, may be the best place to look to see what it's going to be like when the REAL ID Act, the 2005 federal law that calls for a higher level of security for driver's licenses, starts going into effect next year.

REAL ID has just about every state, including Colorado, up in arms. It's not that states dispute the need for a more secure license. They are well aware that numerous institutions rely on licenses as identity documents. Their beef is with the U.S. Department of Homeland Security and its proposed rules for closing security holes using the state licensing process. The DHS rules, which finally surfaced this past March, ask the states to take on an immensely difficult task—some say an impossible one—and to pay for the privilege of doing it.

From *Governing,* June 2007.

124

There are rumblings in Congress about repealing the law. But as things now stand, the proposed DHS regulations for a new or renewed license call for all drivers to go to a DMV office in person and show original identity documents. DMV employees will have to verify those documents—birth certificates, Social Security numbers or other credentials. An impact analysis done jointly by associations of state legislators, governors and motor vehicle administrators figure that REAL ID requirements will more than double the workload of motor vehicle offices.

Estimates on the cost of the program are even more daunting. The National Governors Association figures states are likely to spend at least $11 billion of their own money over the next five years to get REAL ID up and running. The largest contributing factor is the more than 2.1 million hours of computer programming states will need to adapt their systems for new requirements for things such as eligibility verification and database design.

Several states have been outspoken about their misgivings over the likely problems. "If we had all the money right now, it couldn't get done in 10 years," says Matthew Dunlap, Maine's secretary of state. "This is bigger than the space program."

It's also a lot touchier, raising as it does politically sensitive privacy issues. To make REAL ID work nationwide, it would have to be supported by a variety of databases and that raises alarms for civil liberties groups over control of personal information. Although DHS claims that REAL ID does not establish a national database of driver information and that states will collect and store information just as they do today, that hasn't eased concerns. DHS's proposed rules, says state Representative Scott Lansley of Maine, "didn't do much for me in calming my fears about Big Brother stepping in and overstepping bounds."

Given those concerns, states have a decision to make: to comply or not to comply. REAL ID is not a mandate. It is voluntary. States can opt in or opt out. If they opt in, they would have to scramble to meet REAL ID's tight and looming deadlines. The first implementations are scheduled to go into effect in May 2008. States such as Colorado and Virginia are preparing themselves for that deadline. States that opt in but aren't ready to meet the 2008 deadline can request an extension, as most states likely will, but it may not make compliance any easier in the long run.

If states decide to opt out—as Montana and Washington have done—it could create major inconveniences for their residents, who would not be able to use their driver's licenses to board planes or enter secure federal facilities. An opt-out could also shatter the federal government's plans for how REAL ID will work.

GETTING READY

Colorado's experience is telling. The state kicked off its efforts five years ago in response to a problem that was rampant in the state: fraud and identity theft and the fake licenses used by criminals to misidentify themselves.

Producing fake licenses is low-tech and brazen. Burglars have used heavy vehicles to ram through DMV walls, windows or doors to steal license-making equipment and paper stock. Colorado DMV offices were burglarized four or five times. Or, identity thieves go "dumpster diving" behind banks, picking up discarded checks with driver's license numbers and names and using that information to apply for new licenses. Five years ago, when people came to a Colorado DMV office and said they'd lost their license, they would be issued a new one with few questions asked. Thieves were using 30 or 40 identities to obtain as many fraudulent licenses.

"When we went into the customer service business," says Joan Vecchi, director of Colorado's Division of Motor Vehicles, "it started costing us." Not that Colorado was the only state with such problems. In an effort to be driver-friendly, Maine cut a deal with Rite Aid pharmacies to issue state licenses—only to find that young store clerks were making fake IDs so their underage friends could buy beer.

When Colorado decided to cut down on the opportunities for license fraud, it convened an identity-fraud working group in 2000. It came out with recommendations on how the state should tighten license-issue procedures, and the DMV started putting them into action, starting with verification of such basic documents as immigration papers.

That was when Colorado's DMV discovered that cracking down is hard to do. People got pretty unhappy. Particularly upset were those drivers who use their cars daily for their jobs. They came in expecting to walk out with a license the same day, as they always had, but some legal immigrants were told that it could take weeks or months while their immigration documents were verified. "We'd say, 'We'll have an answer in three weeks,'" Vecchi says. "They'd say, 'What are you, crazy? We need to get to work.'"

The DMV soldiered on. It started using facial-recognition technology, taking pictures and checking them against 12 million photos to see if any other documents were on file under a different name. To cut down on the theft of supplies from local DMV offices, it set up processing of licenses at a central facility in another state.

Today, when applicants come into DMV offices, employees check Social Security numbers against a federal Social Security database and naturalization certificates against a U.S. Citizen and Immigration Service database. The electronic Social Security verification system has provided quick answers, but the USCIS's electronic system for verifying the status of immigrants has been slow and clunky, and sometimes information is incomplete. In part that's because the USCIS system was created for a handful of federal agencies to use to verify whether legal immigrants are eligible for certain benefits. It was not built to handle additional requests from the states, and certainly not the millions of hits expected to come its way once all states go live under REAL ID.

There are other documents that also need verification under REAL ID, such as birth certificates. As Vecchi sees it, the only reasonable way to do that would be for the federal government to create a database. Otherwise, states would have to hit 56 different state and territorial databases during the checking process. Yet, if a state opts out, its database would not be available, thus undermining the whole REAL ID system.

As to offering advice to others, Vecchi says "there's not a whole lot you can do to plan except be ready for an onslaught. We're holding our breath to see what DHS is going to tell us has to happen."

THE HOLDOUTS

The May 2008 REAL ID deadline may be less than a year away, but no one knows exactly what the rules will say. States were alarmed at what they saw as unrealistic timetables, unreasonable demands and huge costs contained in the proposed regulations issued in March. The rules were open to comment until early last month. DHS promises that its final regulations will address questions, complaints and suggestions received during the open comment period and, says Russ Knocke, a DHS spokesman, "provide the way forward for implementation of an absolutely vital initiative."

Knocke considers it vital because of terrorists' misuse of state driver's licenses to board airplanes before the September 11, 2001, hijackings. Admitting that REAL ID may be burdensome, Knocke notes that "there is a known vulnerability with state-issued driver's licenses. Shame on us if we don't take steps to fix it."

Early in the REAL ID process, DHS contacted some state officials so it could run proposals past them as they were being finalized. The department was not expecting the response it got. "The greeting that these proposals received was like something you'd see at Lexington and Concord," says Maine's Dunlap, who was one of the contacted officials. "Not surprisingly, after that the Department of Homeland Security went on radio silence."

But the states are speaking out. In addition to the two that have taken a stand by statutes, Maine and more than 30 other states have passed or are considering bills to protest REAL ID.

Knocke calls non-compliance a bad decision—not only in anti- terrorist terms but as an inconvenience to residents who will have to find another sanctioned ID in order to board planes. One sanctioned ID is a passport. And this is where some DMV officials get really ticked off. While the federal government is demanding hypersecurity for state licenses, it doesn't apply the same rule to federally issued passports.

Most people view the U.S. passport as the gold standard for security, but the passport office is not required to verify all state birth certificates. Even if a person applying for a passport can't provide proper identity documents, such as a previous passport or government ID, that person can appear with a witness to corroborate identification. Moreover, passports can be issued in any name as long as someone submits public records to establish the exclusive use of an assumed name for a long period of time. As one DMV expert put it, "If you've been living as Minnie Mouse for the past five years, you can get a passport in the name of Minnie Mouse."

States could not do the same under REAL ID. DMV administrators say they'd have to turn away a person without proper documents. "There's debate whether a passport is any more verifiable than a Sam's card," says Dunlap, referring to the bulk warehouse shopping chain. He calls the security weaknesses in passports and other federal documents a "huge hole" that no one's addressing. "The idea that we're going to solve the problem with state driver's licenses is a fantasy that leaves all these things unaddressed."

Federal officials have told DMVs that a passport is only a travel document, not a national ID. But security personnel use it to let people on airplanes under the assumption that it is a secure identity document. "Fine," Vecchi says, "but don't say the passport is the premier identity document, then beat me up for having higher standards and not wanting to use it." Her DMV's problem is that when it turns customers down because they don't have the documents the state demands, "they come back with a passport. Then a passport with a different name." When DMV employees ask for a second document, in addition to a passport, people, she says, "go nuts."

MOUNTAINS TO CLIMB

There are many problems with the proposed rules, starting with an unrealistic deadline. States seeking an extension have until February 2008 to do so. It would give them until January 1, 2010, to start issuing compliant licenses. By spring 2013, all licenses in states doing REAL ID need to be compliant.

The catch is, states that start on time have five years to complete the task, but those that start later don't get extra time to finish. The final deadline of 2013 remains the same for all. "We're rushing into something that can't be done," says D.B. Smit, commissioner of Virginia's DMV. "It's scary."

Another problem is the technology. It's not ready for prime time. If someone moves to Virginia, for instance, and comes to its DMV with a license from her former home state, Virginia has no way to check if the out-of-state license is legitimate. "Someone's got to tell me how to do that," Smit says. "We're not arguing whether we should improve security. If the Department of Homeland Security has a better mousetrap, we're willing to use it."

DHS officials are more positive. They see it as a matter of developing rules for data exchange for state-to-state queries.

But there also are in-state documents DMVs may be asked to validate. Drivers can corroborate their residency now with utility or phone bills that have their home address on them. To verify those electronically, a state would have to surf the databases of power and telephone companies, which are unlikely to allow state snooping. "They're saying, 'Not so fast, my friend,'" Smit says.

Along with those problems, REAL ID interferes with carefully developed funding cycles for DMVs. The number of DMV locations, employees and IT resources are based on the number of years in license renewal cycles. Twenty-four states now have renewal periods longer than five years. REAL ID telescopes that cycle to five. States are flinching at the predicted hardships in complying. Under the proposed rules, nearly 30 million additional people would show up at DMV offices over the next five years. DMV workloads would increase by 132 percent on average.

Virginia figures REAL ID would bring an additional 250,000 people into each of its 73 DMV service centers. "It would pretty much break the seams," Smit says, affecting transaction times and adding more stress on centers.

To ready his agency for REAL ID, Smit plans to move as much non-licensing work out of customer service centers as possible. For instance, some auto dealers currently bundle a day or two of car-buying paperwork and stand in line with everyone else. When they get to the counter, they do 15 transactions at once. Smit has been meeting with auto dealers asking them to use online services or go to franchises known as DMV Selects, which can issue titles, registrations and handicapped placards. "I'm telling them, 'We love you very much, but we don't want you in our service centers.'"

Smit invited an official from DHS to come across the river to Virginia so he could try to make him understand why REAL ID demands are so hard to meet. "The people across the Potomac think it can be worked out easily," he says. "We can't get them to understand. It's frustrating."

Maybe a light bulb would go on if federal officials took a look at the logjam the passport office faces each spring when the number of applications picks up as people get ready for overseas vacations. At these busy times, passport offices deal with several million more people than usual and use a well-tested system. States would be faced with re-licensing 245 million people in five years, all of whom would have to show up in person.

Right now, Dunlap sees Maine's non-REAL ID driver's license as being as secure as a passport, perhaps more so. The problem is that non-compliant licenses will create hassles for residents trying to get through airport security gates after REAL ID goes into effect. "That's one of the great dichotomies," Dunlap says. "Your less-secure passport will be just fine."

25

Going after GASB

Penelope Lemov

A change in accounting rules
could unbalance the books
for state and local
governments.

W hen public finance officers met this summer in Anaheim, their association's outgoing president kicked off the convention with an all-out assault on an accounting board. Thomas J. Glaser spent the lion's share of his opening-day address ticking off the follies of the Government Accounting Standards Board's recent rules and what the Government Finance Officers Association intended to do about them. GASB's "time has come and gone," Glaser told the 3,000 or so members in attendance, some of whom interrupted the speech with their applause.

The attack on GASB was more than a little ironic, given that when the organization came into being in 1984, the finance officers' group played a major role in persuading the Financial Accounting Foundation, which oversees financial reporting standards for the private and nonprofit sectors, to set up a special branch for government accounting. In subsequent years—especially in the early years when it really mattered—GFOA worked to build its membership's respect for and acceptance of GASB and the standards it set.

Today, GASB is a powerful entity. Its financial-reporting rules have the potential to bring a government's budget to crisis. Refusal to follow its accounting precepts could lead to a downgrade in a credit rating or a shunning by the financial community.

But it is also an agency under pressure—and not just from GFOA. There is a threat to its financial-reporting hegemony: At least one state and several of its localities are set to defy a major GASB accounting rule. What's more, the chairman of the Securities and Exchange Commission has suggested that the SEC participate in the selection of some GASB board members. Such a move could impinge on the organization's independence and bring it, along

From *Governing.com*, November 2007.

with state and local accounting rules, closer to federal purview.

There is a lot at stake in this debate. If the effort to put GASB out to pasture were to be successful or if the other attempts to undermine its independence or hegemony were to prevail, it could have a profound effect on the way state and local governments do business.

THE SCOREKEEPER

The creation of GASB, which replaced the National Council of Governmental Accounting, was a sign of times: The mid-1980s was an era when the finance markets were taking an ever-increasing interest in governments and their bonds, and states and localities needed to modernize and harmonize the way they kept their books. "We knew we needed an independent standard-setter," says Relmond Van Daniker, who was executive director of the National Association of State Accountants, Comptrollers and Treasurers. At the same time, Van Daniker adds, "there was always a very large concern about federal involvement."

By having the FAF add GASB to its empire, state and local governments would have an independent standard-setter that understood, as GASB's current chairman, Bob Attmore, puts it, "government financial reporting is very different from the business environment. Governments don't exist to generate wealth or net income but to provide services to citizens."

Furthermore, an entity such as GASB also would understand the financial-reporting needs of Wall Street and the investors who put their money into municipal securities. "Financial reports are like a scorecard," says Parry Young, former director of the public finance department of Standard & Poor's Corp., the credit-rating agency. "You need a consistent methodology for keeping score so you can compare and look at an entity on an absolute basis and relative to others."

In the past 23 years, GASB has issued 50 "statements"—accounting rules—on how states and localities should report their revenue streams and account for various assets. Some statements clarified current practices. Most dealt with mundane issues, such as how to report food stamps as revenue. Then, in 1999, came Statement 34.

Unlike previous statements, 34 stirred up a great deal of angst. In effect, it turned the way governments kept

their books upside down. Statement 34 called for accrual accounting, which measures not just current assets and liabilities but also long-term assets and liabilities—including infrastructure. In short, 34 was a demand for an inventory of fixed assets and the costs of taking care of them.

At GFOA's annual meeting following the issuance of 34, a huge ballroom designated for a discussion of the latest GASB statement was packed—not only was every seat taken but every inch of floor space was filled with finance officers sitting on their haunches and taking notes. The concern among many of them—and certainly within the leadership of GFOA and other public-interest groups—was that the statement would be prohibitively expensive to implement and would deal with information nobody would want and that no one had ever asked for.

Glaser, who was the chief financial officer for Cook County, Illinois, before taking his current position as chief operating officer with its Bureau of Health Services, estimates that it cost Cook County $2 million to implement the infrastructure dictates of 34. Moreover, he claims that the information the $2 million produced has never been used by anyone making public policy decisions.

Statement 34 went into effect in 2001 for large governments; small governments had until 2003 to adjust. But just as finance officers and their governments were coming to terms with 34, along came 45. Statement 45, approved by the GASB board in 2004, says governments have to account for the liabilities of other post-employment benefits (OPEB) just as they do for pensions. The bulk of OPEB is retiree health benefits, and it turns out those liabilities are huge—billions of dollars for some states and cities.

At this point, most governments are still trying to figure out the extent of those liabilities and how they will deal with such complex details as "implicit rate subsidy." Only a handful of agencies have decided how they're going to pay for an expense they always had but never booked. CalPERS, the huge California pension plan, is setting up a trust fund. Others may issue bonds or notes or use a pay-as-you-go approach.

But one state—Texas—is refusing to comply. This past summer, its legislature decreed that the state does not have to report OPEB liabilities nor do its localities—a change that was, in fact, more moderate than the original draft of the bill, which would have prohibited localities from reporting OPEB liabilities.

Nevertheless, it represented an in-your-face defiance of a major GASB statement. Some Texas legislators questioned the legitimacy of GASB, and Texas Comptroller Susan Coombs and other Texas officials tried to persuade other states to follow their lead.

What the non-reporting of its OPEB obligations will mean to Texas and its standing in the financial community remains to be seen. "To the extent that that information is not provided or is ignored," Parry Young says, "that would leave a hole in the information process from that government. It is not a very good thing."

For Bob Attmore, who has headed up GASB for the past three years, the Texas defiance came down to whether the fire would spread. "If others had followed, I'd be concerned," he says. "But most folks recognize that when they incur obligations and make promises, they should be accountable."

For now, the Lone Star State stands alone.

SEA SCRAPE

No one has fully adjusted to 45—and yet, this past April, GASB announced another major initiative: reporting on Service Efforts and Accomplishments, which is voluntary but still represents another burden.

The SEA project is developing protocols to help state and local governments set up performance measures and report on them. It does not say what services should be measured or how. That would be left up to each individual government. "What we're talking about is a sliver of what's referred to as performance management," Attmore says. "We're focusing on reporting the actual accomplishments back to citizenry. We're interested only in public reporting."

Nevertheless, the SEA initiative set off a firestorm. Along with GFOA, several of the major public-interest groups feel GASB is trying to take control of the performance management process, and that what's voluntary today will be mandatory tomorrow. "Even though they would argue they are not trying to require it," says Don Borut, executive director of the National League of Cities, "the moment a body known to be a standard-setter talks about recommendations, people will say, 'these are standards, and we have to follow them.'"

Van Daniker takes a more sanguine view. From his current perch as executive director of the Association of Government Accountants, which represents federal, state

and local financial officers—he is willing to give GASB the benefit of the doubt. "We agree with GFOA that there should not be standards," he says, "but we are willing to accept GASB's word that they will not develop standards in this area. I don't think GFOA is. That's what it comes down to."

It also comes down to a belief that, by entering the SEA field, GASB is impinging on political and budgetary decisions. "Focusing attention on SEAs is not an appropriate role for GASB," argues Borut. "GASB plays a positive, fundamental role in terms of financial standards, and that's where its expertise, talent and skill sets ought to be directed."

Esser is less tactful. He considers the board's move into SEAs nothing short of mission creep. "To a man with a hammer," he likes to say of GASB, "everything looks like a nail."

Despite all the tension last summer, GASB is moving forward with its project and has gathered allies from the public sector, such as the Association of Government Accountants and the National Association of State Accountants, Comptrollers and Treasurers. Meanwhile, GFOA and the International City/County Management Association are working with several other public-interest associations to set up an advisory commission that, according to Michael Lawson, director of ICMA's Center for Performance Measurement, "would look at performance management and the role it plays in larger organization leadership." The new association, however, is not necessarily in competition with the GASB effort. In fact, Lawson was among those attending a GASB presentation on its SEA effort this fall.

OIL ON TROUBLED WATER

Much of the overt tension between GASB and GFOA seems to stem from the SEA project, which surfaced in an environment of frustration with previous dictates. For localities, however, the issue may be further compounded by growing pressures that have nothing to do with GASB—namely, unfunded mandates and state and federal preemptions that have given cities and counties the feeling of not being in control of their purse strings or their destiny.

There are other theories for the ill-will toward GASB. Van Daniker, who has no problem with the board being the national standard-setter, thinks the problem may lie in the early history of the organization. When GASB was being developed, many finance officers thought they were going to have an accounting board that would write so many standards and be finished. "Well, they've written 50 now, and they have a big work list," he says. "What some people may be thinking is, 'Jiminy Christmas, we never thought GASB would be around this long, and all these standards cost money—maybe we should just get rid of GASB.'"

However frustrated the public-interest associations and their members—mayors, county executives, legislators and finance officers—may be, the tone of the argument has been more muted this fall. Jeff Esser is careful to say that his first choice is not the demise of GASB. "GFOA supports having an independent standard-setter," he says. "We prefer to have GASB continue with its original mission."

The softer tone may also reflect a coming together against a common "enemy." With the SEC making noises about trying to participate in the naming of some GASB board members, representatives of the big seven public-interest groups and GFOA went to see SEC Chairman Christopher Cox. "We indicated to him—and he acknowledged—that states have sovereign rights," Esser says. "He acknowledged that, specifically, setting financial and reporting standards is one of those." Esser feels reassured by a Cox speech in July that acknowledged the sovereign rights of states.

Nonetheless, the threat is there. And the SEC's vetting of GASB board members could lead to federal oversight of state and local financial reports. That's something GASB was formed to avoid and GFOA clearly opposes.

26

Duo Takes Public Service 'from Cotton Fields to Congress'

Charles Taylor

The baby boomers are leaving the public sector. Can a public service academy help replace them?

With baby boomers on the cusp of retiring in record numbers, where will the next generation of public servants come from?

If Chris Myers Asch and Shawn Raymond have their way, many will come from the U.S. Public Service Academy, a West Point-style university that, instead of requiring military service after graduation, will have a five-year public service obligation.

Its graduates would fill public service positions at all levels of government, from federal to state and local. NACo has enthusiastically endorsed the concept.

"It's been nearly 47 years since President Kennedy appealed to Americans with his 'ask what you can do for your country' call to public service," said NACo Executive Director Larry Naake. "The U.S. Public Service Academy will make it possible for thousands of young Americans to answer the call."

The proposal was the subject of a recent forum at the American Enterprise Institute, a conservative think-tank in Washington, D.C. Speaking at the forum, John Bridgeland, a former director of the White House Domestic Policy Council, called the concept "one of the most transformative ideas" he's seen in a generation.

"We face a growing crisis in public service because of the retirement of the baby boomer generation," Asch—the son of two public servants, a diplomat and a civilian physician at a military hospital—said in an interview. "We have tremendous shortages cropping up, particularly in rural areas, and at the state and local level, as well as at the federal level all around the country."

For evidence, one need look no further than Travis County, Texas, where according to a recent *Austin American-Statesman* arti-

From *County News Online,* January 2008.

cle, "Many of the county's six department heads and managers who work for them could retire with full benefits next year. A quarter of the 4,000 employees will be eligible to retire within five years."

Asch said, "Local governments that find that they are having trouble recruiting or retaining good people could apply to the academy and get graduates who would come and serve for five years."

It's an idea that germinated in Sunflower County, Miss., where Asch and Raymond, now in their 30s, met while working in the Teach For America program. Today, Asch says the idea has traveled "from the cotton fields to Congress."

BIPARTISAN LEGISLATION PENDING

Last March, bipartisan legislation was reintroduced in the House and Senate supporting the concept, the Public Service Academy Act of 2007. The Senate bill, S. 960, was cosponsored by Sen. Hillary Clinton (D-N.Y.) and Sen. Arlen Specter (R-Pa.). The House version, H.R. 1671, has more than 90 bipartisan cosponsors. The measures are currently in committee.

The proposal also has the support of three previous superintendents of West Point, Asch said. Among them, Lt. Gen. Dave Palmer, U.S. Army (Ret.) has said, "It stands without question that our country sorely needs a source of leaders of character dedicated to selfless public service in the civilian sector."

Modeled on the nation's five military academies, the U.S. Public Service Academy would provide a "service-oriented, leadership focused education" to more than 5,000 undergraduates, funded as a public-private partnership with Congress appropriating $164 million annually—or as the founders like to point out, less than 60 cents per American. Asch said the five existing military academies cost the federal government about $1 billion-plus per year.

Spots for nearly 1,300 incoming freshmen would be allocated by state, following a congressional nomination process similar to the one used for admission to the military academies.

The institution would be a bricks-and-mortar campus in the nation's capital. Its proponents have suggested the site of Walter Reed Army Medical Center, which is being shuttered by the Base Realignment and Closure Commission.

TODAY'S YOUTH EAGER TO SERVE

In addition to the impending boomer drain, Asch and Raymond note an equally compelling reason for the academy: an increasing interest among today's youth in public service—especially after 9/11 and Hurricane Katrina.

They cited in their "proposal for America's first national civilian university" that more than two-thirds of the 2005 college freshman class expressed a desire to serve others, the highest rate in a generation, according to the Higher Education Research Institute.

In his presentation at the American Enterprise Institute (AEI), Asch said a survey of 2007 Coca Cola Scholarship winners found that more than half would have applied to a U.S. Public Service Academy, had one existed.

Rising interest aside, academy proponents say many public service-minded students have a hard economic calculus to consider upon graduation.

"…[T]he reality is that most young people are forced to abandon their dreams of giving back to their country because their college loan burdens price them out of public service careers," according to the academy proposal. The cost of college tuition has increased dramatically over the past decade—up 47 percent at private schools and 63 percent at public institutions.

The average college graduate owes about $20,000 in student loans, an increase of more than 50 percent in the past decade, according to the Project on Student Debt.

"The federal government should provide at least one undergraduate institution that will insure that all students, regardless of economic background, will be able to pursue public service," the proposal states.

OPPONENTS QUESTION NEED

The Jan. 9 AEI forum considered both sides of the issue, and opponents questioned the need for a civilian West Point, when existing colleges can produce committed public servants. Stephen Joel Trachtenberg, president emeritus of George Washington University, and Phil Levy, an AEI resident scholar presented the opposition view.

"I'm a great believer in what would be functionally a civilian ROTC," Trachtenberg said in an interview, "that is to say, programs that funded training, education in public administration and public policy, but did it in all 50 states."

The academy's proponents counter that a stand-alone campus is the only way to create a "unique, unified campus culture" that develops a strong sense of mission around the public service.

Asch explained, "Having a college campus with sharp uniforms, and the kind of order and unity and *esprit de corps* that you associate with the military, but having it in pursuit of civilian public service goals, I think would be very inspiring and appealing to a lot of young people." In addition, he said the nation's military academies remain about 85 percent male, and the academy would provide an option for young women who are interested in public, but not military, service.

Levy, a former Yale University professor, said before the forum the problem isn't "an inability of the educational system to train people for the government," but rather the nature of government service, especially at the federal level.

"With the federal government there's some ossification, that you can enter the government and find that as a young person there's a very long, slow grind to get anywhere," he said. "You come in with no vacation days. And you look and there are people who are 20 years senior to you who may be working half as hard with three times the vacation days and many times the salary."

In a 2007 contrarian article titled, *The Pitfalls of Public Service U.,* Levy wrote that those disincentives to public service could be addressed by making government employment more competitive—"where talented civil servants are rewarded and promoted." He also suggested that government scholarships could be awarded to students to attend existing universities, with the requirement of public service after graduation.

Raymond, the academy's cofounder, says he's "all for scholarships." However, "There is no proposal for these types of scholarships, and there is a proposal for the academy."

"Scholarships are pretty easy to take away," he continued. "And so, if the political winds change, it's something that can be discontinued. I think it's much more difficult to do that for an institution that exists...."

GRASSROOTS ADVOCACY NEEDED

Asch believes the academy is "the kind of big idea that requires presidential leadership." To that end, he's working to win the endorsements of the current crop of presidential hopefuls. However, he adds that any American can help advance the concept.

"It's really old-fashioned grass roots stuff. The old 'contacting your congressman' is tremendously important—writing, calling. We have volunteers all around the country who are helping. They can help us win endorsements from local leaders."

Raymond added, anyone interested in helping "can take 20 seconds" to visit *www.uspublicserviceacademy.org* and sign a petition asking Congress to pass the pending legislation.

Asch said, "Building this institution will send a very powerful message to young people about the value that we as a nation place on public service." And Raymond is convinced "that the more people that hear about this idea will see the intrinsic value of what we're trying to do."

"I'm confident how good this would be for our country," he added. "And frankly I think this could be our generation's Peace Corps, this defining American institution following 9/11 and Katrina, that tells young people that service matters and that this country is going to stand behind young people that want to give back to their communities."

27

The Young and the Restless

Zach Patton

There are proven strategies for state and local governments to recruit and retain the younger generation. If only state and local governments knew about them.

T wo years ago, the American workforce passed a major milestone. A majority of the nation's workers now come from Generation X, born between 1965 and 1977, or Generation Y, born between 1978 and 1990. This shouldn't come as a shock to many people—baby boomers can't stay on the job forever—but for many, it takes some getting used to. Nevertheless, it's reality.

Except in state and local government. There, it's a very different scene. The average age of local managers has actually risen dramatically over the past several years. In 1971, 45 percent of local government managers were in their thirties, according to the International City/County Management Association. By 2000, only 16 percent were. Thirty-five years ago, 26 percent of managers were under 30, but by the turn of this century, only 2 percent were. The story at the state level is similar.

It's not that older government employees are refusing to leave their desks. Quite the opposite. States and localities are starting to lose experienced workers by the droves. But they aren't finding young people to fill the jobs the way private companies are. Most governments are concerned about this to one extent or another; many are scrambling to draft succession plans to determine their needs a decade or two down the road. But even the best succession planning efforts face one major dilemma: Boomer retirements leave an enormous gap to be filled, but will younger people, especially those in Generation Y, even want to fill it? How do governments recruit them, and then how do they keep them? This is the problem that the most sophisticated workforce specialists are currently focused on. And it's a very frustrating problem: A series of talks I

From *Governing*, September 2007.

recently conducted with a sampling of younger workers in both state and local agencies made clear just how complex the problem is.

For example, I had a long conversation with a young man I will call Mike Taylor. He works as a mid-level manager for the state of Tennessee. In his early thirties, Mike already has held a number of different positions at the state and local level, focusing on fiscal analysis. He has liked them all, more or less. But he's thinking of leaving. "I'd get into a job, learn it and get bored," he says. "When you're working for the government, it's easy to start thinking, 'I know this stuff. It isn't going to change. I need a new challenge.'"

In many ways, Mike Taylor sounds like a match for the Gen X-Y stereotype. Both cohorts are widely viewed by their management elders as being impatient, demanding, tech-addicted, narcissistic and needy. Some of that may be true of Taylor. But he's not selfish, or lazy or flippant. He's not a slacker. It's not even that he doesn't like government work. "I feel like I need something new and exciting potentially happening every couple months," he says.

All the academic experts who study these issues say Taylor is typical of his contemporaries. "I've definitely seen a shift in my students in recent years," says Paul Light, a professor at New York University's Wagner School of Public Service. "They're more interested in jobs that have significant opportunities for impact as well as skill development and personal growth. In the 1970s, people were looking for a 30-year career that would lead to stable retirement. Today, there's very little stated interest in spending 30 years in any one organization. Gen Y workers expect to shift jobs often, and they look forward to it."

TIME AND FEEDBACK

Jen Parks, a 31-year-old social worker who does substance abuse training for the Massachusetts Department of Public Health, is a little different from Mike Taylor. She feels fulfilled by her job in state government. But she worries that it will somehow come to define her, and she doesn't want that. She says she needs time for hiking, bicycling, making pottery and volunteering. "I see some other people working crazy hours," Parks says, "but I've just very purposefully decided to avoid that. I'm not going to let myself get consumed by my job."

Younger workers are looking foremost for flexibility, says Sally Selden, who teaches management at Lynchburg College in Virginia and is a nationally respected workforce planning scholar. Selden says agencies that offer flexible schedules, where an employee can work longer hours most of the week in exchange for Fridays off, are much more attractive to younger workers. "They enjoy their time. Having the option of flexibility—even if they don't use it—is a very, very attractive tool for young people." Once managers begin to understand just how vital time is to Generation Y, they have a much better chance to compete for talent.

If that were the only problem, the public workforce shortage, as serious as it is, might be amenable to some relatively painless solutions. But it's not that simple. The newest generation of workers wants more than time to explore personal interests. In many cases, they want immediate influence and access to decision making. "You need to get them on board, up to speed and owning some valuable task quickly," says Bruce Tulgan, the author of several books on managing younger workers and an expert on the Gen X and Gen Y workforce. "They think short-term and transactional. 'What do you have for me today? Tomorrow? Next week?'"

Tulgan attributes some of that need for constant feedback to the child-rearing methods of 20 years ago. Anybody who raised a child in the mid-1980s—or was one—knows how fashionable the concept of self-esteem was both in parenting and elementary education. Today's entry-level workers grew up with T-ball games where nobody was allowed to strike out. In Tulgan's view, this has helped many of today's young people feel good about themselves. But it has also led them to want praise from others—and reassurance that they're having an impact.

One way to offer that reassurance is to adopt a merit-based system for salaries and promotions. But this is something state and local governments have been extremely slow to do, and it is costing them. Selden, in fact, declares flatly that this is the most important thing governments need to change if they want to attract young people. "The biggest mistake they can make," she says, "is not providing performance-based pay. Younger people have come up through very competitive output-based programs. They have grown accustomed to rewards and pats on the back."

"I'm not interested in being an Analyst 1, and then an Analyst 2, and then the special assistant to the deputy director," says Tanisha Briley, who is 28 and is a management analyst for the city of Davenport, Iowa. "I just want to know that I'm valued and recognized. My generation is excited and committed, but we want to get started now. If you can't do that for us, then that's what's going to continue to turn young people away from government."

At the moment, private consulting groups and even nonprofits seem to have a better handle on the desire for feedback than government agencies do. Public-sector recruiters say this comes up when they compete with the private sector for young talent. Private firms, of course, can usually pay salaries much higher than government wages. Nonprofits can't do that, but frequently they offer focused work with a specific, well-defined mission—and benchmarks that make it possible for a new recruit to see what he or she is actually accomplishing. State and local governments haven't done very well at offering similar enticements.

But there may be more to it than that. Cuong Nguyen, a 28-year-old scheduling director for the borough president of Manhattan, thinks governments don't even do very well at promoting the advantages they possess. Born in Vietnam but raised mostly in California, Nguyen became interested in government work after a Peace Corps assignment in Honduras, then came back to the states and got a master's degree in public administration at NYU. He was an easy sell for the city—he knew he wanted to work there. But if he hadn't actively sought a job in local government, Nguyen says he might never have even heard about jobs that were available in the field. "I think that's really the area where governments could improve," he says. "They're really lacking in areas like HR and recruiting. A lot of folks don't know how to get connected. And if you're in school, just weighing your options, you would never even think about government."

Some of the steps that would improve public-sector recruiting are actually rather simple. Market research shows that Generation Y spends an average of 12.2 hours per week online—28 percent more even than Gen X. And the first place Gen Y goes to in seeking out employment is the Web. But many of the Web sites run by governments are simply lists of available jobs with links to applications. There's no effort to discuss why someone might wish to work for the government—or why the government needs them. "If you want people to come work for you, you need to let them know you want them," says Selden. "If you're only being reactive and not proactive,

you're not going to get the workers you want. They need to feel like they're being pursued."

There are some striking examples of governments that seem to be doing it right. Visitors to the Vermont state hiring site first see a banner reading, "Great jobs—an even greater purpose… When you work for the State of Vermont, you and your work matter… You are contributing to the betterment of the people, places and traditions of Vermont." But the site also emphasizes how a public job will help in professional development, with language expressly geared toward Gen Y. The jobs site talks about challenges and personal growth, and promises help "finding your path." It touts government as a "stepping stone" where you can gain significant experience early in your career before moving on.

There's another recruitment example for states and localities that's blunter, more aggressive and extremely effective: the military. Their entire marketing strategy is built on the idea that if you join as a young person, the armed forces will shape you into the person you want to be. As Bruce Tulgan puts it, "They say, 'Come work for us, and we will be the best managers in the world for you. We'll coach you and train you and make you into someone great.'" It's simplistic, but it seems to be the kind of message that resonates with Gen Y in civilian as well as military life.

IMAGE PROBLEM

Beyond recruiting strategies, of course, there's the much larger question of image. "Local government isn't really seen as sexy among people of my generation," says Briley, the Davenport management analyst. "I can't imagine a 20-year-old in college right now saying, 'I can't wait to be a sanitation engineer.'"

Briley didn't grow up dreaming of sanitation work, but somehow she did end up choosing local government for a career. She attributes that in part to her childhood in a housing project in Cleveland. "We were very much dependent on public services of all sorts," she says. "That's probably the thing that led me to where I am now."

Initially, Briley wanted something different: a business career where she could make a lot of money. "I fell in love with the women I saw walking around downtown, in their power suits and tennis shoes, carrying their briefcases. They seemed to have a purpose. They seemed so important." A year of study in Africa changed her mind. "I realized those were all the same issues people were struggling with in the neighborhood where I grew up," she says. Even so, she makes essentially the same criticism of public service recruiting that Cuong Nguyen does: If she hadn't been looking for a job in government already, it's unlikely she would have been attracted.

Fairly or not, Gen X and Gen Y continue to perceive government as a bureaucracy mired in paperwork, where new employees won't be able to make a difference until they've put in their time and moved up through the ranks. In many cases, the fact is that states and localities offer a better shot at instant impact than the private sector. But they don't communicate that. As Briley says, "local government has not done a good job of explaining what it does."

Part of the perception that governments aren't a place for social impact is rooted in the notion that governments are by their very nature inefficient, ineffectual and wasteful—an idea that has been drilled into Gen Y members for their entire lives. "The respect for the institution of government is so low," says Selden. "You've heard all the negative rhetoric, so why would you ever work there? There has to be a general shift in perspective, to see that government's not bad. You need for government to be perceived as worth your intellectual energy."

If any public employee would seem a likely counterpoint to the restlessness of the younger generation, it's Klint Johnson, in Maricopa County, Arizona. With a father in the military, Johnson attended 13 schools before he went to college. He doesn't need any convincing that stability is valuable. And as a 32-year-old fiscal policy analyst for the county, with a wife and a seven-month-old daughter, Johnson is quite a bit more career-oriented than many people his age. He even thinks seriously about his retirement package—something few workers in his cohort seem to do, either in the private or public sector.

Perhaps ironically, though, it's the retirement issue that is giving Johnson concerns about being locked into a government job for the rest of his career. In particular, Johnson worries about the defined-benefit programs that Maricopa, like most public entities, still offers its employees. With its written guarantees of fixed retirement income, one might expect a defined-benefit system to provide a form of reassurance. But after watching problems nationwide with underfunded pensions, and with the boomer retirement all but certain to exacerbate those problems, Johnson says he would happily opt out of his retirement system if he were allowed. He says he's beginning to view his pension the same way he views Social Security—that is, with fear that he'll never see it.

So, as much as Johnson values stability, he also wonders if betting too much of the future on one public employer might be a mistake. "Defined-benefit programs are designed to reward only those with lengthy stays within a particular political geography," Johnson says. "These programs discourage mobility within the workforce. My peers in the private sector have a lot more flexibility to move around."

Local Government

Local governments do not have the power or visibility of state and federal governments. Yet while they might lack the legal punch, the revenue sources and the headlines of other levels of government, they do not lack for responsibilities.

Traditionally those responsibilities focus on providing public services such as education, law enforcement and fire protection to a defined, sub-state geographic area (like a county, a municipality or a specialized school, sewer or water district). Local governments still provide all of those things and a lot more besides.

Increasingly, however, local governments are also dealing with issues that stretch far beyond the concerns of a neatly defined geographical area. Some of these issues are the making of localities themselves. Urban sprawl, for example, tends to have environmental, economic and social implications that do not respect local or even state boundaries. Other boundary-crossing issues have consequences but not causes at the local level; global warming and illegal immigration are current high profile examples.

The readings in this section highlight the wide variety of these non-traditional, boundary-crossing issues that various levels of local government are dealing with.

WHAT LOCAL GOVERNMENTS ARE

Local governments come in three basic forms: counties, municipalities, and special districts. Counties originated as, and to a considerable extent still are, local outposts of state government. For governing purposes, states historically subdivided themselves into smaller political jurisdictions called counties, and turned over to these basic local functions such as road maintenance and law enforcement.

Municipalities are public corporations, created to provide basic governance to defined geographic jurisdictions. Municipalities include familiar political entities such as towns, villages and cities. They differ from counties in that they tend to be more compact geographically, are more urban, and legally exist as independent corporations rather than being the local office of state government.

Special districts are something of a miscellaneous category that include everything else, and when it comes to local government there is a lot of everything else. The most obvious difference between counties, municipalities and special districts is that the former two are general governance units. They provide a broad range of programs and services. Special districts, on the other hand, are created to provide a specific program or service. School districts are the most common form of special district—they exist solely to provide public education. Other examples include water treatment and sewage management districts.

That said, it should be kept in mind that these definitions are fairly loose. For example, what constitutes a town or a village or a city is governed by state law and the powers and policy responsibilities of these different categories of municipality may vary considerably. Municipalities, counties and special districts are not even clearly separated by geography, but piled on top of each other, which can be confusing to citizens and create coordination and control problems for public officials. A county may be almost completely covered by a municipality, or a series of municipalities. There may be several school districts crossing over county and city boundaries. Fitted across these jurisdictions may be other special districts. Local governments fit together like some sort of three-dimensional jigsaw puzzle with some pieces missing. Given this, it should not be surprising to hear that local governments sometimes get into arguments about who should be doing what.

Though local governments can seem to be something of a confusing jumble from a big picture perspective, there is a fairly clear difference between the vast majority of local governments and state government. Generally speaking, state governments are sovereign governments and local governments are not. What this means is that state governments get their powers and legal authority

directly from citizens—this power and authority is codified in the state constitution.

Most local governments, however, get their power from state government, not directly from citizens. Their powers and legal authority are mostly set by state law, which is to say the state legislature. And what the legislature gives, it can take away. So unlike the relationship between the federal and state governments, which at least in theory is a relationship of equals, the relationship between state governments and local governments is legally a superior-subordinate relationship. Some states grant local governments broad powers, others reserve much of these powers to themselves and delegate comparatively little. Even in the states that grant local government considerable independence, however, the state technically is still the sovereign government, while the local government is not.

This hierarchy is codified legally in what is known as Dillon's Rule, which is the legal principle that local governments can only exercise the powers granted to them by state government. The independence and power of local governments thus varies enormously not just from state to state, but from locality to locality within states. Some municipalities are virtually city-states, powerful political jurisdictions with a high degree of self rule. Others are little more than local extensions of state governments.

RECENT TRENDS

The readings in this section highlight a range of complicated issues that government is grappling with at the local level, even though the causes, consequences and policy responses cut across different geographic and political boundaries. Zach Patton's essay takes a look at urban sprawl, a particular problem for sunbelt cities that have pursued years (even decades) of low density development. This growth has left in its wake pollution, traffic congestion, and a dislocated sense of community. Some cities are taking a fresh look at how to keep the growth while limiting the problems.

Christopher Swope's essay looks at the micro-level implications of global warming. While global warming as a policy issue is typically from a planetary perspective, its impacts are most noticeable at the local level. Local governments have little in their policy arsenal to slow global warming; the policy challenge is to manage the effects.

Sean Slone examines a new holistic approach to community and regional planning that is designed to promote healthier citizens. Originally developed in Europe, this approach is now paying dividends in the Untied States.

Finally, a second essay by Zach Patton highlights the paradox of cities that, for the most part, get everything right. Good location, good schools, good parks, good communities, good jobs; these are the sort of places people want to be. Cities with this good fortune, however, are not so sure they want everyone to know about their good fortune.

28

Back on Track

Zach Patton

Cities in the Sun Belt try new directions for growth.

Tracy Finch would prefer to show visitors around the south side of Charlotte by train. But the city's first light-rail line won't open until this fall, so for now, Finch is stuck criss-crossing the tracks in her Audi. Stopped at an intersection, she cranes around in her seat, fishing through a mess of rail maps, budget documents and development plans in the back of the car. As she grabs the paper she was looking for, some artist renderings of new buildings, a car honks. Finch sees the green light and heads off, navigating a maze of construction sites strung along the rail line.

"That's going to be 400 apartments with stores on the ground floor," Finch says, pointing to an empty lot hugging the tracks. "And that," she says of a low-slung industrial building a little father down, "is going to be 11 stories of mixed-use residential and retail." Although the line is still months from opening, developers have been staking their claim along it for a few years. In the South End alone, the city is adding nearly 4,000 residential units and almost 400,000 square feet of commercial space. "There's just so much going on down here right now."

Finch should know. As Charlotte's transit-oriented development czar, she has a focused mission: to ensure that dense, pedestrian-friendly villages cluster around rail stations. In a sprawling Southern city of 600,000 people that has grown up entirely around the automobile, that's a radical new mindset. And it's working surprisingly well. Developers are investing more than a billion dollars in projects centered around Charlotte's transit stations—and the trains haven't even carried a single passenger yet. When the 9.6-mile South Corridor line opens, it will be the first leg of a regional system planned to crisscross Charlotte and surrounding Mecklenburg County with

From *Governing,*
June 2007.

142

more than 75 miles of light rail, commuter trains, streetcars and bus rapid transit. With a price tag inching toward $5 billion, it's by far the single biggest infrastructure project in Charlotte's history.

Charlotte isn't the only low-density city pegging its future on the rails. Sun Belt cities are building out light-rail systems, in an historic break from the car-bound past. Planners in these cities hope transit will ease traffic congestion and help residents travel more efficiently. But if you think this movement is about getting more people to the office during rush hour, you're missing the point. Places such as Charlotte view transit as a tool for redefining the very nature of the city and how it will continue to grow. These cities are banking on rail to help create a walkable, urban cityscape—a sense of place in the Land of Sprawl.

Managing this cultural shift can be a challenge. Critics complain that light rail is an expensive way to move relatively few people around, and that it hasn't been proven to reduce congestion on the roads or pollution in the air. In Charlotte, cost overruns and missed deadlines have soured some residents on the whole program. Now, a well-financed ballot drive aimed at cutting off funding for rail construction threatens to cripple the bold experiment before it even starts. Tracy Finch acknowledges that embracing transit-oriented development is an exercise in education—for a city, for developers and for residents. "There simply hasn't been this kind of development in Charlotte," she says. But, as Finch points out while zipping from one construction site to the next, the phenomenon is already changing the face of the city.

A LONG-TERM INVESTMENT

Older cities, such as Boston, Chicago, New York and Philadelphia, have been shaped by their subways and "els" for more than a century. Then there were the "streetcar suburbs" of the early 1900s, places such as Brookline, Massachusetts, or Shaker Heights outside Cleveland, which lured city dwellers with the promise of an easy commute back downtown. In those days, nobody thought of trackside row houses or downtown skyscrapers as "transit-oriented development" per se. It was just how things were done before the era of suburban sprawl.

More recently, transit-oriented development has emerged as its own discipline within the urban planning profession. The tenets are fairly simple: Development should encourage walking and riding transit and discourage automobile use. To achieve those goals, projects feature pedestrian-friendly design elements such as ground-floor retail, limited parking, outdoor public spaces, enhanced streetscapes and buildings set close to the street. And, of course, easy access to transit stations. Ideally, these projects aim for a dense mix of uses within a half-mile radius of each station.

Portland, Oregon, is the most famous follower of this approach. Light rail in Portland has stimulated $3 billion in new development near stations over the past two decades. And a city-owned and -operated streetcar line has brought in $1.4 billion in new projects along its downtown loop since it opened in 2001.

Now a lot of places besides Portland are talking about transit-oriented development. Denver and some of its suburbs are building out a $4.7 billion transit system with 137 miles of light-rail and bus-rapid-transit lines. Salt Lake City is expanding its light-rail system, to stretch over 130 miles—it's already triggered hundreds of millions of dollars in new development. Other cities, including Austin, Dallas, Minneapolis-St. Paul, Phoenix and Sacramento, are all constructing new light-rail lines. "Everybody talks about smart growth now," says Robert Dunphy, a transportation and land use expert with the Urban Land Institute. "These cities understand that transit is a huge part of that."

But transit-oriented development is more than just the latest buzz phrase, its advocates say. Growing concern over air pollution and traffic congestion has policy makers looking for ways to reduce driving and to give people alternatives to an auto-only lifestyle. Meanwhile, changing demographics are fueling demand for this type of development. Many baby boomers want to trade the house in the suburbs for a more urban way of life; an AARP study found that 71 percent of older Americans want to live within walking distance of a transit station. The same is true among the young generation of "Echo Boomers" who will soon make up more than a third of the country's population. All totaled, predicts the Center for Transit-Oriented Development, a nonprofit clearinghouse for information on the subject, national demand for living above the tracks could double by 2030.

In Charlotte, it was the city's rise as a national banking center that began discussions about finding a new way to grow. In the early 1990s, Bank of America relocated its corporate headquarters to Charlotte. Other banks, including what is now Wachovia Corp., also proliferated there. With the banks came an influx of employees transferring from cities such as Philadelphia, New York or San Francisco. "These were people used to an urban lifestyle," says Finch. "They didn't want to live on a half-acre lot at the end of a cul-de-sac. They understood the value of a walkable neighborhood." At the time, Charlotte didn't have many of those to offer; Finch says that a lot of bank employees refused to make the move.

Planners began thinking about transit by mapping where population growth was already occurring around Charlotte. What they came up with was a five-armed figure, a slightly askew star with downtown at its center. The city council adopted this "Centers and Corridors Vision" in 1994. From that, planners started to see how they could use trains or rapid buses to channel future growth along those corridors. "We always saw transit as a means, not an end," says planning director Debra Campbell. "The real impetus for transit was how it could help us grow in a way that was smart. This really isn't even about building a transit system. It's about place making. It's about building a community."

Nobody worked harder than Mayor Pat McCrory to sell Charlotte on this vision. A Republican elected in 1995 and now Charlotte's longest-serving mayor, McCrory excelled at translating planner-speak into terms that resonated with everyday people. "Planners use acronyms and words like 'density' and 'R6 zoning,'" McCrory says. "People can't relate." The mayor liked to present two competing images of Charlotte's future. One included tidy tree-lined streets with bikeways and sidewalks. The other showed "traffic lights every 15 feet, strip malls and unlimited pavement." More than anything, McCrory stressed the idea that a transit system isn't intended to be a quick fix but rather a long-term investment.

McCrory's argument worked. In 1998, residents in Mecklenburg County voted for a half-cent sales tax increase to help pay for transit. That would cover the 25 percent local share of the overall cost; the state pays 25 percent and the federal government pays half. Voters also approved $50 million in bonds to pay for infrastructure improvements related to light rail. In 2005, the federal government approved funding for the first segment of the system. All the while, the city was focused on bringing in development along the proposed South Corridor route. It wasn't easy. Developers were skittish about com-

mitting to the project until the federal funding came through.

Charlotte did two creative things to build momentum, turning its effort into a national model for transit-oriented development. First, the city ran a commuter trolley along existing freight tracks in the South End—the same tracks the light-rail trains will use. The trolley opened in 2001 and ran for only a couple of years along a relatively short section of tracks. But as a public relations tool, it helped residents and developers taste the potential. Campbell calls the trolley an "instrumental catalyst" for showing what this transit thing was all about.

Second, the city created Tracy Finch's job. Finch's position—coordinator for station area development—is evenly split between the city's economic development office and its transit agency, and may be the only such dual-purpose position in the nation. Finch collaborates with developers to make sure projects in the transit corridor match the city's new sensibilities. When one developer wanted to open a Lowe's hardware store a block from the rail line, Finch worked with him to wrap the big-box store in street-front residential units, move half the parking lot to the back of the store and put the rest of the parking on the roof.

NEW SUBURBANISM

Huntersville is a suburb 15 miles north of downtown Charlotte. Twenty years ago, 3,000 people lived there, and locals jokingly called it "Hootersville," after the tiny town from "Green Acres." Today, it's home to 40,000 residents, and remains one of the fastest-growing cities in North Carolina. Signs of transition are everywhere. At the homey, wood-paneled Toast Cafe, customers are still greeted by name, but the breakfast specials on a recent weekday morning included an asparagus-and-brie omelet and a ham-and-gruyere quiche.

Huntersville is positioned to get a rail station on its main street, a block down from the Toast Cafe. Unlike the soon-opening line to Charlotte's south, however, the North Corridor line still exists mostly on paper. Nevertheless, Huntersville planners are eager to use the line to help re-orient the town's runaway growth. In the late 1990s, Huntersville and a few other northern suburbs brought in Andres Duany, the New Urbanist guru, to sketch out a vision for development along the corridor. Duany called the stations "a string of pearls," and he encouraged the towns to design for a rail line, even though it hadn't been officially proposed at the time.

That's exactly what's happened. All along the proposed northern route, builders have made plans for high-density development. Huntersville is already moving forward on an ambitious plan to create a 400-acre transit village, a walkable mix of housing, retail and office space. Mecklenburg County plans to spend over $30 million to reroute the existing tracks so that the new development can straddle both sides of the future station. Huntersville expects the development to bring more than half a billion new dollars to the region.

Not all of Charlotte's suburbs have been as enthusiastic about transit-oriented development as Huntersville. The town of Pineville voted against having the South Corridor line extended there because, the mayor said, Pineville couldn't handle the density required to make light rail work. And commissioners in Iredell County, just north of Mecklenburg, recently voted to stop the commuter-rail tracks at the county line. Generally, though, suburbs are eagerly preparing for the train. "What they wanted to happen is happening," says Nate Bowman, a Huntersville developer who's already working on some other high- density projects in town. "All the developers have already lined up all the way up the line." In the old center of Huntersville, business leaders have erected a booster-ish sign on the spot where the station would go, urging residents to "Ride the Rail!"

But the rail may never come to Huntersville. Opponents are building a campaign against transit that threatens to undermine the future of the entire plan. The problems began last fall. Cost overruns, due partly to the skyrocketing price of cement and steel, pushed construction of the South Corridor line up to $463 million. That's $36 million over budget and more than double the original projection when the line was first proposed.

The news galvanized opponents of the transit plan. A loosely organized but deep-pocketed group of local business leaders is mounting an effort to repeal the half-cent sales tax passed in 1998. They hired a private company to gather enough signatures to force a vote on the repeal this November. For these critics, rising costs were merely the final straw. They never believed transit was a good fit for such a spread-out place as Charlotte in the first place.

"The whole thing has been a colossal mess from the start," says Don Reid, a former city council member who is helping to run the tax- repeal effort. "We don't have the density to support transit, and you can't force the density unless you spend considerably more money. Yes, transit is bringing development, but only at a huge expense to taxpayers." Reid and others would like to see the money Charlotte is spending on transit used for other purposes. "We don't have enough people to fight crime; we don't have enough room in our schools; and our roads are in their worst shape in 30 years."

Those are common arguments against transit-oriented development across the country. Many people believe funds would be better invested by expanding and maintaining existing roadways. "It can be tough," says the Urban Land Institute's Dunphy. "The forces of business-as-usual are strong to overcome." Especially in cities where residents have always driven everywhere they need to go, transit can seem like an affront to the accepted way of life. "Many people still think of 'density' as a bad word," says Tim Halbur of the Center for Transit- Oriented Development. "They think it means 'projects' and public housing."

Charlotte's transit boosters are confident they'll prevail in November. Voters have supported transit several times in the past, and city officials, from the planners to Mayor McCrory, have worked hard to build support within the community. Tina Votaw, a planner with the city agency in charge of light rail, says it's important to convey a big-picture message to the public. "You have to be honest and say, 'You're right. This transit line might not help you. But it might help your neighbors. It might help your children.' " Votaw adds that traffic congestion isn't going away, and that adding lanes to busy freeways is a short-term solution to traffic problems. "We're not traditionally good at taking the long view," she says. "But you've got to impress that upon people one by one."

MORE THAN TRAINS

Even without political opposition, it's difficult for cities to get transit-oriented development right. Most cities are stuck with outdated zoning codes that strictly prohibit the kind of mixed-use development that is critical to success. And even with the proper zoning in place, a city may find itself facing what planners often call transit-oriented development's evil twin—transit-adjacent development.

Just because a building is located near a transit station does not mean it's "transit-oriented." For example, look at what's happened around Atlanta's Lindberg metro station, in the ritzy Buckhead area. City plans called for a mixed-use village of residences, ground-floor retail and office space. While it looked good on paper, the end result didn't work as the city had hoped. The mix of uses wound up segregated into distinct areas near the station, connected by lifeless pedestrian walkways. Visitors to Lindberg can feel intimidated by the looming corporate towers and parking decks.

Another challenge is what Tim Halbur calls the "island problem." By focusing so intently on the area immediately surrounding a transit station, a city may end up with a well-designed station area that can't relate to its surroundings. That was the problem in Beaverton, Oregon, seven miles west of Portland. The city worked hard to make the area around its light-rail station, which opened in 2001, accessible to pedestrians. "They put a lot of thought into the station area," Halbur says, "and it's beautiful. But it's surrounded by automobile- oriented development. The hope is that the station area becomes a catalyst that will spread out. But it won't spread if you don't also invest in the necessary infrastructure improvements to link it with the rest of the city." That means sidewalks and through-streets that connect the station to the blocks around it.

Because transit-oriented development represents such a radical break from standard practice, it's best to get planners, residents, developers and transit managers talking at the earliest stages of planning. That's been the biggest lesson learned in Denver. The city's first light-rail trains began running in 1994, but it took another decade for the development side of the equation to catch on. "When I first started talking about transit-oriented development then, nobody knew what it was," says Bill Sirois, who manages development issues for the growing rail system. "It really has exploded in the past two years. But the earlier you can get involved in the process, the better."

That's certainly been the mantra in Charlotte. For the past 15 years of development planning, the city has worked to have as many players involved as possible. And from the beginning, transit was seen as much more than the trains on the tracks. It's the tool for building the Charlotte of the 21st century. That's hard work, but for Tracy Finch, the underlying idea is pretty simple. "You can't just put the transit line in and expect development to come."

Note

This article has been modified from the printed version, which incorrectly listed Orlando as constructing a light-rail system. The new commuter-rail system in the Orlando area will use existing railroad tracks, without light rail.

29

Local Warming

Christopher Swope

Local governments cannot stop global warming, but they can start dealing with it.

It's a blue-sky morning in Seattle, which means that Ron Sims can see the Cascades all the way from his downtown office. The mountain range cuts a long, jagged shadow on the eastern horizon, before heaving upward to the surreal snow-capped heights of Mount Ranier. It's a nice view, but there's nothing pretty about what Sims, the King County executive, knows is going on up in the mountains: Temperatures there have nudged higher in recent decades and, as a result, the snowpack has declined by as much as 60 percent in some places.

Historically, the pattern has been that each winter, snow piles up high in the Cascades, and each spring and summer, that snow gradually melts. Cities depend on the runoff for drinking water, farmers depend on it for irrigation and hydroelectric dams depend on it to generate almost all of the region's power. In other words, modern human life here is calibrated to one grand assumption: that complex cycles of water, ice and slush will keep working pretty much as they always have.

The problem is, they aren't. And that's what has Ron Sims concerned. Temperatures are up one-and-a-half degrees from a century ago. And as global warming heats up, that trend is expected to accelerate. Scientists at the University of Washington predict that local temperatures will rise another 1.9 degrees by the 2020s and 2.9 degrees by the 2040s. What that means for weather this winter, or for any specific year in the future, is hard to say. But scientific modeling points to a couple of inescapable conclusions that have huge implications for how King County plans its future.

One is that a lot of the water that used to fall as snow in the Cascades instead is going to fall as rain. So rather than trickling from

From *Governing.com,* December 2007.

the mountains for months, that water will rush down the valleys, surge into floodplains and strain levees that were designed for cooler times. Flooding events such as the one last November, which caused $34 million worth of damage, are likely to become more frequent. The other conclusion is directly related to the first. Less snow in the mountains means less snowmelt in the spring and summer. And that means water for drinking, farming and generating power will be a lot harder to come by.

The science has pointed Sims to a conclusion that many of his peers will find hard to swallow. No matter how many hybrid cars they buy for government fleets or energy-efficient light bulbs they install in government buildings, some degree of climate change is inevitable. The amount of greenhouse gas already in the atmosphere is simply too great to avoid any consequences. "With all the discussion we've had on global warming, I am stunned that people haven't realized that it's actually going to occur," Sims says. "The ice caps are melting now. They're not going to refreeze next year because we reduce our emissions. We're going to live in that world. So plan for it."

Sims is not saying that governments should give up on reducing their carbon footprints. In fact, both King County and the city of Seattle are national leaders in reducing emissions through the use of biofuels and other measures. However, if most of the talk about global warming—and all of the controversy—have been about mitigation, Sims believes that governments must also start thinking about adaptation.

So King County has begun looking out to the year 2050 and planning backwards. County staffers are working with scientists to understand what the local impacts of climate change are likely to be. They expect coastal-erosion problems associated with rising sea levels, health crises associated with new infectious diseases and heat stroke, public-safety difficulties associated with more frequent forest fires and ecological issues associated with endangered habitat for salmon. Climate change won't affect every region in the U.S. in quite the same way, but every region will be affected somehow. That's why King County also published a guidebook for local, regional and state governments. It's called "Preparing for Climate Change," and it's essential reading for government managers everywhere.

King County is building climate-change risks into all of its long-term planning and policy-development processes.

Last month, the county council agreed to a tax inspired by the looming dangers of climate change—a down payment on Sims' $335 million plan to bolster levees and reduce flood risks during warmer, wetter winters. "We're learning to define ourselves not in 2007 terms or 2009 terms but in 2050 terms," Sims says. "It's a gamble. We're making decisions based on something that has not occurred yet, but we believe from the science that it's what will be.

"I don't think we're being unreasonable," Sims goes on. "But I don't know how you divorce your immediate issues from 2050. If you get there by accident, fine. But if you know you need to plan and don't, to me that's negligent."

ADAPTATION PLANNING

There's a paradox about climate change that you can easily miss, even if you accepted all the arguments in Al Gore's documentary, "An Inconvenient Truth." For a problem that is global in scope and whose politics reverberate internationally, the on-the-ground consequences of climate change are entirely local. And local governments, by and large, will be the ones stuck dealing with floods and drought, fires and storms, infectious diseases and invasive species.

Ron Sims' call for municipal officials to adapt for global warming may sound daunting. It shouldn't. Most cities and counties are accustomed to doing land-use planning, natural-hazards planning and, since 9/11 and Hurricane Katrina, disaster planning. Most of global warming's local perils are familiar problems, only magnified. And although environmentalists don't like to talk about this, some regions stand to gain. Longer warm seasons for agriculture and recreation could be a boon for some northern climes.

What's difficult about adaptation planning is that it casts doubt on many long-held assumptions.

Take the concept of the "100-year flood." That benchmark is deeply ingrained in local planning documents, building codes and the federal flood insurance program. Yet a 100-year flood today may not mean the same thing just 20 or 30 years from now. Scott Shuford, a city planner who has worked in St. Petersburg, Florida, and Asheville, North Carolina, says climate change essentially voids the historical record. "Basically, we're looking at changes to our climate that have not been witnessed for centuries or millennia," Shuford says.

The other cognitive leap with adaptation is a matter of acceptance. This isn't the old debate about whether or not global warming is for real—that is settled. Rather, the debate is among environmentalists and others who never doubted the problem. Until recently, adaptation was something of a dirty word. Some greens believed that time, money or resources dedicated to planning for a warmer world only distracted from the hard work of preventing warming in the first place. Some still see adaptation as waving the white flag. "It's kind of depressing," says Anne Marie Holen, who coordinates a global warming task force in Homer, Alaska. "It's hard not to see the need for adaptation as a sign of failure. If we'd begun serious mitigation measures when scientists first began warning government leaders about global warming and climate change, we wouldn't be in such a pickle."

COMPANION EFFORTS

Despite Holen's misgivings, Homer is one of a handful of communities around the country that have begun thinking about adaptation. Homer, a coastal town of 5,000, is feeling vulnerable to nature's whims. A recent run of warm, dry summers brought an invasion of spruce bark beetles that ravaged millions of acres of forest. Then this summer, about 75 square miles of the weakened timberland caught fire. Homer also is susceptible to sea-level rise: The city's port and its major tourist draws are located on a low lying spit. Many locals noticed when the Anchorage Daily News ran a front-page story in October about three Alaskan villages that must relocate, at a cost of $330,000 per person, because of coastal erosion. "That's just the beginning," Holen says.

Holen's task force is looking at how to scrutinize coastal development more closely, account for wildfire risks, bolster storm-water infrastructure and develop new sources for drinking water. The goal is to go back later and inject that thinking into the city's comprehensive plan. "The advice I'd have for other communities is take it seriously now," she says. "Because the challenges and the costs will only increase the longer we wait. And the impacts on families and on city budgets will only increase."

A few larger localities also are paying attention. Boston Mayor Tom Menino recently asked for an adaptation plan for the city. He also ordered that any construction or renovation of public facilities include an evaluation of the project's climate-change vulnerabilities and a description

of how to manage those risks. A climate-change task force in Chicago has been studying adaptation questions such as what kinds of trees will thrive in a warmer climate and how to handle warm-weather pests such as termites.

In Miami-Dade County, the big worry is a rise in sea level. Harvey Ruvin, the county clerk and a longtime activist on climate change, is grim about accelerating ice melts in Greenland and the Arctic Ocean. His biggest fear is what scientists call the "albedo effect." That's where solar energy is absorbed into the seas where it used to reflect off icepack, creating a feedback loop of melting and warming. In the worst-case scenario, sea level would rise quite suddenly, not imperceptibly over a long period of time.

Ruvin, who chairs a climate-change advisory task force, ordered maps of what Miami-Dade would look like with the sea level one, two, three and five feet higher than it is now. At the upper end of that range, most coastal areas, including Ruvin's home in Miami Beach, are underwater. But even the low end of the range shows salt water intruding into the county's drinking-water sources. "We've got to reduce our use of fossil fuels, but at the same time we have to deal with adaptation," Ruvin says. "Those are companion efforts."

SHARING THE SCIENCE

Almost everything Ron Sims knows about global warming he learned from scientists at the University of Washington. The Climate Impacts Group brings together climatologists, hydrologists and experts in aquatic, coastal and forest ecosystems. If scientists are often caricatured as insular and aloof, this group defies the stereotype by making public engagement essential to its mission. No entity has done more to explain to people and policy makers in the Pacific Northwest how global climate patterns are playing out in their backyard.

The Climate Impacts Group gets much of its funding from the federal government. But many of its clients are state and local agencies. Water systems and utilities have been particularly interested in the researchers' work on the Cascades' retreating snowpack. "In the last two years, the demands on our time have really shot through the roof," says outreach specialist Lara Whitely Binder. "Local governments are saying, 'Okay we get it.' They're asking us to share the science with them because they're ready to take action on it, and they're trying to bring themselves up to speed."

As state and local leaders begin thinking about adaptation, the first people to find are the nearest climate scientists. Most of what's known about global warming is, not surprisingly, global in scope. Somebody has to "downscale" the data to local conditions to make it useful for communities to plan around. Climate scientists may, in fact, become every bit as crucial to state and local policy making as demographers and economists. Because if you accept the idea of planning for a warmer future, then you also must accept the idea of making decisions based upon scientific modeling rather than historical observation.

That's a big leap. Politicians usually want certainty before they stick their necks out. Yet there is much about climate change that scientists are still unsure of. For example, changes in precipitation are notoriously hard to predict. That's because so many forces, from ocean currents to topography to vegetation, drive weather patterns, and each responds slightly differently to rising temperatures. When it comes to temperature, on the other hand, scientists are dead certain that the whole planet is warming. They disagree only on the question of how much.

As Sims sees it, the fact that scientists are still debating details is no reason for government not to act now. After all, governments are accustomed to building highways based on traffic projections or schools based on projections of school-age children. "Here's what I say: I don't need perfect, I need approximate," Sims explains. "I'll never be a scientist. I'm a policy maker. Our job is to ask, 'Do you think this might happen?' and when the answer is yes, that's sufficient for me."

Perhaps the biggest problem with the science is that there's not enough of it to go around. "Local warming" is something of an emerging field. And government at all levels has failed to fund enough downscaling work, given the stakes. The Climate Impacts Group is one of only eight such teams around the country—and not every region has one of its own. "We've been working for years to show there's a problem" with global warming, says Josh Foster, a program specialist with the University Corporation for Atmospheric Research. "Now we've convinced everyone there's a problem and overnight they want much greater certainty. We haven't invested enough resources into the questions for which answers are now being demanded."

Building research capacity is a crucial matter and one that states might be well suited to help with. Washington State, for example, has contracted with the Climate Impacts Group to model climate changes across the state down to a scale of six kilometers. And California produces a biennial report on climate impacts across the state. By revisiting the issue every two years, California is recognizing the importance of keeping policy makers up to date with the latest understanding of what's going on.

On the national level, Shuford is working with scientists at the National Climatic Data Center to develop another climate change handbook for local planners. He's hoping to pull together a detailed national picture of what urban and rural communities across the country can expect from global warming. "One of the challenges is to identify these resources and translate them into something useful," Shuford says. "As we get further into it, it may be that we find it's not possible to break it out at a county or community level. But I'm fairly convinced that for most of the areas we can get information out there summarized in a way that will be effective for them."

NO REGRETS

If climate adaptation is still a nebulous field, Sims has come up with a way to navigate the fog. King County is focusing first on "no regrets" policies. In other words, policies that would make good sense to implement whether or not the year 2050 turns out as wet and wild as Sims fears it will be.

A good example of what "no regrets" means can be found in an industrial zone southeast of Seattle. Hundreds of warehouses and light manufacturing plants, including a Starbucks coffee-roasting facility, are situated in a flat river plain that goes on for miles. In late October, the Green River looks tamely confined within its earthen levees. But it was a different scene in November 2006, when unusually heavy rains soaked the whole region, including the Cascades. Muddy runoff came to within a foot of overtopping the Briscoe levee, which began cracking and sloughing under the strain of holding back the waters. Mark Isaacson, director of the county's water and land resources division, walks atop the levee as it undergoes repairs, recalling the economic disaster that almost was. "The engineers asked me if I thought the levees would hold," he says. "And I said I can't promise you that."

As Isaacson explains, there are 119 miles of levees in King County. And many of them date back to the 1930s and '40s, when farmers protected their crops by heaping piles of sand, rocks and tree stumps along the river banks. The Army Corps of Engineers shored up many of the levees back in the '60s. But development that followed in the flood plains raised the stakes. Boeing, for example, makes 737s at a plant adjacent to the Cedar River in Renton. When the river floods, new airplanes can't get to the runway to take off.

Now, climate change is layered into the calculations. The Climate Impacts Group tells King County to expect more flooding events in the future, especially during November. So Sims ordered a countywide flood-control plan, and persuaded the county council to replace numerous small flood-control districts with one that serves the whole county. The real test came last month, when the council funded the first phase of the plan with a property-tax hike.

"No regrets" thinking is simple enough to grasp when it comes to levees, especially after Hurricane Katrina. But King County is now applying the same logic across all areas of government. County officials are promoting the use of reclaimed water as a drought-proof source of summer irrigation water. Health officials are plotting responses for non-native diseases such as the West Nile and hanta viruses. And planners are looking at ways to reduce the urban heat-island effect, as a hedge against heat waves. That last measure may sound particularly odd in a cool region where most homes don't even have air conditioning. But that's exactly the point. "You don't want to believe anything's going to change," Sims says. "You want to say we're going to reduce our emissions, and everything's going to be okay.

"I won't be here in 2050," Sims goes on. "But I believe that whether it's my children or their grandchildren, future generations will look back and say these were prudent investments."

30 Building Healthier Communities

Sean Sloane

A new planning approach helps cities promote healthier communities.

Cities around the country are using a new planning tool that could lead to health benefits for residents. Urban and rural areas used a community engagement approach to address such issues as safe streets, secure housing, water quality, crime prevention and physical activity promotion.

San Francisco boasts the most expensive housing market in the country. But it also leads the nation in the use of a city planning tool that is garnering attention from state legislatures around the country.

From November 2004 through May 2006, the San Francisco Department of Public Health conducted a process to assess the health benefits and potential burdens of new development in three San Francisco neighborhoods.

The Eastern Neighborhoods Community Health Impact Assessment (ENCHIA) made use of methods that emerged from Europe in the 1990s, promoted by the World Health Organization. A Health Impact Assessment (HIA) is defined as "a combination of procedures, methods and tools by which a policy, program or project may be judged as to its potential effects on the health of a population, and the distribution of those effects within the population."

Both a process and a document, the HIA can be used in advance as a predictor of health impacts that may result from proposed roadways, housing developments or shopping malls due to things like increased traffic, fewer opportunities for people to walk, and greater air and noise pollution. In the case of ENCHIA, the HIA was used in a broader context to assess the impact of overall ongoing development policies. It also sought to generate public dialogue about how land use planning affects health, influences future city land use

From *State News,*
August 2007.

152

policies and improves interdepartmental cooperation and consensus-building.

"The ENCHIA process was really sparked by a lot of community organizations and residents of San Francisco who were feeling intense development pressures," said ENCHIA project coordinator Lili Farhang of the San Francisco Department of Public Health. "They had a sense that health and social impacts of development weren't adequately being considered through the formal regulatory process … and by our planning department."

SAN FRANCISCO'S EXPERIENCE WITH HIAS

The ENCHIA was launched to address the effects of changes in three diverse city neighborhoods: the Mission, South of Market and Potrero Hill. Farhang said the neighborhoods were concerned about housing affordability, the availability and adequacy of public infrastructure, and the impact of recent changes on access to parks, safe streets, traffic, air pollution and pedestrian injuries.

"And a lot of groups felt like our application of the health impact assessment would be able to highlight some of the equity or disparities between neighborhoods and how they were growing or changing," she said.

The ENCHIA process, with the help of community organizations, developers, attorneys and public agency representatives, produced the Healthy Development Measurement Tool (HDMT).

"So what I think (the neighborhoods) can expect to see (next) is that we apply this tool that we've developed to land use plans and the plans hopefully change in a way that reflects some of the issues that we've identified through those assessments—improving environmental quality, housing accessibility and affordability, public infrastructure, access to child care, parks, schools and retail services, and improving public transportation and decreasing automobile use," Farhang said.

But it's not just urban areas that can benefit from these kinds of processes. The rural community of Wabasso in Indian River County, Fla., recently used a similar community engagement approach to address such issues as safe streets, secure housing, water quality, crime prevention and physical activity promotion. The community used a tool—the Protocol for Assessing Community Excellence in Environmental Health (PACEEH)—to

address core problems and the holistic relationship between places and health.

Farhang believes the use of the health impact assessment in San Francisco has provided some much needed structure, specificity and authority to a set of ideas about land use planning and the impact of man-made surroundings on public health.

"I think what we found is that health impact assessment provided a concrete methodology that you can go through, a set of steps that are internationally accepted to be able to quantify and qualitatively describe impacts and then share them with relevant stakeholders," she said.

Unfortunately, Farhang said, the health impact assessment is still not producing what it could due to the lack of political support.

"Our experience has been that it can be really hard to try and compel your sister agencies to accept your findings," she said. "I definitely feel that having at a state level acceptance for acknowledging that there's a relationship between health and land use and supporting agencies working together would make our lives at the local level much easier."

That kind of state level acceptance may not be a dream for long.

State legislators around the country are taking notice of the promise of health impact assessments and what they can do to improve local planning and zoning processes. For example, urban sprawl, some public health advocates contend, dominates the natural landscape and increases the use of cars, decreases opportunities for physical activity and thus contributes to chronic diseases like obesity and asthma.

California Assemblyman Mark Leno has introduced legislation that would expand statewide the principles his home city of San Francisco has embraced.

House Bill 1472, the California Healthy Places Act, would establish the Health Impact Assessment Program in the Department of Public Health to guide and support the practice of conducting HIAs around the state. Under the legislation, the state would provide training and technical assistance to local agencies conducting HIAs, create a grant program to fund HIAs, evaluate all HIAs implemented in the state, and maintain a database of all those conducted.

Leno sees the HIA as an idea whose time has come.

"I think it's a very clever way to approach some of these issues of health, and what I think looms to be one of the most serious epidemics that we're going to face both in California and nationally in the next generation … is obesity and diabetes," he said. "All of these elements are clearly connected to one another. So this health impact assessment is coming at just the right time."

INCREASING PHYSICAL ACTIVITY IN WASHINGTON STATE

Washington state Senate President Pro Tempore Rosa Franklin, a retired registered nurse, is an effective advocate for improving the walkability of communities to improve physical activity.

"Over the years I've been very much concerned about the health of our population because of what was happening in the built environment," she said.

In 2005, Washington legislators passed Senate Bill 5186, which seeks to promote policy and planning efforts that increase opportunities for exercise. The law directs county and city comprehensive plans to incorporate urban planning approaches that take into account physical activity whenever possible.

"(Kids) need to be able to bike to school if they want to," Franklin said. "They need to be able to walk to school safely. I've seen increased traffic and increased urbanization take a toll on our population not only in the number of accidents but on the physical health (of the population) in general."

Since the bill was adopted, Franklin said she's already begun to see improvements in the placement of bike paths and walking trails and the development of safe routes to school for kids.

Last year, Franklin also proposed, and the legislature approved, legislation to create an interagency council to establish state policy on eliminating health disparities. The council is authorized to work with the state Board of Health in completing health impact reviews of state projects, which can be requested by any state legislator or the governor.

"When we speak of planning, when we speak of safe places to walk, for me it means taking a comprehensive look, not a piecemeal look," Franklin said. "We need to do it in a comprehensive way because each time we do things individually, it has collateral impact and we have to come back and try to fix it. Certainly planning is local but we have a state growth management plan in which local communities also must plan and conform to that."

ENVIRONMENTAL JUSTICE IN MASSACHUSETTS

Disparities are also a concern for Massachusetts state Sen. Jarrett Barrios.

Research has shown that lower income communities and communities of color in Massachusetts are exposed to ecological hazards more often than higher income and predominantly white communities. A 2005 study, "Unequal Exposure to Ecological Hazards 2005," found links between exposure to environmental toxins and carcinogens and the racial disparities in mortality rates in the state.

Barrios has proposed legislation to establish a community environmental health disparities program in the Department of Public Health. It would create a communities health index and require certain proposed projects to complete HIAs. The communities health index would compare indicators like emergency room visits, asthma prevalence in children and heart attack hospitalizations with rates for the entire state and with such environmental indicators as particulate matter in the air. A health impact assessment would be required if a proposed project, such as a factory or power plant, is in or might affect a community deemed vulnerable by the communities health index data.

"If a development were to go in and it (could) demonstrably impact the environment in a negative way, as part of getting state approvals, it would have to indicate how community health would be remedied," Barrios explains. "This is similar to an existing program that we have in the state and that most states have for environmental remedies … If you're going to have additional traffic, well show us how you're going to get the cars out of there, how you're going to ameliorate the traffic impact.

"Now we're going to say 'OK, if you're going to have additional particulate matter put in the atmosphere, show us how you're going to ameliorate that impact to public health so that in the aggregate it's no worse than before you chose to locate here,'" he said.

Barrios believes HIAs can be important tools not only in improving public health but also in achieving environmental justice.

"I have for a number of years with colleagues filed environmental justice legislation and seen that legislation die, ultimately because the very strong real estate lobby in Massachusetts has been able to overwhelm public support for such a bill," he said. "After six years of some frustration, the tack I chose to follow this year with my advocacy partners was, rather than focus on race and economic background for additional environmental protections, we would focus on public health … Those health statistics speak much louder in many forums than race and economic background do. It's my hope to use the plain facts of the health data to amplify the voices of these community members during these development processes."

ENCOURAGING 'SMART GROWTH'

Massachusetts is also taking a different approach to influencing planning and zoning.

Legislation passed in 2005 allows cities and towns that establish "smart growth zoning districts" to receive additional reimbursement of the cost of educating students in those districts. The term "smart growth" refers to a set of land use and transportation principles that often include mixed land use, decreased automobile dependence, increased availability of transportation alternatives, increased density, and preservation of green spaces. Smart

growth advocates believe those principles can get people to walk more, improve air quality and create a greater sense of community than the bland, unconnected suburbs that contribute to the rising prevalence of chronic disease today.

More than 30 states have enacted some form of smart growth legislation. Over the last decade, Maryland has pioneered a statewide program that targets state assistance to locally chosen priority funding areas. Lawmakers in California and New York have also recently sought to provide planning grants, incentives and other assistance to local governments to promote more constrained smart growth development patterns.

FEDERAL SUPPORT FOR HEALTHY COMMUNITIES

States and localities could get some much needed help from the federal government if legislation introduced by Sen. Barack Obama and others is successful. The Healthy Places Act would establish a program at the National Center for Environmental Health (NCEH) within the CDC focused on advancing the field of health impact assessment. The program would provide grant funding,

States Can Play a Role

Efforts of states like Massachusetts, Washington, California and Maryland attempt to impact a process that has traditionally been and continues to be a mostly local one around the country.

State governments rarely get involved in specific local land use and development decisions. But a number of states, including Washington and Maryland, have established statewide, comprehensive growthmanagement frameworks. They have recognized that fragmented local land-use decisions, relatively unchecked and uncoordinated development and the haphazard growth patterns can have consequences for the state as a whole and can create large hidden costs.

The problem is that despite efforts like smart growth incentives, municipalities often have limited resources with which to manage land-use issues.

According to author Joel Hirschhorn, a powerful "sprawl industry" has stepped in to shape local planning and zoning processes to its own advantage. In his book, "Sprawl Kills," Hirschhorn writes that the industry includes not only land developers, builders and real estate agents, but also national fast food and big box chains and

even the pharmaceutical companies that benefit from selling drugs to manage the chronic disease that results from too much physical inactivity in the country.

"With some state governors promoting smart growth, activities to influence state legislators have become more important to the sprawl industry," Hirschhorn writes. "By keeping the role of the state as small as possible, it is easier to influence decisions of local governments."

Hirschhorn points out that the states can be broken down into "Dillon Rule" states, which limit the control of land use and planning by local governments, and "Home Rule" states, where local governments control land use and planning.

"In Dillon Rule states the sprawl lobby must corrupt state legislators; in Home Rule states it must corrupt local officials. The sprawl lobby is adept at both," Hirschhorn said in the book.

That, some say, makes state legislative efforts to bring some order, consistency, and accountability to planning and zoning processes and to encourage the use of tools such as the health impact assessment all the more important.

technical assistance and training to state and local government jurisdictions to undertake HIAs.

Obama has also introduced legislation to create an advisory committee to assess the impact of federal laws, programs and practices on environmental health and environmental justice around the country. The committee would also assist in the development of a grant program to aid communities most at risk for adverse health outcomes from environmental pollutants.

All these state and federal efforts aim to bring public health into the conversation about community design and renewal and to help Americans lead healthier lives.

31

Do You Really Want to be the Best?

Zach Patton

We're number one! But keep that to yourself.

Spend a morning walking around the historic pedestrian mall in downtown Charlottesville, Virginia, and you'll want to move there. Cafes, bookshops, art galleries and theaters line the brick-paved thoroughfare, which the city closed to automobile traffic in the 1970s. And it's not just tourist kitsch. Along with the clothing boutiques and handmade pottery stores are hallmarks of a workaday downtown—a jewelry repair shop, a pharmacy and banks. A couple of years ago, the city helped build the Charlottesville Pavilion, a concert venue that now attracts national acts. The pavilion's swooping white tent roof anchors the mall's east end.

On warm nights, the whole mall teems with local families and students from the University of Virginia, whose campus—with its life-sized statue of its founder, Thomas Jefferson—is just a few blocks away. But even on a bone-chillingly cold morning in January, the mall is filled with residents bustling to work or running errands, stopping to chat or to warm themselves briefly at an impossibly cute espresso cart. Looking up over the roofs of the brick buildings lining the mall, you spot the rolling, steel-blue foothills of the Blue Ridge Mountains.

This, you're thinking, would be a great place to live.

As it turns out, you could back up that opinion with empirical proof—or as empirical as this kind of stuff gets. The Charlottesville area was named the best place to live in the 2004 edition of "Cities Ranked and Rated," a hefty compendium cataloging more than 400 metropolitan areas throughout the country. The book, by Bert Sperling, praised Charlottesville's clean air and water, good schools, healthy economy and manageable cost of living. The city cheered the recognition. Retail and housing developments 30 miles away started

From *Governing.com,* February 2008.

flaunting their location "in Charlottesville." The chamber of commerce printed bumper stickers touting "America's #1 community."

For this city of 40,000 and for surrounding Albemarle County, which has an additional 90,000 residents, the ranking has been a boon, according to Charlottesville city council member David Brown, who served as mayor for four years until he stepped down last month. "The good growth we've achieved—being able to attract the creative class—has been fueled by that ranking," he says over a cup of coffee at the Mudhouse, a cozy hangout at the west end of the mall. "We've improved as a destination, and I think there's some connection to the ranking. It's been helpful, and it's something we're really proud of."

Others in Charlottesville weren't so happy with the designation. "I wanted to strangle Bert Sperling," jokes Jack Marshall, the president of a nonprofit group called Advocates for a Sustainable Albemarle Population, which pushes for a stationary population size in the region. "We'd rather keep it a secret what a nifty place this is. It's transparent that [the ranking] has exacerbated our growth problems." Reactions to the rankings, he says, fell into two camps. "A lot of the city fathers and mothers thought this was the best thing to hit Charlottesville since Thomas Jefferson. Those of us on the other side thought it was the kiss of death."

That tension seems to play out in any city or town that earns a "best of" ranking. Of course it's nice to be called the greatest town in the country. Economic development boosters plug the rating in hopes of attracting individuals and businesses interested in relocating. But such recognition can spark fears of a flood of incoming residents, sprawling growth and skyrocketing housing costs. Residents worry that their town's newfound attention will erode everything that made it a great city in the first place. Locals start blaming every civic ill on their city's best-in-the-nation status. Depending on who you talk to, being called the best place to live is an honor, a nuisance, a curse or a wash.

DOUBLE-EDGED SWORD

These days, you can find city rankings based on just about any criteria imaginable. If you are so inclined, you can move to the Healthiest City for Women (San Francisco), the Best City for Dogs (Colorado Springs) or the Most Romantic City for Baby Boomers (Pittsburgh). It seems

that every week, another magazine or news Web site has found a new "best of" niche.

But the most venerable and most well known is Money magazine's "Best Places to Live" issue. Published almost every year since 1987, it's the go-to guide for civic rankings. Bert Sperling provides the data for the magazine's report. Sperling, a former accountant and software designer in Oregon, has made a career out of compiling data on cities. In addition to his partnership with Money, he consults with various other magazines, such as Self and Ladies' Home Journal, on more narrowly tailored city lists. He runs Sperling's Best Places, a constantly updated online resource where visitors can access a trove of city data, and where municipalities, organizations and even neighborhoods can create their own profiles. And Sperling has also published two editions of "Cities Ranked and Rated."

To keep these lists fresh—and to stoke ongoing interest—Sperling and other researchers change the factors they use to determine city rankings. One year, crime statistics may be given more weight. The next, education is treated as a bigger concern. The focus depends, Sperling notes, on what current issues resonate with the public. As a result, these lists can vary widely from one year to the next. For that reason, many people view these kinds of rankings as arbitrary. But the methodology doesn't really matter to the cities themselves. The effect is the same: Someone's called you the best place to live. You'd better be ready to deal with the title.

Sperling himself is the first to admit that his rankings can have a downside. "When cities appear in the top 10, it has a very significant effect on the interest they get from businesses and individuals. But a lot of places do see this as a double-edged sword. They're flattered by the attention overall, but they also feel like, 'Please don't tell anyone else about us. We like our town the way it is.'"

There's no way to track exactly how many people move to a city based on its best-place ranking. Although a list-topping city might see a subsequent population increase or an uptick in interest from businesses, it's impossible to pinpoint what role a high ranking plays. Still, according to Census figures, 39 million Americans, about 14 percent of the population, move every year. And—anecdotally, at least—some of them do seek out a city specifically because it has sat atop a best-of list. That's been the experience of David Cieslewicz, the mayor of Madison, Wisconsin, which has garnered several "best place" nods, including Money magazine's top spot in 1996. "I do anecdotally hear from people who say they moved to Madison sight unseen because they did an Internet search for the best place to live," he says. "But obviously, that doesn't contribute to any appreciable growth."

Tell that to the citizens of Rochester, Minnesota, a place that's quite familiar with this kind of notoriety. The city of about 100,000, home to the Mayo Clinic, has been a steady fixture on Money's list, nabbing the No. 1 spot twice in the 1990s and consistently ranking near the top. During that decade, the populations of both Rochester and surrounding Olmsted County surged about 20 percent. Growth and sprawl became a concern. Violent crime jumped 150 percent. Minority populations increased, and racial skirmishes made headlines. Long-time residents linked the city's problems to the Money rankings. In a 1996 survey, 47 percent of people who had lived in Rochester for 15 years or more said they blamed these problems largely on the "best places" list. Moreover, they believed Rochester had become a welfare magnet as low-income families, attracted by Rochester's high marks, swarmed the city looking for jobs.

But, as an investigation by the Rochester Post-Bulletin discovered, those perceptions didn't match reality. True, the population had expanded, but Rochester's growth rate was low compared with similar cities around the country. Yes, more minorities had moved to Rochester, but that trend had begun before the city showed up on Money's list. Overall crime was down. The number of people on welfare had declined. Basically, the newspaper found, the Money rankings hadn't really had that much impact.

Despite fears such as those among Rochester residents, the truth is that cities receiving national attention all seem to go through the same pattern of phases. Initially, they're deluged with inquiries from out-of-towners. When, for example, Gainesville, Florida, found itself at the top of Money magazine's list in 1995, the local chamber of commerce had to hire an additional receptionist to help handle the calls. But that flurry of interest soon dies down, and cities are left wondering if the ranking had any effect at all.

Fort Collins, Colorado, about 60 miles north of Denver, is home to Colorado State University and about 130,000 residents. After it was named Money's best place in 2006, Fort Collins experienced the same arc as other

previous winners. "Our personal relocation requests went way up, with people from around the country calling, walking in or e-mailing the chamber," says David May, president and CEO of the Fort Collins Area Chamber of Commerce. "But has the notoriety and expressed interest translated into actual relocations of people? We have no evidence one way or the other." May adds that business recruiters had the same experience. "Their inquiries went up also. Being named as the best place to live in a prominent publication immediately puts your area on site-location lists for companies, because quality of place matters. But has the No. 1 ranking flooded us with new companies moving to the area? No, just more inquiries."

The same has been true for Charlottesville, notes the president and CEO of its regional chamber of commerce, Tim Hulbert. Over a lunch of crab soup and iced tea, Hulbert looks around Siips, a new bistro and wine bar that's set up shop on the downtown mall. This, he says, is certainly an example of a business that was attracted in part because of Charlottesville's ranking. But he adds that the bistro probably would have come anyway. "So then what's the impact of a No. 1 ranking?" he asks. "I would say none. I don't want to dismiss it, really. But mostly it was just acknowledging something that was already known."

NO. 1 IN EVERYTHING

Maybe these rankings don't result in a population explosion or an influx of new businesses, but cities say there's fallout nonetheless. As happened in Rochester, the biggest impact may be a shift in perception.

Take Moorestown, New Jersey. When you picture "hometown America," you're probably thinking of someplace like Moorestown. A relatively sleepy burg of just over 20,000, the town has a tree-lined Main Street dominated by a Quaker meeting house and school. The quaint feel of the place—coupled with the fact that it's only a 15-minute drive from center-city Philadelphia—earned Moorestown Money magazine's top spot in 2005. Moorestown celebrated the news with block parties, a parade and the town's first fireworks show in 30 years.

Councilman Dan Roccato says he was happy to hear about the ranking, but he also braced for potential fallout. "Almost overnight, Moorestown went from this quiet, modest town to being in the national spotlight." Moorestown's strength, Roccato says, is that it's been able to maintain its historic character against "the tide of pressure" to build new developments. "That pressure has only ratcheted up since the national recognition." The moment Moorestown was crowned the best place to live, real estate developers descended on town hall, Roccato says. "We had a flood of development offers, and each one was from someone who said he had the best way for us to capitalize on the ranking." Roccato says the town has politely declined them all.

The pressure came from residents, too. Moorestown citizens started using the No. 1 rating as justification for any number of pet projects, everything from repaving the sidewalks to building better ball fields to lowering taxes. "They'd come to us and say, 'For the best town in America, we should really have this,'" says Roccato. "From a public official's point of view, there was some irony and perhaps some downside to being recognized as No. 1. Everyone suddenly thought every single thing about us should be No. 1. And that's, of course, impossible."

Sometimes even municipal employees start trying to trade in on a town's supposed newfound cachet. That's what has happened in Middleton, Wisconsin, a 17,000-person suburb of Madison and Money magazine's 2007 pick for the best place to live. Mayor Kurt Sonnentag says his town's rating hasn't had much of an impact so far, except in one area: "City employees are coming in to ask for a raise. They'll say, "Hey, you're No. 1. You can afford to pay better.'"

Ask Jeff Werner about the effect the No. 1 ranking had on Charlottesville, and he starts groaning before you can finish the question. Werner is the Albemarle County land-use field officer for the Piedmont Environmental Council, a smart-growth group focused on a corridor stretching from Albemarle County north to the Washington, D.C., suburbs. PEC has won some high-profile land-conservation battles—this was the group that led the fight against Disney's plan in the early 1990s to build a 3,000-acre history theme park in the middle of Virginia. Werner admits that he doesn't see a correlation between a best-of ranking and growth, but he bemoans the added attention all the same. "It's sort of a local joke for cities. 'Oh my God, what can we do to keep from being named a best place to live?' " When Moorestown was picked as a top city, Werner called a friend of his who lives there and told him, "Better you than us."

For Werner, the main result of a No. 1 ranking is something akin to a communal crisis of conscience. "If there's a spike in anything after these best-places designations, it's local discussion. What kind of a place do we want to be? It's almost more of an exercise in psychology than land use."

That's an exercise Charlottesville is undertaking right now. Funded in part by money from the city and the county, Advocates for a Sustainable Albemarle Population is launching a sweeping research effort to determine the area's "optimal sustainable population"—that is, finding out what kind of city Charlottesville wants to be and the ideal population it should have to maintain that character. The project will examine a host of environmental, fiscal, demographic and philosophical issues, bringing together officials, advocates, academics and statisticians—including Bert Sperling. "Growth is good, up to a point," Marshall says. "But there's a point where it ain't. Or, more articulately, there's a point where the costs outweigh the benefits." Being named the best place to live, says Marshall, has given Charlottesville the impetus to start asking where that point might be.

Last May, Sperling released a second edition of "Cities Ranked and Rated." Charlottesville was no longer No. 1. The city had fallen to 17th place, largely, according to the book, because of its escalating housing prices. Predictably, there were some who cheered the fact that the city no longer held the top honor. One chamber of commerce staffer said she was happy to learn that Charlottesville wasn't No. 1. After all the attention, she told a newspaper reporter, "maybe things will come back to the ground." On Internet message boards about the rankings, Charlottesville residents posted comments such as, "Thank God Charlottesville has fallen out of the 'number one' position. The ranking was a curse on our fair city. The cost of living skyrocketed and [we] attracted a boatload of people who apparently rely on someone else's assessment of a 'good place to live.'…Good riddance to that ranking and the rubbage that follows."

Even David Brown, the former mayor who was bullish about the ranking's ability to help attract the creative class, acknowledges a little relief over Charlottesville's lower rating. "There are a lot of great reasons to move here," he says. Being at the top of someone's rankings isn't one of them. "To the degree that people would move here simply because they saw us on a list, I'm glad we're not No. 1 anymore."

In Sperling's latest book, Gainesville, Florida, has taken over the top spot—and the media attention, internal disagreements and philosophical hand-wringing that come with it. The recognition has meant a lot of good buzz, says Bob Woods, the city's communications and marketing manager. The city is experiencing renewed interest from families thinking about making a move.

And economic development officials are eagerly promoting the ranking in an effort to bring in new businesses. "But it's important for us to maintain the environment that got us named the best city in the first place," he says. "That's the tension we're constantly working with."

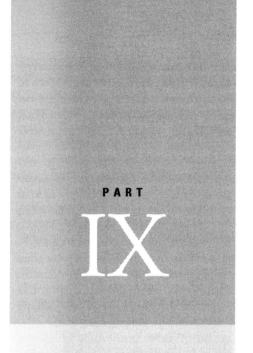

IX

Budgets and Taxes

There's a well-known piece of doggerel that sums up every government's dilemma on budgets and taxes:

Don't tax you,

Don't tax me,

Tax that feller behind the tree

As these lines succinctly put it, nobody likes taxes; not the tax payers footing the bill and not the politicians who pay at the ballot box if they dip too far and too often into their constituents pockets. Those lines also convey the harsh reality that somebody has to be taxed. It's just that everybody prefers it be somebody else. The paradox underpinning government finances is that everyone likes at least some government expenditures, but nobody likes paying for them.

Many people say they are for cutting government spending, and even more are for cutting taxes. But when it comes to specifics—exactly what programs are going to be cut, exactly who is going to pay how much for what remains—there is considerably less agreement. Who gets what and who pays for it are among the central questions of democratic politics, and are at the heart of much of the political conflict in states and localities. As the readings in this section will show, the reality of state and local government finances revolve around trying to find acceptable solutions to the difficult problems these issues present.

RAISING AND SPENDING MONEY

According to the most recent estimates, state and local government expenditures total more than $1.8 trillion.[1] By any measure, that's a lot of money. Where does it all come from?

State and local governments rely on six major sources of revenue: sales taxes, property taxes, income taxes, motor vehicle taxes, estate and gift taxes, and grants and transfers from the federal government. Of the taxes state and local governments levy, the biggest revenue producers are sales taxes (about $414 billion), property taxes ($369 billion), and individual income taxes ($275 billion). Grants from the federal government add $358 billion to state and local coffers.[2] Other sources of revenue include everything from fees for licenses to hunt, fish, or marry to interest earned on bank deposits. There is enormous variation from state to state—and even locality to locality—in how governments raise their money. Some states (for example, Texas and Florida), have no individual income tax and rely more heavily on sales taxes.

There are pros and cons to employing different forms of taxation. Property taxes, for instance, are one of the most hated forms of taxation. They are typically levied as a portion of the assessed valuation of property such as a house. They are most often paid in a lump sum once or twice a year, and thus tend to be stark reminders to taxpayers about how much government takes from them. For most homeowners, property taxes work out to be about 1.55 percent of the house's value. So someone who owns a house worth, say, $200,000, will pay about $3,100 a year in property taxes. Writing a check that big can be painful.

While property owners are never going to be enthusiastic about them, property taxes historically have had clear advantages for state and local governments. Most importantly, they are a relatively stable form of income. Income and sales taxes will rise and fall along with the ups and downs of the economy, while property values were seen as less vulnerable to wilds swings during an economic downturn. That historical perspective, however, was severely challenged in 2008 by tough times in real estate. A property bubble pumped up by easy credit and the development of exotic financial instruments backed by shaky mortgages burst and the fallout was not pretty. Property values fell, foreclosures increased; this meant property tax receipts also got squeezed.

As a softening economy led to belt tightening by many, sales tax receipts also took a hit. Budgetary shortfalls were expected in many states in 2008.[3] So much for property taxes insulating state and local government coffers from economic downturns.

RECENT TRENDS

Facing a softening property market and the prospect of a full-blown recession, many states are currently contemplating reforms of their tax systems. As Katherine Barrett and Richard Greene point out in the first essay of this section, state tax systems do not reflect twenty-first century economic realities. This not only hurts the public treasury, it acts as a drag on the economy.

Bert Waisanen's essay focuses on property taxes, perennial winner of the least loved tax competition, and a special concern to those living on fixed incomes. States are moving to reform property taxes to deal with these issues, though whether the reforms can keep up with the gyrations of the property market is an open question.

In a second essay, Barrett and Greene take an in-depth look at one of the most pressing financial issues facing state and local governments: public pensions. For decades, state and local governments have made generous retirement promises to public employees. Keeping those promises is going to be tough, especially when public pension funds are billions in the hole.

Finally, Ron Snell takes a look at an untraditional economic development and revenue source that states are beginning to pay increasing attention to: the elderly. Though traditionally thought of as consuming rather than supporting public services (think Medicare, Social Security), state governments have suddenly recognized retirees are also a group that is mobile and has money to spend. The "gray gold rush" is on.

Notes

1. U.S. Census Bureau, *Statistical Abstract of the United States,* 2008, Table 417, http://www.census.gov/compendia/statab/tables/08s0417.pdf . Accessed April 29, 2008.

2. Ibid.

3. National Association of State Budget Officers. *The Fiscal Survey of the States.* Http://www.nasbo.org/Publications/PDFs/Fiscal%20Survey%20of%20the%20States%20December%202007.pdf. Accessed April 29, 2008.

32

Growth and Taxes

Katherine Barrett and Richard Greene

Twentieth-century tax
structures slow a twenty-
first century economy.
States are trying to revamp
their revenue sources to fit a
new age.

From *Governing.com*,
January 2008.

It's been known for a long time that obsolete state tax systems are not producing the revenue states need. But what's becoming clear today is that those tax systems are not only failing to keep up with the dramatic shifts in the U.S. economy. They are a drag on economic growth.

The new economy is more than a swing from manufacturing to services. Thanks to new technology and telecommunications, products can be purchased as easily from an outlet 3,000 miles away as from one down the block. Small businesses are increasingly vital—they now account for about a third of the value of U.S. exports. Moreover, the service economy is moving toward a further evolution: It's becoming increasingly knowledge-based. Where managerial and professional jobs accounted for roughly one-fifth of total employment in 1979, such jobs are now moving past the one-third mark.

And yet, state tax structures, developed at a time when computers—"thinking machines"—were the stuff of science fiction, and the American economy flourished with the automobile industry, have failed to evolve. They are "completely inefficient," says Ray Scheppach, executive director of the National Governors Association. They stifle economic vitality by creating an environment that's inhospitable to businesses.

To take one example, there is the outmoded way in which telecommunications companies are taxed. A reliable, high-quality and affordable telecommunications system is essential to the economic competitiveness of states—to say nothing of the nation. And yet, these systems are subject to very high taxation rates in a number of states—by a tax approach set when the industry, dominated by one telephone company, was highly regulated. The result is a damper on

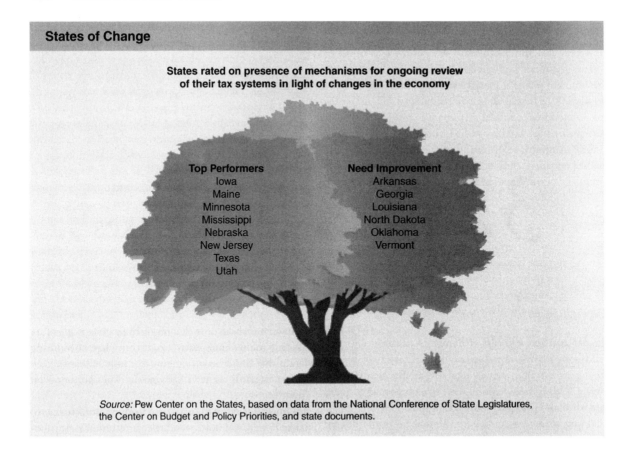

States of Change

States rated on presence of mechanisms for ongoing review
of their tax systems in light of changes in the economy

Top Performers
Iowa
Maine
Minnesota
Mississippi
Nebraska
New Jersey
Texas
Utah

Need Improvement
Arkansas
Georgia
Louisiana
North Dakota
Oklahoma
Vermont

Source: Pew Center on the States, based on data from the National Conference of State Legislatures, the Center on Budget and Policy Priorities, and state documents.

the telecom industry. According to a 2004 report by the Council on State Taxation, the average effective rate of state and local transaction taxes for telecommunications services is around 14 percent, compared with about 6 percent for general businesses nationwide.

That's not the only fallout from antiquated state tax systems. They are often unfair—undertaxing one portion of the economy at the expense of others. In many states, for example, a number of services—including things such as tattoo parlors, car washes and gardeners—are free from any sales tax, while tangible goods—things such as pencils, cars and garden hoes—are subject to a higher tax rate to make up for the slack.

Over the past year, the Pew Center on the States has researched the question of how state tax systems can adjust to a new economy in which fundamental business rules have been changing. The report that follows looks not so much at the basic principles of taxation but at specific tax systems and practices that are critical to promote economic vitality.

Those tax systems are no longer a parochial matter of interest to each of the 50 states as an independent entity. That is, the battle for economic growth is not a civil war among the states anymore. It's a world war. The U.S. is already at a huge disadvantage in competing internationally based on cost. Wages in India and China, for instance, are as much as 90 percent lower than those in the U.S. The competitive strengths in the U.S. are in innovation, productivity, marketing and entrepreneurship. All of these things can be either helped or hurt by the nature of the states' tax systems—as can the revenue base, which states need to make the investments necessary to succeed.

"States are aware that their tax structures aren't up to snuff," says Michigan Governor Jennifer Granholm. "The question for us as the state of Michigan, is, 'What is it that is going to make us competitive?' If it's not going to be price, then perhaps it's going to be quality, and that means investing in your talent. If you have class sizes of 37, then you're going to be uncompetitive."

At Your Service

States that tax professional services and states that tax more than 55 of the roughly 143 different services susceptible to taxation

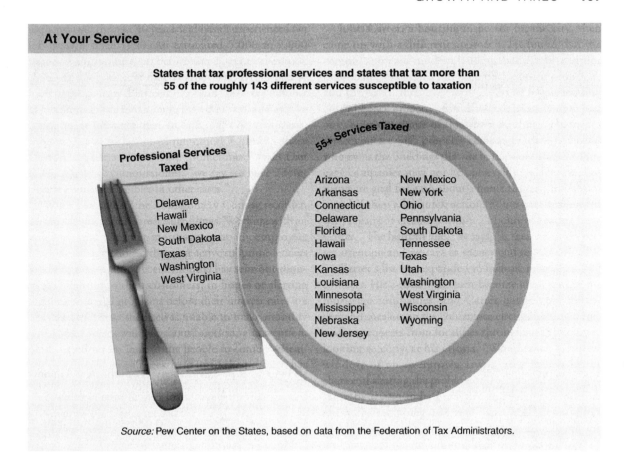

Professional Services Taxed

Delaware
Hawaii
New Mexico
South Dakota
Texas
Washington
West Virginia

55+ Services Taxed

Arizona	New Mexico
Arkansas	New York
Connecticut	Ohio
Delaware	Pennsylvania
Florida	South Dakota
Hawaii	Tennessee
Iowa	Texas
Kansas	Utah
Louisiana	Washington
Minnesota	West Virginia
Mississippi	Wisconsin
Nebraska	Wyoming
New Jersey	

Source: Pew Center on the States, based on data from the Federation of Tax Administrators.

Since 2000, virtually every state has commissioned at least one major tax reform panel to study the issue and develop proposals for modernization. Seventeen states now have in place at least an informal mechanism for continuous review of their structures. Much of this action has been propelled by fiscal shortfalls or the realization that various revenue streams are declining relative to spending pressures. In more than a handful of states, the property tax—which has tended to rise inexorably to make up for some of these gaps—has led to citizen rebellions. Both Florida and New Jersey, for example, have been responding to public fury about the property tax by considering major tax restructurings.

The tax questions the states will need to grapple with in coming decades are ones that lie at the heart of the new economy. How can states reshape and modify their tax systems to encourage greater interstate, federal-state and state-local cooperation—and still retain the autonomy of each level of government? In an age of globalization, how

do states compete with other countries, yet minimize tax competition among the various levels of government? How do states generate revenues from the intangible products of knowledge-based firms? How do they capture business activity within state borders when borders are increasingly irrelevant in conducting business?

There's a shortage of proven solutions for dealing with a borderless, knowledge-based economy. But some good ideas have emerged—and are already being tested by some states—to deal with the most basic, underlying issue: creating a tax structure that encourages economic vitality.

The material in the pages that follow has been informed not just by predictions of the world to come but by respect for the deep-seated fundamentals of a solid tax system—one that is simple and transparent, with broad-based taxes that provide a balanced revenue stream, spread the tax burden fairly and heighten the chance of compliance.

Our research acknowledges the idea that some powerfully held beliefs about appropriate tax policy have little

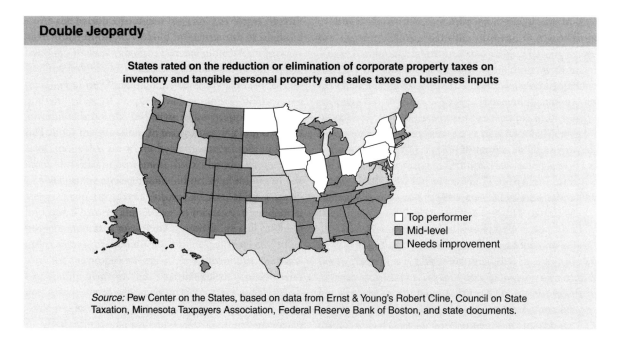

Double Jeopardy

States rated on the reduction or elimination of corporate property taxes on inventory and tangible personal property and sales taxes on business inputs

☐ Top performer
■ Mid-level
☐ Needs improvement

Source: Pew Center on the States, based on data from Ernst & Young's Robert Cline, Council on State Taxation, Minnesota Taxpayers Association, Federal Reserve Bank of Boston, and state documents.

chance of prevailing. For example, some tax policy experts believe there should not be any corporate income taxes, because they raise a relatively small amount of money, are complex and end up being passed along to consumers anyway. Politically, however, it is unlikely that taxpayers will stand for an abolition of the corporate income tax. "Most economists come down saying corporate income taxes are really bad ideas for states," says William Fox, director of the Center for Business & Economic Research at the University of Tennessee. "But then they have to talk about the real world." Similarly, many people believe that tax incentives to corporations are a zero-sum game and potentially unproductive as an economic development tool. But incentives are not going away.

One cluster of questions addresses tactics that pertain to specifics of the new economy: the transition to services; the rapid growth of untaxed Internet sales; the need to encourage newer high-tech industries while not overburdening old-time manufacturing; an adjustment of telecommunication tax rates and complexity to a world in which telecom companies are no longer monopolies; and strategies to tax multi-state and multi-national corporations in a fair way. Those tactics have grown increasingly critical in order to preserve any kind of equity between large multi-state or multi-national firms and smaller, in-state businesses.

Four areas pertinent to vitality in the new economy are examined in the stories that follow. Fifty-state evaluations inform these articles on the transparency of tax incentives, the efficiency of tax collection, the stability of revenue streams and the tax flexibility states allow their localities—which provide many of the key services that support the new economy.

THE RATE DEBATE

Much of the argument over reform has tended to focus on the notion that a tax increase to any segment of the economy will drive away business, while a tax cut will do the opposite. This was the point Wisconsin state Senator Alan Lasee made during the 2006 campaign season. "High taxes," he told voters, "are driving our employees and businesses to move to other states for higher paying jobs and lower taxes."

Tax rates doubtless play some role in creating a fertile economic climate—and if all other things were equal, businesses might choose to settle in lower-tax realms. But in the real world, all things are never equal. Some states have better-educated workforces, a better-developed network of roads or nicer public amenities. These elements, all of which require steady flows of tax revenues, are crucial to the equation.

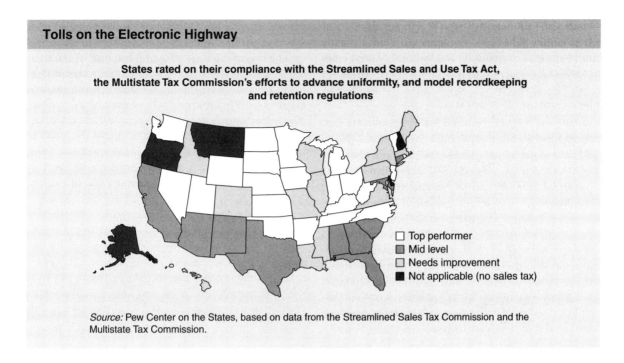

Tolls on the Electronic Highway

States rated on their compliance with the Streamlined Sales and Use Tax Act, the Multistate Tax Commission's efforts to advance uniformity, and model recordkeeping and retention regulations

☐ Top performer
▨ Mid level
☐ Needs improvement
■ Not applicable (no sales tax)

Source: Pew Center on the States, based on data from the Streamlined Sales Tax Commission and the Multistate Tax Commission.

There is now evidence that low tax rates by themselves are not a silver bullet. In his New Economy Index, Rob Atkinson, president of the Information Technology and Innovation Foundation, measures the progress of states in adapting to the new economy by looking at factors such as workforce creation, entrepreneurial activity and patent creation. Five of the eleven lowest-scoring states on his list are among those having the lowest tax burden: Alabama, Montana, Oklahoma, South Dakota and Wyoming. As Tom Clark, executive vice president of the Metro Denver Economic Development Corp. and the Denver Metro Chamber of Commerce, puts it, "If low tax rates were the only factor, Wyoming would be the economic epicenter of the world."

It is theoretically possible to use low tax rates to drive economic vitality. Robert G. Lynch, chair of the Department of Economics at Washington College in Maryland, points out that academic studies on tax rates "suggest that state and local tax cuts and incentives may help economic growth, provided that government services are not reduced to pay for the tax cuts."

But as Lynch makes clear, in reality, lower taxes tend to lead to service reductions, some of which inevitably fall in areas that fuel economic vitality. Bruce Johnson, a former lieutenant governor of Ohio and head of economic

development for that state, notes that "ground zero for economic development is a high-value workforce." That requires a considerable investment in education as well as in quality of life to enable states to compete effectively in the worldwide market for talent. Then there are investments in R&D at a time when innovation is key to economic development and in infrastructure, including broadband access, bridges, airports and, of course, roads.

TAXING SERVICES

One of the tectonic shifts that marks the new economy is the long-term transition to a service economy. In 2005, service industries accounted for some 68 percent of the total U.S. gross domestic product and 79 percent of growth in the GDP. Yet, only a handful of states tax more than 80 of the 143 or so common services, according to Federation of Tax Administrators' data. "We've ignored services in the past," says Tennessee's Fox. "But with all the new forms of technology available to expand the service sector, that's no longer a reasonable idea."

A number of obstacles stand in the way. The power of interested or affected parties is high on the list. They can and do lobby their legislators effectively. Last summer, a potentially forward-looking reform in Maine failed to pass the Senate largely because a slew of services—everything from haircuts to car towing—would become subject to tax. "Expanding the tax base to consumer services is good tax policy," says George Washington University professor David Brunori, "but the service providers rarely see it that way."

When it comes to the taxation of professional services—such as those provided by lawyers, accountants, financial advisers—things get even tougher. About 20 years ago, Florida attempted a bold experiment aimed at vastly broadening its taxation of services—to professionals and just about every service in the state's economy. When the state's newspapers and magazines realized that meant that advertising would be taxed, they mounted a full frontal assault. The state backed off, the governor suffered politically and ever since there have been very few states with the fortitude to move in the same direction at full force. Only last month, the Michigan legislature repealed a new service tax—mostly on business-to-business transactions but also on such things as manicures and ski lift tickets—just hours after it went into effect.

Even states that consider adding service taxes in a more marginal way have to deal with the knotty problem of taxing business inputs. The issue is sometimes called pyramiding—at an extreme, a state could tax the services an accountant provides to a law firm, and then tax the services the law firm provides to a car manufacturer, which either builds those taxes into the price of a car or reduces its investments in the state. Most tax experts agree that placing sales taxes on assets or services purchased by businesses is a form of double taxation and to be avoided.

States are making progress in reducing or eliminating the taxing of business inputs in an arena other than straightforward sales taxes. States that tax inventory and tangible personal property are dwindling in number. Ohio eliminated its taxation of tangible personal property, Indiana is on its way to doing so, and Michigan has enacted a 35-to-40 percent reduction in its tangible property tax.

Meanwhile, the rise of the high-tech and services-based economy has ushered in another trend: The reliance of corporations on customers who are remarkably mobile and geographically widespread. The steadily growing number of sales transactions over the Internet—Jupiter Research Online Retail Forecasts anticipates growth of 10 to 15 percent per year over the next decade—puts local retailers at a disadvantage. Those that sell their wares electronically often escape the sales tax. That, in turn, is contrary to the precept that taxes should be levied over as broad a base as possible so that states and localities can generate the revenue they need at the lowest possible rates.

The biggest obstacle to taxing Internet transactions has been the wide variety of sales tax structures used by the individual states (and their localities), which make it extremely difficult to coordinate a means of taxing them. The Streamlined Sales Tax Project is the clearest effort by states to deal with the complications of this world in which there are virtually no physical barriers to commerce. The ultimate goal of the project is to create an environment in which transactions conducted over the Internet could be easily taxed by states. The agreement would simplify state and local tax returns and the administration of exemptions; it would also provide for streamlined tax returns and a centralized electronic registration system for all member states. Nearly half of the states have made a commitment to either fully or partially comply with the Streamlined Sales and Use Tax Act, which requires uniformity in state and local tax-based definitions and sourcing rules for all taxable transactions.

CATCHING CORPORATE DOLLARS

Even as the technological complexity of the world has advanced, so too has the capacity of large companies to create business forms designed, in part, to shift tax burdens from high-tax states to low- or no-tax states. Many states allege that interstate income shifting amounts to little more than tax evasion, while corporations argue they are legally taking advantage of competing state tax systems. The state courts are divided on the issue, and the U.S. Supreme Court has yet to rule on it.

As a remedy, states have been adopting combined reporting as a more comprehensive approach to curbing artificial interstate income shifting. Combined reporting forces corporate parents and their subsidiaries to add profits together. This enables the state to tax the percentage of an out-of-state subsidiary's profits that can legitimately be attributed to the corporation's in-state operations. Many big corporations, obviously, are not advocates of combined reporting. For one thing, it closes a loophole that many enjoy. In addition, there are potentially significant compliance costs for companies required to alter their bookkeeping. Despite these drawbacks, there is no evidence that the economies of combined-reporting states have suffered compared with those without combined reporting.

Among the states that don't use combined reporting is Iowa. "Our state," says Peter Fischer, professor of urban and regional planning at the University of Iowa, "loses a

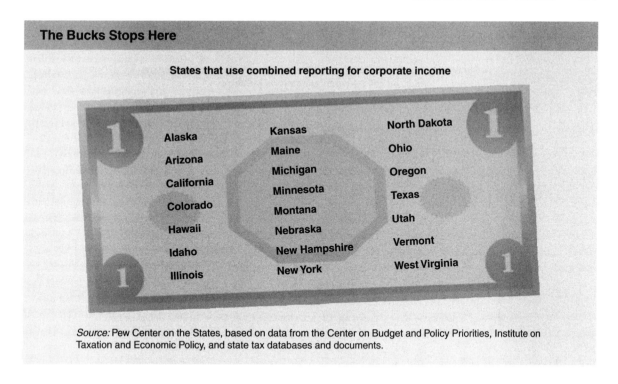

The Bucks Stops Here

States that use combined reporting for corporate income

Alaska	Kansas	North Dakota
Arizona	Maine	Ohio
California	Michigan	Oregon
Colorado	Minnesota	Texas
Hawaii	Montana	Utah
Idaho	Nebraska	Vermont
Illinois	New Hampshire	West Virginia
	New York	

Source: Pew Center on the States, based on data from the Center on Budget and Policy Priorities, Institute on Taxation and Economic Policy, and state tax databases and documents.

pretty big chunk of corporate taxes because of its unwillingness to take on combined reporting." Fischer thinks it may be that people who are simply anti-tax see it as a tax increase. Whatever the reason, it has been proposed in Iowa a number of times, but the legislature has not moved on it.

An aligned area in which states are gaining some control is in taxing a growing array of new business structures. James Edward Maule, a professor at Villanova University's School of Law, was one of the first to study the tax treatment of limited-liability companies, limited-liability partnerships and S corporations. The new entities are similar to corporations but have a more flexible ownership structure. His initial findings on the tax picture made Maule reflect that they were in a state of "chaos."

Take S corporations. The simple problem is that they pass all their profits through to shareholders and are essentially immune from corporate taxes. These profits are taxed by a state personal income tax imposed on the individual shareholders. There are now some 3.6 million S corporations in the United States. Obviously, this means that whenever a company elects to use this form, the state may lose some revenues—and the problem is even more intense for the nine states that don't tax income.

Like S corporations, limited-liability corporations and limited-liability partnerships are also "pass-through entities"—states generally don't impose tax at the corporate level but instead collect taxes by imposing the personal income tax (if they have one) on individual members and partners.

The chaos to which Maule refers came from states having no model for how to tax these various new business forms that aren't exactly corporations but aren't individuals, either. Without guidance, confusion reigned in the states over how to apply their tax structures to these alien new business forms. Until the states got a handle on the very concept of what these new business forms were, they couldn't properly capture taxes duly owed, if they captured any taxes at all. Fortunately, the states have gained a large measure of control in recent years. There is now a Model S Corporation Income Tax Act that provides states with a template for how to tax S corporations and is endorsed by both the American Bar Association and the Multistate Tax Commission. It gives state lawmakers and tax administrators a way to think consistently about state tax treatment of pass-through entities.

As for LLCs and LLPs, one breakthrough came when states, en masse, determined that they would no longer

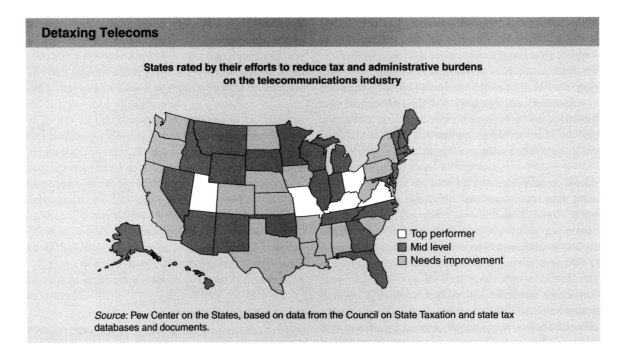

Detaxing Telecoms

States rated by their efforts to reduce tax and administrative burdens on the telecommunications industry

☐ Top performer
■ Mid level
☐ Needs improvement

Source: Pew Center on the States, based on data from the Council on State Taxation and state tax databases and documents.

allow the owners of these new business forms to elect to be classified as one type of entity for federal tax purposes but another for state taxation, which might have given them more favorable treatment. A number of states also now require LLCs and LLPs to withhold taxes on the distributive state share of nonresident members' and partners' earned income. This helps ensure that the taxes properly owed to the state don't slip away as they did in the past.

MARCONI'S LEGACY

Telecommunications was once an industry dominated by telephone companies that were monopolies—and states taxed them accordingly. This was a quid pro quo for the lack of competition.

But today's industry is totally different. Not only don't telecom companies have monopolies, there is bitter competition over a business that has changed dramatically from just supplying phone lines to one that permits transfer of data through a variety of technologies—technologies undreamt of when the codes were written. But states continue to apply the old, outdated tax regimes. Only a handful of states have undertaken telecommunications tax reform over the past decade, and in many of those states, the primary reform has been in centralizing return filing.

Telecommunications companies are also hampered by major administrative burdens. Many states still require telecom companies to file more than 500 returns. This area would be another beneficiary of the streamlined sales tax movement, which requires centralized filing and payment of local taxes—including local telecommunications taxes—to the state governments. The agreement also contains uniform telecommunications sourcing rules and definitions. And if the states succeeded in resolving nexus questions for Internet-based sellers, the change would, for the first time, put telecommunications companies on a level playing field with Internet-based companies that sell essentially the same products and services to customers.

These taxing issues are germane not only to the economic vitality of a state but to its compact with taxpayers—be they individuals or businesses. The way in which revenues are raised—the fairness and transparency—is fundamental to the trust constituents have in their government. Right now, most of the states need to modernize their tax policies to encourage growth, and to do that they need to look beyond immediate and purely political considerations. "The biggest problem we have is policy makers making decisions in a vacuum," says Utah state Senator Howard Stephenson. "Overcoming that is crucial to making good tax policy."

33

The Property Tax Shuffle

Bert Waisanen

States seek to ease the property tax burden for some, even as slumping property values squeeze government coffers.

"Property taxes are issues No. 1, 2 and 3 for the residents of this state," says New Jersey Assemblyman John McKeon.

That sentiment has echoed across the country the past two years as rising assessments and higher tax bills have caught up with rapidly accelerating home prices.

Home values, up 55 percent over the past five years, boosted personal wealth for homeowners, many of whom took advantage of the growth in equity. Sales of vacation homes and investment properties pumped up real estate values in coastal and resort areas. At the same time, homeowners on fixed incomes or with stagnant paychecks faced new financial pressures as property taxes soared. In popular parts of the country, working-class people can no longer afford houses in their hometowns and cities. The imbalance between housing economics and pocketbook economics has taxpayers demanding relief.

At least 21 states are working on property tax cuts this year and many others enacted property tax relief in 2006, using a variety of tools. This year in New Jersey, where homeowners facing the highest property taxes in the country were discussing a constitutional convention, legislators turned to homestead credits and tax limits.

The New Jersey Legislature last year created four joint legislative committees to review ideas for property tax reform including alternatives for funding schools and the possibilities of consolidating local governments. Next they secured voter approval to increase the sales tax by a half cent in exchange for property tax relief. The four committees reported recommendations in November 2006, and legislators entered 2007 still in special session to work on delivering property tax reform. The final package signed into law in April reduces property taxes by 20 percent for homeowners with incomes

From *State Legislatures,*
June 2007.

173

The Tax We Love to Hate

Americans detest the property tax and they aren't alone. Swedes rate their real estate tax as the most unpopular in that nation. England's version of the property tax—the council tax—is the most scorned there.

So why is the property tax so maligned by the taxpaying public? The Tax Foundation, a research organization in Washington, D.C., points to three principal reasons. First, taxpayers cannot control the property tax bite because it is based on neighborhood property values and assessment levels. They are frustrated with their inability to rein in their tax tab by changing their behavior or buying habits. Second, property taxes are not based on a homeowner's ability to pay, but on the property's value. This is particularly burdensome for elderly homeowners whose home values have risen but whose incomes have not. Finally, the tax is highly visible. Unlike the sales tax, which is paid in small increments with each purchase, the property tax is billed all at once. For the roughly one-third of Americans who own their homes outright, the annual lump-sum

bill can be staggering. Even homeowners who pay their property taxes through their monthly mortgage payments receive an annual property tax bill that shows the amount due, revealing just how much their property tax burden really is.

"One of the great ironies of tax policies is that people hate the tax that's easiest to see, not necessarily the one that costs them most," says the Tax Foundation's Andrew Chamberlain. He points out that state and local governments actually collect more in sales taxes than in property taxes.

But that fact hasn't swayed irritable taxpayers in their demand for property tax relief or weary state and local officials in looking for ways to provide it. "No one likes the property tax," says David Brunori, a professor at George Washington University who specializes in property tax issues. "And no matter how much a person pays, he thinks he pays too much."

—*Corina Eckl, NCSL*

up to $100,000 and phases down to 10 percent for homeowners with incomes up to $250,000. The plan trims the average homeowner's property tax bill by $1,000. It also requires doubling the renters' rebate for 800,000 tenants.

The package restricts annual property tax increases to 4 percent for school districts and local governments, down from a recent average of nearly 7 percent, and requires voter approval to exceed the limit.

The proposed state budget calls for increased state aid so local governments can continue to reduce their reliance on property taxes. And a commission has been created to study how to consolidate New Jersey's myriad local governments, which include 567 municipalities, a third with fewer than 5,000 residents.

Assembly Speaker Joseph J. Roberts Jr. says the package "provides historic levels of property tax savings, cutting property taxes for the overwhelming majority of New Jerseyans."

GOING WITH THE SWAP

Other states recently swapped one tax for another. Texas lawmakers cut property taxes as part of a school finance reform package. The revenues were partially replaced

with a combination of a $1 per-pack cigarette tax increase and a business margins tax, which broadens the business taxpayer base. Both Idaho and South Carolina have eliminated school maintenance and operations taxes by increasing the general state sales tax by 1 percent.

South Carolina's reforms include a sales tax increase tied to the elimination of school taxes plus a cap on property taxes. It limits assessment increases to 15 percent over the next five years, averaging 3 percent a year, but only for owner-occupied homes, not secondary or investment property. Since vacation-home buyers drove up property values, voters were all too happy to approve a November referendum calling for the cap.

SHIFTING BURDENS

Those who do not share equally in property tax relief are quick to point out that it shifts property tax burdens onto them. Yet as recent state actions demonstrate, the trend right now is to focus more relief for the residential taxpayer over the commercial taxpayer, and the primary homeowner over the investment owner.

Florida began this trend in 1992 when voters passed the Save Our Homes ballot amendment that placed a 3 percent assessment cap on residents' primary homes.

Per Capita Property Tax Bills, 2004

Rank		Per Capita	Rank		Per Capita
1	New Jersey	$2,098.90	27	Indiana	$975.40
2	Connecticut	$1,943.90	28	Minnesota	$965.30
3	New Hampshire	$1,939.70	29	Oregon	$963.30
4	District of Columbia	$1,855.60	30	California	$962.50
5	New York	$1,677.00	31	Nevada	$920.40
6	Rhode Island	$1,628.80	32	North Dakota	$919.20
7	Maine	$1,596.50	33	South Dakota	$914.60
8	Massachusetts	$1,531.80	34	South Carolina	$882.40
9	Vermont	$1,530.50	35	Georgia	$879.70
10	Illinois	$1,407.20	36	Arizona	$848.10
11	Wyoming	$1,351.70	37	Idaho	$777.40
12	Wisconsin	$1,349.70	38	Missouri	$747.30
13	Alaska	$1,305.60	39	North Carolina	$713.50
14	Texas	$1,253.80	40	Utah	$689.40
15	Kansas	$1,187.50	41	Mississippi	$641.10
16	Michigan	$1,185.50	42	Tennessee	$608.40
17	Nebraska	$1,148.20	43	Hawaii	$571.20
18	Maryland	$1,082.30	44	Delaware	$546.00
19	Iowa	$1,079.90	45	West Virginia	$540.00
20	Florida	$1,064.20	46	Kentucky	$515.80
21	Montana	$1,034.30	47	Louisiana	$502.20
22	Virginia	$1,031.30	48	Oklahoma	$464.70
23	Washington	$1,028.90	49	New Mexico	$441.40
24	Colorado	$1,026.10	50	Arkansas	$400.30
25	Pennsylvania	$1,010.00	51	Alabama	$367.30
26	Ohio	$981.00		**National Average**	**$1,085.80**

It worked for a while. But as population growth and housing demands sent home prices soaring, its flaws flared up. The cap doesn't transfer, so people are reluctant to move because they'll be bumped into the current market value of their new residence. The cap does protect those who remain in their homes, but newcomers, out-of-state owners of vacation houses and especially businesses have been hit with higher and higher taxes. (A similar situation exists in California where a 2 percent cap benefits those who stay put.)

"Runaway property taxes threaten the standard of living of millions of homeowners and renters and the bottom lines of businesses big and small," said House Speaker Marco Rubio as lawmakers rolled up their sleeves to tackle reform. But the regular two-month session, which ended May 4, wasn't long enough to sort through differences in competing House and Senate plans. Lawmakers were forced into a special session scheduled for June 12 to 22.

"The issue is too important to our state and to our taxpayers for us to give them a product they would not be proud of," said Senate President Ken Pruitt in announcing the special session. "We have laid a great foundation."

Rubio said some broad agreements had been reached and the sides were "very close" on a compromise measure that would provide significant relief to homeowners, renters and commercial property owners.

The biggest difference between the chambers is how deeply to cut property taxes. The House plan rolls back

Tax Relief Toolbox

States generally choose among three approaches when crafting property tax relief.

- **Targeted Relief:** Tax cuts for certain populations based on age, disability or income levels. Most states have homestead exemption programs for seniors and disabled taxpayers, which remove part of a house's value from tax calculations. Many states also offer incomebased circuit-breaker programs that provide a safety valve against an overload of property tax burdens, and often include rental households, who pay taxes indirectly through their rent. A less well-known solution allows eligible taxpayers to defer or put off paying property taxes until they move, sell or die, helping them to remain in their homes. Some

states have offered rebates on property taxes when state funds were available.

- **Tax Limits:** Caps on the amount of revenues that can be levied by a local government. Some states freeze taxes at certain levels, impose levy limits, tax rate limits or limit assessments, often called "appraisal caps" for either all property, or just certain classifications (residential, commercial, farm, etc.).

- **Property Tax Swaps:** An intergovernmental trade that increases state taxes such as the sales or cigarette tax to provide aid to local governments. Some states do this by providing certain taxing authority to local governments that are then required to reduce property taxes.

taxes to 2001 rates and replaces the portion of property taxes used to fund schools with a 1 percent increase in the sales tax. Counties could chose to eliminate the rest of the taxes on homesteaded property, exchanging it with another sales tax increase of 1.5 percent. The plan would save homeowners as much as 19 percent. The House deal would also save owners of second homes and commercial property owners.

Senators are opting for relief to a broader range of property owners, that phases in over several years and does not raise the sales tax. Their plan rolls back tax rates, slows growth in future taxes, doubles the homestead exemption for first-time buyers and makes the Save our Homes tax cap portable. It offers $11 billion in relief while the House version offers $25 million or more, setting the stage for negotiations on what kind and how much property tax relief might be achievable.

Both chambers are considering rollbacks as well as providing businesses relief for the personal property taxes they pay on equipment and furnishings. Whatever the final agreement is in the Sunshine State, it will be crafted into a proposed constitutional amendment for voters in 2008.

READING THE TEA LEAVES

How much states decide to reduce reliance on the property tax is also critical to local governments, which depend heavily on this stable revenue source to deliver local services. Since property taxes support chiefly schools and local governments (72 percent of their revenues on average), cities, counties and school boards are concerned about new limits or rollbacks of property taxes without the revenue being replaced.

For now, targeted relief, tax rebates and tax swapping will likely remain the preferred solutions for reducing dependence on the property tax as a revenue source.

And change could be ahead. Although house values nationally declined only slightly in March, resales suffered their biggest monthly decline since the late 1980s. Foreclosures are up. Prices are dropping.

But it will take some time for the slowdown to show up in property tax assessments. So until a different solution for paying for government services presents itself, the ubiquitous property tax bill, unpopular as it is, will continue to show up in homeowners' mailboxes.

Housing Slump Stings State Coffers

Property taxes are tied to assessment rates and house values, so rapidly escalating prices in recent years have intensified appeals for property tax relief. But by all accounts the housing boom is over. The supporting evidence is considerable.

- According to the U.S. Department of Housing and Urban Development, single family housing starts have fallen dramatically since early 2006. After reaching just over 1.8 million starts in January 2006, they dropped to about 1.2 million in February 2007.
- CNN reported in February that new house sales saw their steepest plunge in 13 years. The decline affected every region of the country, from an 8.1 percent dip in the Midwest to a 37.4 percent drop in the West.
- The growing glut of new houses triggered a drop in prices. In February, the median price of a new home fell to $239,800, a 2.1 percent dip from a year earlier. Builders are offering potential buyers attractive incentives like upgrades to granite countertops and finished basements to lure them in.
- The National Association of Realtors reported that existing home sales plummeted in March, falling 8.4 percent compared to February figures. This was the largest one-month decline in nearly two decades.
- As reported in *The New York Times,* the states that benefited most from the housing boom are expected to get hit the hardest in the current slide. From late 2005 to late 2006, the number of existing home sales fell by 21 percent in California, 27 percent in Arizona, 31 percent in Florida and 36 percent in Nevada.
- Serious mortgage delinquency rates—loans that are more than 90 days delinquent or in foreclosure—are rising. Although much of the national media focus is on subprime mortgages offered to borrowers who

could not qualify for conventional loans, Douglas Duncan of the Mortgage Bankers Association notes that local economic factors are more important than loan type in evaluating mortgage delinquency rates. As a side note, residential mortgage payments are estimated to jump $10 billion as subprime teaser rates adjust from their low starting points.

Although the housing market is only one sector of the economy, its strength—or lack thereof—has far-reaching consequences. John Peterson of the Congressional Budget Office reports that because home values have fallen, there is a lack of home equity to tap for consumption and remodeling, which further weakens the economy. "But our economy today is more flexible and better able to absorb shocks than in the past," he says.

In addition to national economic impacts, state coffers are affected, too. Sales tax collections are adversely affected as consumers reduce their purchases of building materials, furniture and big household items like stoves, refrigerators, and washers and dryers.

Other state tax categories also are being hit. Slowing home sales and lower prices are curtailing collections from real estate transfer taxes; in several states collections are well below original estimates. In Connecticut, for instance, real estate conveyance taxes were nearly $26 million below expectations at the end of February.

Will the slumping housing market and the resulting impact on state revenue collections stem the demand for property tax relief? Probably not. It will take a while for property tax assessments to reflect the slowdown. And even when they do, other factors propelling property tax relief concerns—like how best to provide equitable and adequate school funding—will remain.

—*Corina Eckl, NCSL*

34

The $3 Trillion Challenge

Katherine Barrett and Richard Greene

Under-funded public pension funds may cost taxpayers billions. Who is running these things? Nobody is really sure.

Texas pensions have a problem. Four-fifths of the nearly 100 public retirement plans are underfunded—not by a thousand dollars here and a million there. All totaled, they're in the hole by $22 billion.

That was enough to catch the attention of Texas Attorney General Greg Abbott. As part of his investigation into the situation, he's found that some of the problem can be traced to mismanagement by the boards of directors. Some boards have been manipulating actuarial assumptions to make their funds appear to be in better financial shape than they are. One board even shifted the interest rate assumption from 7 percent to 10.25 percent, allowing it to reach its goal of increasing benefits and decreasing contributions. But that action also increased the pension fund's long-term liability substantially. In other instances, there were conflicts of interest—some board members had been hired by investment managers after these firms had contracted with the retirement board. In addition, 10 percent of the plans had failed to file or were late in filing legally required financial reports with the Pension Review Board.

"Inadequate governance," Abbott says, "will cause a pension fund to nose-dive and crash." The risks are great in states and localities that have fallen into arrears. Connecticut, Indiana, Rhode Island and West Virginia just start the list of states with dramatic pension fund problems. In Illinois, the state pension systems face a $41 billion shortfall, and that's after bonding out some $10 billion in liabilities just four years ago.

Even governments that don't have dramatically underfunded pension plans are facing unprecedented problems in paying for their liabilities, largely as a result of prior years' decisions to put off

From *Governing,* October 2007.

actuarially required contributions and a more recent phenomenon: the growth in the number of retirees.

Here's one way to understand the current funding pressure: A decade ago, the amount paid out annually by state and local pension plans was $60 billion. Today, it's closer to $150 billion. Here's another calculus: In 1988, Kentucky paid an amount equivalent to 8.2 percent of employee salaries into its retirement fund. For the current fiscal year, it's 16 percent; in five years, it will be 30.7 percent.

The growing anxiety over pension plans and their funding has been exacerbated lately by a new accounting rule that makes clear the huge liabilities states and localities have built for post-retirement health care. There isn't a direct link between pensions and other post-employment benefits but the funding comes from the same place, leading to tension between funding pension plans and funding other post-employment benefits.

Clearly, pension boards are functioning in a more challenging environment than ever, with more sophisticated and varied responsibilities and roles. For instance, statutory or constitutional restrictions on investments other than those with minimal risk—such as bonds—have been lifted. That means that public-sector pension plans can place their assets in a broader range of investments. So today, 70 percent of funds are invested in equities, compared with only 39 percent in 1990. Along with the dramatic shift to equities, a growing number of states are trying to juice up returns by putting some of their money in other alternative investments such as hedge funds, which can be a high-risk, high-return investment. "It's not that investing in something with an expectation of higher return is necessarily bad," says Susan Mangiero, president of Pension Governance, a consulting firm. "But you need to do even more in terms of assessing the risk."

Public funds are responsible for managing more than $3 trillion in assets—money that will or already does pay retirement benefits to as many as 14 million public servants and 7 million retirees and their family members. How that money is managed stands to affect not only those retirees but also the coffers of states and localities themselves, since investment shortfalls put pressure on general budgets to make up the difference. And yet, very little is known, either in or out of government, about the boards—how they're governed and who's in charge of overseeing the many calculations, estimations and fac-

Money at the Ready
Financial status of selected public employee pension plans, FY 2006

Plan	Acturarial funding level	Liability or surplus (in thousands)
Florida RS	105.6%	+$6,181,784
Oregon PERS	104.2	+2,088,600
North Carolina Local Government	99.4	−84,359
Vermont State Employees	99.3	−9,044
Georgia ERS	97.2	−378,301
Idaho PERS	95.2	−461,700
California PERF	87.3	−26,630,000
Texas Teachers	87.3	−13,693,000
California Teachers	87.0	−19,635,000
Alabama ERS	84.0	−1,699,618
Virginia Retirement System	81.3	−9,256,000
New Jersey Teachers	78.0	−10,016,478
Nevada Regular Employees	76.5	−4,778,029
Ohio Teachers	75.0	−19,362,974
Mississippi PERS	73.5	−6,607,401
South Carolina RS	71.6	−8,591,961
Kentucky ERS	61.3	−3,681,411
Illinois SERS	52.2	−9,974,688
Oklahoma Teachers	49.3	−7,673,000
Indiana Teachers	44.3	−9,199,594

Source: National Association of State Retirement Administrators.

tors that go into managing a public pension fund. When he looks at what's happening in his state, Abbott sees a need to make improvements before things get worse. "Caution flags," he says, "are being raised."

A BALANCING ACT

Boards with five, 10 or even 20 members run the pension show in the states and most large cities and counties. There are exceptions: New York State's plans are managed almost exclusively by the state's comptroller—a situation that Governor Eliot Spitzer and Attorney General Andrew Cuomo are questioning.

Money in Markets
Average asset allocation for state pension plans, 2006

Asset Class	Allocation
U.S. equity	42.3%
U.S. bonds	27.2%
Non-U.S. equity	17.1%
Real estate	4.8%
Private equity	4.4%
Other	3.2%
Non-U.S. bonds	0.9%

Source: Whilshire Association Inc.

While specific board functions vary from state to state, in general boards are in charge of overseeing pension operations, guiding investment policy, hiring investment consultants, making determinations on individual pension issues and approving changes in actuarial assumptions. Aside from periodic cases of outright fraud, most board members are men and women who genuinely wish to do a good job. Often, however, they don't have the necessary skills. As one observer put it, boards tend to be "incompetent groups of competent individuals."

As the funds have grown larger, the choice of individual board members should reflect that need for expertise. But the selection of individuals is often under the control of a pantheon of politically motivated individuals and groups—seats are reserved for employees, retirees, union members, elected officials and other subsets of groups— and does not lend itself to careful recruitment of an appropriate mix of different skills. It's much harder for a public board than it is for a private one to look at its current composition, see the potential holes in expertise and go after the skills that are missing.

The various groups from which members can be appointed each have positives and negatives. Union-selected trustees will certainly watch out for the retirees, but they may be less financially savvy. And trustees who hold political office may have a greater incentive to reduce state contributions to pension plans, freeing up money for other endeavors.

On many boards there's an air of foxes guarding the henhouse since many board members are pension recipients themselves. In Illinois, for example, employees and retirees make up more than half the members of most pension boards. In Texas, Abbott found that state and local pensions were dominated by employees. And that's a problem, Abbott says. There is a danger that they will "intentionally or inadvertently game the system."

Bottom line: A balance of representation is desirable, and it's critical to include citizen representatives—someone outside of government. "When you're not benefiting from the money, you have a different take on it," says Lynn Reed, a board member of Minnesota's Center for Public Finance Research, which came out with a critical report on Minnesota's pension performance last year. "The people who are involved are people of good will, but they don't ask the taxpayer kinds of questions."

THE SWAY OF MISINFORMATION

Many pension board members simply don't have the appropriate training to understand the plethora of numbers that only an actuary could love. It's not so much a case of cooking the books, as being unable to read the books with any degree of skill. When the Mississippi Public Employee Retirement System conducted a survey of other state systems on behalf of the National Association of State Retirement Administrators, it found that, among the 25 or so systems that responded, only nine plans had any formal education policy for board members, only six had mandatory educational requirements and only one had a mandatory certification program.

Things get particularly tricky when it comes to the nitty-gritty investing decisions. How much money can appropriately be placed in hedge funds? Stocks of local companies? What are the trade-offs in the short term and the longer stretch? Boards are frequently presented with a variety of options by the investment managers they've hired, and millions of people will be affected by these decisions. But one of the integral roles of the board is to apply appropriate oversight to these recommendations.

"Without a level of sophistication, these boards can get swayed by misinformation," says Lance Weiss, senior manager with Deloitte Consulting. Board members may have the right intentions but lack the knowledge or background to make good decisions. "These are people," he says, "who were teachers or state employees and have been retired for 20 years. You start talking about alternative investments, and they're lost."

Investment decisions aren't the only thing that's complicated here. Boards are presented with a wide array of assumptions including projections of investment returns,

"The $3 Trillion Challenge" was written by *Governing* correspondents **Katherine Barrett** and **Richard Greene**, based on research by the Pew Center on the States (PCS), a division of the Pew Charitable Trusts. PCS conducts research and analyzes states' experiences to find nonpartisan solutions for emerging problems. Online at *www.pewcenteronthestates.org*. Girard Miller, commentator and consultant on public finance issues, and Parry Young, the recently retired director of Standard & Poor's Ratings Services, assisted with research and review of the material.

Pew Center on the States:
■ Susan K. Urahn, Managing Director
■ Kil Huh, Project Manager, Research

"The $3 Trillion Challenge" is the first in a series of reports about post-retirement benefits emanating from research by the Pew Center on the States and is part of a larger Pew Center report on pensions and retiree health care that will be released in November at *www.pewcenteronthestates.org*. Other reports will include a 50-state review of the status of pensions and other post-employ[m]ent benefits, with newly developed sets of data about state pension plans and the liabilities states are facing from their post-retirement health benef[it]s. The final report will examine the ways states and school districts are planning to deal with post-retirement health care liabilities for teachers.

retiree life span and inflation rates. Each of these is based on enormously complex calculations and can have dramatic impact on the way plans are managed.

Consider the figure used for inflation. The higher that number, the higher the rate of return investments have to achieve to adequately fund a plan. According to the National Association of State Retirement Administrators, of 117 entities surveyed, the range of inflation rates used recently varied from 2.5 percent to 5 percent. Thirty-five based their calculations on an inflation rate of 3 percent or less and 43 believed it would be 4 percent or more. That single percentage point may not seem like a lot, but it can represent hundreds of millions of dollars to a large plan.

CONFLICTS OF INTEREST

Of all the problems that surround pension plan governance, the ones most likely to get attention are conflicts of interest: either on the part of the pension board members themselves or the investment managers they hire.

Pension boards in such localities as Chicago, Philadelphia and Milwaukee County, and such states as Ohio, Illinois and California have encountered conflict-of-interest problems over the past six years as members were accused of accepting perks from investment firms and using influence to procure contracts for campaign donors. Illinois' two-year-old problems involved a former trustee for the Illinois State Teachers' Retirement System who was indicted on charges he sought kickbacks from investment firms. The TRS board subsequently adopted new restrictions and disclosure requirements.

In California, the problem centered on allegations that two high-ranking state officials had steered pension business for the state's teachers' fund to companies from which they received sizable contributions. The retirement fund trustees took relatively dramatic action. They voted to halt business dealings with financial investment firms that contributed large sums to the governor or other elected officials. The new rule limits to $5,000 the amount that firms can give to board members (including the controller, state treasurer and governor) in campaign cash annually, if they want to qualify for investment business.

A Massachusetts commission report looked at this issue in the Bay State and found many red flags. Massachusetts board members were allowed to receive honoraria for participation in conferences financed by investment vendors and sometimes received compensation from individuals or firms that do business with the boards or allowed family members to provide services to the board. Moreover, many members of the more than 100 pension boards overseen by the Public Employees Retirement Administration, according to the Massachusetts commission, "do not possess a full understanding of the importance of competitive bidding and the need to negotiate contracts aggressively." For example, boards were retaining vendors for long periods "without entering the marketplace to ascertain if the vendor remains competitive with others."

MR. FIX-IT

While few states can boast solid pension-fund governance, a growing number are taking positive steps toward reform. Ohio, for example, increased education and training of board members. It also changed the composition of the board to remove a couple of elected officials while adding an additional retiree representative and three appointed investment experts.

Some states are looking into ways to cut back on the diverse responsibilities that boards undertake. In a handful of states, the investment function has been separated so that the oversight for all long-term state investments is placed under another entity. The benefit here is that such an arrangement provides focused attention on a very complex topic by men and women with sufficient training.

Arizona took particular care to outline and document the different functions performed by the board and the staff, concluding that it was the top-level functions in which the board needed to be most engaged. "The board's responsibility is to oversee the decision making of management," explains Paul Matson, executive director of the Arizona State Retirement System. But, for that dichotomy to be effective, the board couldn't just get its information from staff. It needed independent sources of information. So the board gets direct feedback from an external auditor, an independent investment consultant and an independent actuary.

In Missouri, continual improvement of pension governance has been an ongoing initiative for the better part of a decade now. It has gotten board members out of the business of day-to-day operations and transferred tasks such as hiring and firing money managers to the staff. This lets the board focus on policy and monitoring performance.

Gary Findlay, executive director of the Missouri State Employees' Retirement System argues that states will be well served by providing a statutory framework that will give boards the capacity to govern in a less political environment. That includes retaining legal counsel separately from the rest of government, hiring independent auditors and setting reasonable compensation levels for the men and women who actually work for the pension system (in an effort to compete adequately with the private sector). As a trade-off for this authority and the delegation of day-to-day tasks to the staff, Findlay says, there needs to be rigorous and transparent reporting of all pension-fund activities so that both the board and the legislature can provide adequate oversight.

The results of such changes in Missouri have been tangible. According to Findlay, the system has reduced turnover in the staff and volatility in its investment returns. It has matched or exceeded the returns experienced by other funds in good markets and has fared considerably better in bad markets.

Maryland is another state that has been making positive changes. In the early days of this decade, its portfolio's performance ranked in the bottom quartile compared with other public-pension plans, according to the Department of Legislative Services of the Maryland General Assembly. One of its investment managers was being investigated by the Securities and Exchange Commission and another was twice indicted for alleged improprieties. The board also had lost $27 million due to a failed computer procurement. After the state hired a consulting firm to make suggestions for reform, the legislature took action to balance the composition of the board—replacing some employee representatives with members of the public—and improve expertise. For instance, it added requirements for minimum experience for investment expert trustees and required all board members to receive at least eight hours of investment and fiduciary training each year.

Others have taken similar steps. San Diego, a city that has been brought to the brink of bankruptcy by pension problems, has removed some of the positions that were designated for active and retired employees in favor of individuals with financial expertise.

Education and training of board members has been a focus of reforms in Ohio, Louisiana and Massachusetts. A Reform Initiatives Advisory Committee Report in Massachusetts, for example, encouraged the Public Employee Retirement Administration Commission to require that every board member meet a basic level of education and be subject to an ongoing, continuing certification process concerning their responsibilities as fiduciaries and trustees.

Of course, it's difficult to attract a board member with sufficient expertise if the compensation isn't sufficient. Even at a big fund like CalPers, for example, members are paid $100 a day for meetings that can go on for 10 to 12 hours. And that kind of compensation is par for the course.

Pensions can no longer be regarded as a footnote to government policy. The stakes are huge, both in dollar terms and in the capacity of the public sector to compete for talented men and women to govern those plans.

Although those running pension plans are appointed, it's the elected officials who are accountable—not for micromanaging pension systems and making decisions but for providing the oversight necessary to ensure that decisions are made honestly and effectively.

35

The Gold in the Gray

Ron Snell

Healthy, wealthy, and retired? States seek a financial advantage by going gray.

When someone says "Americans are aging" bad news usually follows—news about labor shortages, funding problems in Social Security, Medicare, Medicaid and state pension programs, inadequate savings for retirement, health issues, and so forth. But for those who see the glass as half-full instead of half-empty, great possibilities lie in the graying of America. They see attractive possibilities for economic development.

Economic development that depends on the aging of America has a solid base on which to build. The number of Americans over 65 will grow substantially in the next five decades. By 2050, the Census Bureau projects, there will be more than 86 million Americans aged 65 or older—almost 21 percent of the population. Around 21 million of them will be over 85.

GRAY GOLDMINES

While it's true that most Americans don't save enough money for retirement (and not enough Americans save any money for anything) it's also true there are many, many reasonably affluent retired people out there. They tend to be footloose, as anyone knows who's encountered their flocks of Airstream Trailers migrating on the highway. That's where the economic development possibilities begin. Although retired people (65 and older) and those near retirement (55 to 64, in terms of Census Bureau categories) are less likely to move their residence than younger people, enough of them do move to be an important target for states that see retired people as gray goldmines. In recent years a number of states, particularly Gulf Coast states and their neighbors to the

From *State Legislatures,* October/November 2007.

north, have regarded this population as an economic treasure trove.

The reasons are straightforward. People who are inclined to move after they retire tend to be among the healthiest and wealthiest of retirees. The sick and the poor stay put. A Florida study on the importance of attracting retired people puts the advantages in a nutshell: "Florida's growth depends on its ability to attract mature residents. The retirement industry is clean, and its benefits are spread to other high job-creating industries such as hospitality, construction and health care." And even though a skeptic might think, well, after all, they will grow older and less healthy, and put a burden on their new state, that's not quite on target.

For one thing, the health care costs of the low-income elderly depend largely on Medicare and Medicaid, one federally funded and the other heavily federally subsidized. And second, the very aged (those over 85) have a tendency, according to the Census Bureau, to return to their places of origin when their health declines, probably to be near family.

As a result, it's not just Florida that's in the business of trying to sell itself to retirees. The study notes with annoyance: "Other states are devoting substantial marketing resources to eat into Florida's share of the market." So what's going on? And what do legislatures have to do with this?

SIZE OF MARKET

First some facts about the size of the "market." In the five years from 1995 to 2000, almost 30 percent of Americans over 65 changed their residence. Like younger people, most of them didn't go far—they stayed within the same county. But those over 65 were more likely than younger people to go to a different state, and they were more likely to go to a distant state—one outside their region. The Census Bureau found 1.5 million people over 65 who moved to another state in those five years, and 835,000 who moved to a state outside their region. It also notes that people who moved had higher incomes than those who did not move, and those who moved across state lines had higher incomes than those who moved within a county. So that's the rough outline of Florida's "market": people willing to move from one region to another, and who, as it happens, tend to have higher incomes than other people.

Two areas of the country are the sources of most of the elderly migrants: the Great Plains, in a swath that reaches from the Canadian border of Montana and North Dakota into northwestern Texas, and a huge Northeastern crescent swinging from New England and Minnesota into the northern counties of West Virginia and Kentucky. Except for Alaska, all the states with net losses of more than 1 percent of their residents over 65 in the late 1990s are in that crescent. Losses of the elderly in Great Plains states tend in most cases to be offset within the same state.

Over the five years of the Census Bureau study, New York suffered both the greatest loss in numbers—about 114,000 people over the five-year period—and the greatest rate of loss—4.5 percent of the population over 65. Although Alaska's rate of loss was almost as high as New York's, Alaska's smaller and younger population meant a much smaller loss in terms of people—slightly more than 1,400 in five years.

Where did they go? Generally speaking they went west and south. Florida, Georgia, the Carolinas and Tennessee are one contiguous catchment area; the other is Arizona, Idaho, Nevada, New Mexico and Utah. These two distinct regions had different sources of migrants. For the Southeastern states, they are the Northeast and the Midwest. For the Western group, the source is primarily California and to a much lesser extent, the upper Midwest.

This reveals an important anomaly: Despite an attractive climate and a low cost of living, the Gulf Coast states west of Florida and their northern neighbors (except for Tennessee) have not been magnets for retirees as states to their east have been. In recent years, however, Alabama, Arkansas, Louisiana, Mississippi, Oklahoma and Texas have launched vigorous efforts to capture some of the retirees that Florida sees as its rightful market. If I-95 takes Northeastern retirees to the Carolinas and Florida, why shouldn't I-35 and I-65 take Midwesterners to the Gulf Coast?

BIG SPENDERS

Retired people's stable and discretionary incomes are an attraction. A Louisiana study notes that the 20 percent of the state's population over 65 accounted for 36 percent of consumer expenditures in the state in 2000. Military

Do Income Tax Breaks Help Retain the Elderly in a State?

A number of states that are losing residents over 65 have studied the issue.

The loss of talent, personal income and tax revenue that migrating elderly people take with them is only part of the issue. States that forecast stagnant or declining populations as a consequence of low birth rates, emigration and aging will have to address almost unprecedented challenges of population and income distribution, health care, service delivery and public finance. A Michigan study, for example, makes a point applicable to many states: The aging of the population means a lower ratio of workingage people to retirement-age people, challenging the state's ability to provide the services it has committed itself to. Policies that favor seniors in terms of both taxes and benefits will make financial problems worse.

The issues are so overwhelming that they tend to circle back to an issue legislators can actually do something about: taxes on the elderly. For years, Northern states have used tax policy to try to retain the elderly, increasingly offering a mix of property tax breaks and income tax exclusions. The former sometimes are phased out at higher income levels; the income tax breaks tend not to be, since their tacit purpose is to retain the high-income elderly. It is hard to know how successful such policies are, since there's no way to know what would occur in their absence, but the debate in two relatively heavily taxed states offers some light on the issue.

One is Maine, a slow growing state in a slow growing region, and the only one of the 50 states to have become more rural over the past 35 years. Its population under 18 is *falling* and the state is on its way to becoming one of the oldest in the country. It is also among the top 10 states in state and local revenue as a percentage of personal income.

Maine's tax treatment of retiree income does not differ much from its treatment of other income. Social Security income is not taxed, but other than that a retired person is eligible for only a $6,000 exclusion minus Social Security income. Maine's highest income tax bracket is 8.5 percent, which single taxpayers reach with taxable income of $18,500. So, the question comes up, does this drive affluent Maine residents to Florida?

Apparently not. A John F. Kennedy School of Government study suggests that more wealthy people over age 55 move into Maine than leave—and that the pattern is the opposite for neighboring New Hampshire, which has no income tax on pension or Social Security income. Though the samples are small, the suggestion is that the effect of taxes on interstate migration is exactly the opposite of what a person would expect.

Wisconsin imposes a lower overall tax burden than Maine (20th by the same measure) and unlike Maine, experiences a net loss of people over 65. Those who leave at the highest rate are those with incomes over $65,000. Does that indicate that Wisconsin should consider reduced taxation for the elderly? The evidence is not conclusive, since from 1995 to 2000, the state lost an average of only 806 people a year out of about 123,000 in the category. A tax break large enough to affect decisions on migration would therefore be extremely expensive in terms of state revenue. The Wisconsin study points out further that Pennsylvania and Illinois, which do not tax retirement income, continue to have higher losses of their elderly population than Wisconsin does.

The implicit contention that taxes on the elderly do not have much effect on a decision to leave or stay in a state is unconvincing to many legislators. The two studies mentioned here make it clear that their conclusions are tentative, being based on insufficient data and small samples. In 2006, Iowa legislators found such reasoning inadequate and voted to exempt Social Security from income taxes and to increase to $32,000 the total income exclusion for seniors filing jointly.

"This bill sends a message that we value and appreciate our seniors," says Senator David Miller. "It will help keep them from leaving Iowa for lower-tax states and taking their financial, philanthropic and civic contributions with them." Given the few tools legislators have to cope with the facts of an aging population and the perceived threat of emigration to other states, it is likely that the few states that continue to tax retirement income like other income will gradually change their policies. But legislators should be aware that hard evidence for the success of retaining the elderly through tax policy is scarce.

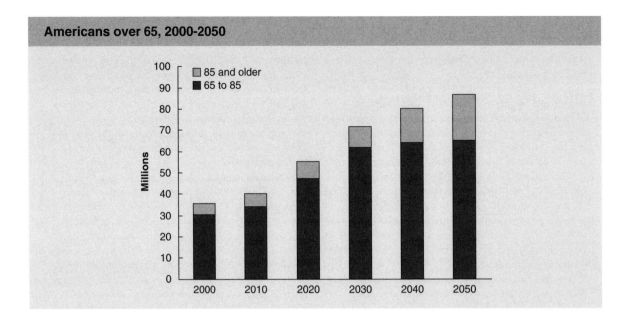

Americans over 65, 2000-2050

retirees alone collect $406 million in retirement pay a year. Arkansas notes that retirees who move to the state generally have higher incomes than average in the communities where they settle.

Moreover, these states note, retiree income is stable and tends to be spent. Retirees buy or build homes; their spending creates new demands for goods and services; they enhance the income, sales and property tax bases; and they can strengthen communities with talent and willingness to volunteer. Their spending may help preserve small town retailers and local health services, and otherwise benefit the local quality of life.

One widespread tactic to attract retirees is publicizing the attractiveness of certain designated retirement communities. Mississippi's Hometown Retirement Cities, for example, are selected because of their cost of living, level of taxes, crime rate, availability of quality medical care, and recreational, educational and cultural opportunities. The Texas Certified Retirement Community Program adds employment opportunities and the availability of public transportation to the mix. In West Virginia, designated retirement communities have banded together to advertise themselves jointly in conjunction with the state Development Office. Alabama's Robert Trent Jones Golf Trail (a set of seven golf complexes financed by the state retirement system) are said to attract the wealthy to nearby retirement housing complexes.

Behind such designations lies careful analysis of the advantages and possible costs of attracting retirees to a state, state government efforts to aid communities in reshaping themselves to attract retired people from beyond the state borders, and sophisticated advertising campaigns. Some states have carefully tracked the origin of the retired people moving into them in order to target potential migrants in states where word-of-mouth and personal relationships may already have advertised their attractions. There is nothing casual about the process, says Matthew Kisber, Tennessee's Commissioner of Economic Development: "We are working to implement programs that would establish retirement migration as an economic development strategy."

TAX ATTRACTIONS

One important element in the competition for retirees is tax policy. Florida's absence of personal income taxes has long been credited as one of its attractions. In recent years it has felt competition from Gulf Coast neighbors that have targeted tax breaks at retired people. Alabama and Mississippi have exempted pensions from state

Where Older People Are Moving

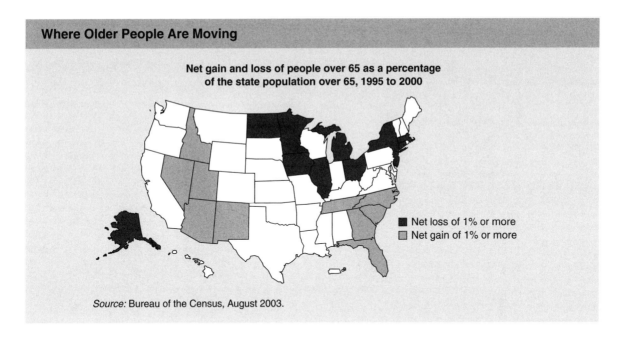

Net gain and loss of people over 65 as a percentage
of the state population over 65, 1995 to 2000

■ Net loss of 1% or more
□ Net gain of 1% or more

Source: Bureau of the Census, August 2003.

income taxes. Georgia's exemption will rise to $35,000 for tax year 2008. Louisiana allows a full exemption for federal civil service and military pensions. Texas has no personal income tax, and Tennessee's is limited to investment income. Arkansas has kept its retirement income exemption at a regionally low $6,000. Oklahoma has raised its exemption to $10,000 for the stated purpose of attracting retired people to the state.

A policymaker then has to ask: Do all these programs actually make a difference? Do advertising, designation of retirement communities, building golf courses, or cutting taxes on retirement income actually bring more people to a state, or are they simply heaping rewards on the heads of those who would come anyway? This is the same tough question that legislators encounter in other economic development activities: do tax cuts bring the car assembly plant to your state, or just reward a company for a decision it would have made anyway? The difference is, of course, that except for the tax breaks for retirement income, existing programs to attract retirees do not cost very much.

Some of the academic work suggests that promotional efforts are not really necessary. While it seems clear that retired people prefer lower taxes to higher taxes—who doesn't?—and that taxes can have an effect on the deci-

sion where people will move, the actual effect seems to be very slight. The same is said to be true of the level of public services—if a county were to increase spending on public safety by 70 percent, that might attract one or two more retired people a year to the county. This suggests that high taxes could be an impediment to attracting people, but that low taxes don't necessarily have much effect. That could especially be so now that most states give very favorable treatment to retirement income.

In fact, what may be most important in attracting retired people are things a state government can't control—climate, mountains, coastlines and general amenities. The Florida study found that what baby boomers most value about a state are weather, natural features, kinship, social attractions, health care and social services, and economic issues. Few of those are very susceptible to government management, although they can be enhanced or damaged. A South Carolina study (funded by the state Department of Parks and Tourism) concluded that "the government's role should focus on providing and promoting the amenities that make South Carolina a desirable state to live in for all age groups, for tourism and attracting industry. Retirees, other migrants and tourists will then automatically find the state." That may be the final word on the subject.

PART

Policy Challenges

If there is any single message to be drawn from the readings in this book it is that state and local governments are expected to do a lot. There is virtually no aspect of social, political and economic life in the United States that is not touched in some way by state and local government policy.

Given their central role it is hard, and perhaps even misleading, to attempt to come up with a short list of "most important" or "high priority" issues facing state and local governments. What is considered "important" and "priority" is often very much in the eye of the beholder. A stressed homeowner upside down on their mortgage may not give a thought to illegal immigration. A college student in their 20s may not spend much time worrying about health care. State and local governments are expected to worry about all of this, and a lot more besides.

Yet while state and local governments are expected to deal with, well, just about everything, they have limited resources. There is only so much time, money and energy to go around. Accordingly, every year it is a smaller spectrum of issues that attract a disproportionate share of government's interest and resources. What are those issues likely to be?

TRENDS

Josh Goodman's essay kicks off this section by providing an overview of the issues currently crowding the top of public agendas. The first is illegal immigration, an issue which is increasingly generating policy action and intense controversy at the state and local level. Faced with a growing backlash against illegal immigration and the federal government's continued inaction, states and localities are being pushed to take matters into their own hands. There are no perfect solutions to this tough issue, just lots of problems. Among other issues, Goodman's essay highlights the growing problem of mortgage foreclosures and the continuing struggle to contain health care costs. Mortgage foreclosures have suddenly become an epidemic and states are scrambling to insulate many of their citizens from financial disasters stemming from property related debt. Unlike mortgages, health care is something that has had the attention of lawmakers for a very long time. That is likely to continue, with concerns about "super bug" epidemics being added to a long list of concerns ranging from how to fund Medicaid to ensuring adequate access for the less well off.

The other essays in this section take one of the issues highlighted in Goodman's essay and examines it more in depth. Alan Greenblatt's essay takes a look at the mortgage meltdown and how state and local governments are dealing with the problem (or not). Some places, like Las Vegas, are banking on more economic growth to pull them out of the property doldrums. In other places, like cities in the manufacturing heartland of the Midwest, explosive economic growth seems less like a solution than a pipedream. The foreclosure crisis in such places is creating nightmares for citizens and policymakers alike.

Josh Goodman returns with a second essay that takes an in-depth look at illegal immigration. This is an issue that combines economics, culture and emotion into a combative and divisive political conflict. It is a conflict that is driving wedges between traditional political allies and reshaping how business is done in state capitols.

Finally, Laura Tobler and Christie Hager take a look at health care reform. More than half the states are either considering or are in the process of reforming their health care systems. New England states have led the way with a series of bold steps designed to rein in costs, improve quality and do so while maintaining access. There are risks involved with these bold moves, but the potential payoffs could spread to other states.

36

Issues to Watch

Josh Goodman

A lot went wrong last year. State legislatures will spend the next year trying to fix things.

In 2008, state legislatures will try to fix everything that went wrong in 2007.

That means focusing on infrastructure funding in response to the bridge collapse in Minneapolis. It also means trying to get homeowners into less-risky fixed-rate mortgages, to combat the wave of foreclosures that spread across the country last year. Water policy will be getting a widespread reassessment, as a result of the severe drought in the Southeast. And legislators will look to combat hospital-acquired illnesses, after reports highlighted the deadly toll of drug-resistant bacteria.

But even with these topics entering the political front burner, legislatures will still debate perennial hot-button issues, including the death penalty, gay marriage and immigration. Each has a new focus this year, however. For the first time, several legislatures are seriously considering extending marriage rights to same-sex couples. They are also preparing for a U.S. Supreme Court ruling on the constitutionality of lethal injection, a decision that could throw execution procedures across the country into doubt. On immigrant policy, perhaps the hottest of hot buttons, states may make it tougher for people in the country illegally to obtain driver's licenses.

So, the 44 legislatures with regular sessions this year will have a lot to do. That's not necessarily a bad thing, though. More than three quarters of legislative seats will be up for election in November. Voters will have an excellent opportunity to judge lawmakers on what they have accomplished.

From *Governing.com,*
January 2008.

ILLEGAL IMMIGRATION

In 2006, Colorado and Georgia each approved bills heralded as the nation's toughest immigration law. Last year, Oklahoma stole the title. The question now is whether the stream of enforcement-oriented immigration initiatives—Tennessee and Arizona also approved notable laws last year—will continue and, if so, where.

That legislators will debate the issue in virtually every state is beyond doubt. But a smaller group of states will consider following the trend established by Colorado: overhauling almost every aspect of state immigration policy at once, rather than taking a piecemeal approach. Legislation proposed in Kansas and South Carolina, for example, would deny government benefits to illegal immigrants, punish employers that hire them and push local law enforcement officers to do more to identify them.

Supporters of these bills have a new argument at their disposal. They say that as immigrants flee neighboring states that have already acted, their states will see an influx of illegal resident[s] unless they pass tough laws now. "Colorado, on our west border, has had legislation for two years," says Brenda Landwehr, a Kansas state representative who is sponsoring the legislation. "Oklahoma on our south border has passed legislation that went into effect November 1. We don't want to become a sanctuary state."

On the other hand, if the laws in Colorado, Georgia and Oklahoma are perceived as faltering, that may put a damper on activity elsewhere. Oklahoma's law faces a court challenge and some local law enforcement officers say they lack the resources to implement it.

The immigration debate will also have a new twist this year, thanks to New York Governor Eliot Spitzer. Last year, Spitzer had to scrap a proposal to allow illegal immigrants to obtain driver's licenses after it set off a political firestorm. States had slowly been moving in the direction of tightening driver's license restrictions, and the New York controversy seems to have accelerated the process.

A few days after Spitzer backed down, Oregon Governor Ted Kulongoski headed off legislative pressure by issuing an executive order requiring proof of legal residency to get a license. A possible sign of things to come: Matt Blunt, the governor of Missouri, a state that already restricted licenses to legal residents, is pitching a measure to create new penalties for acquiring a license illegally.

INFRASTRUCTURE REPAIR

The I-35W bridge collapse in Minneapolis last summer prompted a reassessment of infrastructure across the country. State after state acknowledged roads and bridges in disrepair and quantified billions of dollars in needs. Those reports set the stage for policy makers to direct substantial revenue to infrastructure.

There's a dilemma for legislators, though. At the very moment that the need for new infrastructure spending seems most urgent, the primary source for transportation funding—the gas tax—is most reviled. Widespread agitation over high gas prices makes an increase in the levy dead on arrival in almost every state. As a result, legislators are looking elsewhere for funding.

In many places, the dollar figures involved are enormous. Iowa's department of transportation estimates that, in a state where the 2008 general fund budget came in under $6 billion, the state and its localities face a $28 billion transportation funding shortfall over the next 20 years. Just the most pressing needs will cost the state $200 million a year. Iowa is one of the few states mulling a gas-tax increase.

Proposals elsewhere run the gamut. Legislatures are looking at toll roads, even in states such as Arizona where they've long faced stiff opposition. Florida is considering following in Indiana's footsteps by leasing existing tolls roads to private companies in exchange for upfront payments. New Jersey Governor Jon Corzine also wants to get upfront payments from toll roads, but his preferred mechanism is a new public corporation that will oversee the roads and issue bonds. Many states are also looking at fee increases for vehicle registration and other transactions.

In addition to the safety risks exposed by the Minneapolis bridge collapse, the rapid rise in construction costs will also loom over each of these discussions. Clark Jenkins, a North Carolina state senator who is serving on a special commission on transportation funding, thinks those increases—fueled by demand around the globe—suggest states should borrow money to build now, before prices go even higher. "The inflation in construction costs itself is putting tremendous pressure on our traditional transportation funding sources," Jenkins says. "The longer you wait, the worse it's going to get."

MORTGAGE FORECLOSURES

In response to the national foreclosure epidemic, legislatures in many states are considering overhauls of the lending industry. The hope of reform-minded lawmakers is that they can prevent the next generation of homebuyers from entering into mortgages they won't be able to afford. However, lending reform generally won't help the hundreds of thousands of homeowners who already have adjustable-rate mortgages and whose interest rates are scheduled to skyrocket.

That reality has many states promoting counseling and education for people in bad loans, in the hopes of alerting them to the danger before their homes are at risk. It has also prompted some states and the federal government to go further and help homeowners in adjustable-rate mortgages avoid ever paying the exorbitant interest payments. "This is the only thing that will have an impact on people in unfair or troubling loans," says Steve Tobocman, a Michigan state representative.

A few states, such as Ohio, already have programs underway to offer refinancing for people in adjustable-rate mortgages. Ohio is contributing millions of dollars in state bonds to move low-income and middle-income households into 30-year loans with fixed interest rates. Some states are investing heavily in the concept, and others are considering doing so. Massachusetts' fund is $250 million—$60 million from state bonds and the rest from Fannie Mae.

The Bush administration embraced a similar idea in December in a deal with lenders. The plan freezes interest rates for five years for many homeowners with adjustable-rate mortgages. The Bush plan also encourages these homeowners to refinance through state and local government programs.

States, including California, are also looking at promoting refinancing through bans on "prepayment penalties." These fees kick in if a home loan is paid off early, effectively serving as a deterrent to refinancing.

Lending reform and refinancing are just two pieces of the response to what has quickly become one of the hottest topics in state government. States also are looking at cracking down on appraisal fraud, overhauling the foreclosure process and assisting communities to reduce unoccupied homes. "The foreclosure crisis," says Steve Driehaus, an Ohio state representative, "is on the magnitude of multiple natural disasters across the United States."

HOSPITALS AND HEALTH

A "superbug" with a tongue-twisting name, methicillin-resistant Staphylococcus aureus (MRSA), made national headlines in October, when researchers at the Centers for Disease Control and Prevention announced that the bacterial infection kills close to 19,000 Americans a year, far more than previously thought. The MRSA report brought twin health care challenges into broader public consciousness: the problem of drug-resistant infections and the danger of hospitals (where most MRSA cases develop) as breeding grounds for these infections.

Many legislators were already familiar with the issue. In the past few years, about 20 states have enacted laws that require public reporting of hospital-acquired infections. And "probably every state that doesn't have a law will be taking up this issue" in 2008, says Lisa McGiffert, campaign director for the Consumers Union's Stop Hospital Infections efforts. The logic behind the laws is that when hospitals know the public will see their data, they are more likely to encourage sanitary practices that reduce infections.

Some states are looking at going further than merely requiring reporting. Pennsylvania, for example, passed legislation last year that will increase funding for hospitals that reduce infections. The pay-for-performance initiative dovetails with a new federal policy. Medicare plans to stop compensating hospitals for the cost of certain infections that occur after patients are admitted. The message: If hospitals allow infections, they, not the feds, should have to pay for them.

Legislators also are increasingly interested in measures that go beyond reporting to mandate that hospital patients be tested for drug-resistant infections. The MRSA scare has invigorated those efforts, as lawmakers discover that many hospitals aren't checking at-risk patients for the infections. New laws in Illinois, Pennsylvania and New Jersey require hospital screenings. Proposals to require reporting of MRSA specifically, rather than just hospital-related infections generally, also are under consideration in many states, including Washington and Virginia.

All of these efforts have, at times, run into opposition from hospitals. They argue that the hospitals that are most studious about gathering data—rather than the ones with the biggest infection problems—may end up looking the worst in the reports. Washington State approved an infection-reporting requirement this year, but Representative Tom Campbell, the bill's sponsor, says, "It took many years of confrontation. There's almost a sickness to be secret." Nonetheless, the idea that hospital-acquired infections are largely unpreventable, which was conventional wisdom in the medical community for many years, seems to be fading away.

Of course, legislators will also discuss a host of other health-related issues, from controlling Medicaid costs to expanding access to care. This could be a landmark year for universal coverage proposals, with several states, including New York, Colorado, Wisconsin and New Mexico mulling ideas to bring health care to all.

The most intriguing possibility is that California will try to cover all 6.7 million of its uninsured. Governor Arnold Schwarzenegger's plan requires employers to contribute to health care and also includes an individual mandate, under which everyone would be required to obtain coverage. The individual mandate concept is receiving attention across the country. How far it spreads may hinge on how well it works in the one state, Massachusetts, that's already trying it.

GAMBLING EXPANSION

After a four-year reprieve from widespread shortfalls, unhappy days are here again for state budgets. This year, policy makers will likely be forced to decide between two distasteful options: to raise taxes or cut spending. Some states, though, are looking at another revenue source to avoid this dilemma: gambling.

In Illinois, budget woes are driving lawmakers to look to a land-based casino in Chicago for revenue. Maryland residents will vote on the legalization of slot-machine gambling in November, after the legislature approved the referendum late last year. A $1.5 billion shortfall served as motivation for lawmakers to finally act on slots, after years of discussion.

Even in states without major budget problems, however, gambling expansion is on the table. For example, Kentucky's new governor, Steve Beshear, is asking the legislature to approve a plan for more gaming. Part of the reason that more and more legislatures have embraced casinos in recent years is that places without them see their residents head across state lines in droves to gamble. "The states are definitely competing for revenue," says Richard McGowan, a Boston College professor and

gambling expert. "I would imagine the competition is going to get a little more fierce."

There's another less obvious factor, too. In some states, federal deals with Indian tribes mean that gambling is coming whether states want it or not. The federal agreements can ignore state revenue interests, creating an incentive for states to preempt them by cutting their own deals with the tribes.

That is the argument that gambling proponents in Massachusetts are making as the legislature mulls allowing casinos. Likewise Charlie Crist, the governor of Florida, opposed gambling during the 2006 campaign. But, faced with the threat of an unfavorable federal agreement, he inked a deal with an Indian tribe to expand gambling at seven casinos in exchange for hundreds of millions of dollars in payments to the state. Crist's decision angered Florida House Speaker Marco Rubio and other lawmakers, who plan to argue in court that it required legislative approval.

GAY MARRIAGE

After Vermont became the first state to approve civil unions for same-sex couples in 2000, the response was at times "uncivil," as state Representative Johannah Leddy Donovan puts it. The backlash briefly cost Democrats control of the Vermont House. Last year, however, neighboring New Hampshire enacted civil unions with barely a peep of controversy. "There's been a sea change on this issue," Donovan says. That shift in favor of gay rights explains why another first may be on the horizon: legislative approval of gay marriage, without the prodding of a court.

Legislatures in a handful of states are looking seriously at taking that step, but it's not clear whether it will happen this year. In Vermont, Donovan serves on a commission evaluating gay marriage, although legislation this year seems unlikely. The California legislature has approved gay marriage twice in three years, only to have Governor Arnold Schwarzenegger veto it. In New York, the key stumbling block is opposition in the state Senate.

The main focus now is New Jersey. Garden State lawmakers approved civil unions in 2006, but many same-sex couples say that employers aren't recognizing the relationships. As a result, gay marriage is back on the table, with Governor Jon Corzine saying he'll sign it.

In some sense, these efforts confirm the predictions of social conservatives, who argued that domestic partnership and civil-union laws would lead to gay marriage. Such a move also could send ripples through the national same-sex-marriage debate because the state courts that have been the key players so far have made for easy targets, often derided as judicial activists. Currently, gay marriages are available only in Massachusetts, where they were prompted by a state Supreme Court ruling. Gay-rights advocates think that action by elected legislators would be more difficult to dismiss.

Most states, of course, aren't interested in legalizing same-sex marriage. Twenty-six states ban it in their constitutions and legislators in a few more, including Iowa and Indiana, could move in that direction this year. Florida voters likely will weigh in on a constitutional ban in November, as a result of a petition drive. State law will require the amendment to receive 60 percent to pass, which is likely to make the vote competitive and closely watched.

WATER POLICY

Parched by a prolonged drought, Southeastern states are reassessing anything and everything related to water policy. The lack of rainfall has hurt farmers and created fears of water shortages—fears that, in some places, already have been realized.

The drought comes in a region unaccustomed to water woes. "Here in Atlanta," says Gil Rogers, an attorney with the Southern Environmental Law Center, "the big problem is that no one is looking at how growth is tied to our water-supply problems." That may be about to change in Georgia, where Atlanta's primary water source, Lake Lanier, has been hit hard by the drought. The Georgia legislature is expected to vote in January on a water-management plan under which the state would evaluate how much water it has and how much it will need. Alabama is formulating a similar plan.

Georgia also is looking at constructing new reservoirs, and states throughout the Southeast are encouraging conservation. North Carolina rapidly reduced its water consumption by 30 percent last year, after Governor Mike Easley called on residents to conserve.

Elsewhere, eight governors from Great Lakes states teamed up with two Canadian counterparts in December 2005 to sign a compact to regulate water withdrawal from the lakes and, most important, forbid it from being diverted to outside the region. The deal, though, has been slow to win required legislative approval. However, the drought in the Southeast and a comment from New Mexico Governor Bill Richardson—"States like Wisconsin are awash in water"—have created a new sense of urgency. "If an alarm bell was needed, it's been sounded," says David Naftzger, executive director of the Council of Great Lakes Governors. So far, Minnesota and Illinois have approved the compact. More states are expected to sign off this year.

Water policy is, of course, a perennial topic in the West. This year, the Oregon legislature will discuss water storage, as global warming creates fears that farmland will go dry. A hot subject for debate in California will be $10 billion in bonds for water projects.

DEATH PENALTY

By agreeing to hear a case on lethal injection, the U.S. Supreme Court has created a de facto nationwide death penalty moratorium and turned the debate from abolition to administration. Once the court rules, at least by the end of June, a flurry of legislative activity is likely, as states try to conform to the edict.

At issue in the case, known as *Baze v. Rees,* is whether Kentucky's use of a three-drug protocol to carry out death sentences violates the Constitution's ban on cruel and unusual punishment. That protocol, which consists of a drug to cause unconsciousness, another to stop muscle movement and a third that causes cardiac arrest, has spread across the country since it was devised in 1977. Today, almost every state with a death penalty uses it.

Critics contend, however, that the drugs can cause severe suffering before they kill. A ruling might force states to try alternative methods, such as the use of a single drug. "The sentence is death, not torture," says Tennessee state Senator Doug Jackson, who chairs a committee studying the death penalty.

Regardless of whether the justices pass judgment on the three-drug protocol, court watchers think the ruling will clarify what constitutes cruel and unusual punishment. That will likely lead states to a broader reexamination of execution procedures, such as training for execution teams and whether medical staff have to be on hand. In fact, that process already has started in

California, Florida and a few other states, as lower court rulings in the past two years called execution procedures into doubt. In some states, these sorts of changes can be made administratively, but in others legislative action is required.

The court is not expected to use *Baze* to end the death penalty permanently, but that likely will be a topic of discussion in Colorado, Illinois, Maryland, New Mexico and New York this year. In New Jersey, lawmakers abolished the death penalty in December.

37

Two Faces of Foreclosure

Alan Greenblatt

Foreclosures are a problem everywhere; in some places the trend is a disaster.

From *Governing,*
April 2008.

The house at 608 Oxford Avenue is in bad shape, but its neighborhood is worse. Next door sit two vacant lots where condemned residences already have been torn down. Like 608, the houses at 602 and 604 are boarded up, while all that's left of the house across the street is a set of concrete steps leading up to nothing. The story is the same on block after block of this old working-class district, just across the Mad River from downtown Dayton, Ohio. Driving around, Dayton City Commissioner Dean Lovelace points to a big empty parcel of land and says, "Even drug dealers are starting to abandon this neighborhood."

Nearly 2,000 miles to the west, in the vast sea of stucco-and-tile houses that surrounds the Las Vegas Strip, foreclosure is, if anything, even more prevalent. Fifteen of the 20 ZIP codes with the highest foreclosure rates in the country are located in Clark County, in and around Las Vegas. The water was turned off six months ago at the bank-owned house at 525 Brown Breeches Avenue in North Las Vegas, while the window frame of the master bedroom at 528 is speckled with droppings from the hundreds of pigeons and sparrows who are starting to reclaim the Creekside II subdivision.

But what Lovelace calls "the visibility of despair" in Dayton is not nearly as acute in southern Nevada. The Creekside homes were built only four years ago, aren't boarded up and haven't been stripped of pipes, doors and gutters like so many houses in Dayton. One real estate company is running a foreclosure bus tour through the Las Vegas Valley in order to expedite bargain shopping. A problem that signals permanent decline to central Ohio is seen in Las Vegas more as a bump on the path to continued growth.

197

In short, what looks from a distance like one national crisis turns out on close inspection to be two very different ones. And the reaction of local leadership presents just as much of a contrast. "We have to come up with some clean-up-the-mess strategies," says Dayton's Lovelace. Phil Rosenquist, the assistant county manager in Clark County, talks a laissez-faire game. "We're really not doing too much, to be honest with you," he says.

It's not just a difference in political philosophy. It's a difference in the reality on the ground. In suburbs and cities throughout the Sun Belt, strong growth and rising prices led to widespread speculation. Second homes and investment properties are empty, with individuals who got in over their heads deciding it's best to walk away and let the banks deal with the consequences. Major sections of Florida, California, Nevada and Arizona that had become dependent on growth are suffering the consequences of robust housing sectors suddenly going bust.

In the industrial Midwest, however, the consequences are more serious. The end of the housing bubble coincides with a weak manufacturing job market, and the loss of jobs, more than anything else, is causing foreclosures to proliferate. "Look at Dayton, Toledo or Akron and you'll find that local depressed economies are just miring the housing economies down," says Sam Staley, a Reason Foundation economist who lives just outside of Dayton. "Since there isn't any job growth, you're not seeing any resilience in the housing markets, and it's not clear when it's going to rebound."

Beyond the drop in sales and property tax revenue—and the effect on the ability of governments themselves to borrow money—the impact of foreclosures includes new challenges in terms of public safety and combating blight. "Vacant property attracts crime," says Michael Coleman, the mayor of Columbus, Ohio. "How do we get the mortgage industry to step up and take care of these properties?"

Home-values are going down in Las Vegas just as they are in Dayton. But the long-term impact will not be the same. In Las Vegas, times are tough today, but multi-billion-dollar projects on the Strip and elsewhere suggest a future filled with thousands of new jobs—and new buyers to inhabit the thousands of empty houses. Dayton's mortgage meltdown marks another low point on a long downward trend, leading some city officials to think more in terms of retrenchment than recovery.

JOBS AND HOUSES

In Ohio as a whole, the foreclosure rate last year was nearly double the national average, and seemingly everybody in state and local government is trying to come up with a fix. The legislature last year dedicated $100 million to help struggling homeowners refinance and hold on to their homes. Governor Ted Strickland is handing out other funds to implement the multiple recommendations of his high-profile task force on the issue. The chief justice of the state Supreme Court, Thomas Moyer, has publicly encouraged lawyers to offer pro bono help in foreclosure cases that are clogging dockets across the state. Attorney General Marc Dann has sued more than a dozen lenders and brokers he believes inflated values as part of what he calls "the largest financial scam in American history." The city of Cleveland is suing nearly two-dozen lenders over public nuisance complaints, seeking to force them to take better care of their thousands of vacant properties.

In Columbus, Coleman is taking a multi-pronged approach, cracking down on landlords with tougher code enforcement, offering to help pay for roofs, furnaces and other improvements to keep homeowners in their properties, and acquiring many more properties directly for rehabilitation or demolition. Coleman says the city has managed to address 600 homes in this way over the past 18 months.

And yet, over the same period, the number of vacant or abandoned properties has nonetheless grown from 3,100 to 4,100. "We're seeing the destruction of entire areas of the city as a result of the mortgage crisis," Coleman says. "There is not a city in this country that can handle the extent of this problem."

Dayton's Commissioner Lovelace is pleased that state officials have "gotten the gospel," but he doesn't forget that the state squashed his efforts years ago to try to head off disaster. He blames foreclosures on the "aggressive predatory lending phenomenon," and sponsored a law in 2001 to curb the worst industry practices. His ordinance was almost instantly challenged in court by lenders, and was soon preempted by a weaker state law. Ohio toughened its approach in 2006, but by that time, Lovelace says, "the damage had been done. These predatory lenders and mortgage brokers have just been feasting."

Dayton didn't need a housing price bubble to create a foreclosure problem. The city has lost roughly 100,000 residents over the past 40 years, and hasn't experienced net job growth since 1990. An estimated 5,000 to 7,000 homes were vacant even before the current crisis took root—and it took root much earlier in Dayton than in most of the country. Between 1997 and 2001, the number of local foreclosure filings more than doubled, and they've continued to rise since then. In each of the past two years, the number of filings in Montgomery County, where Dayton sits, has topped 5,000. "Sometimes," jokes Dan Foley, a county commissioner, "we say we have a foreclosure court that dabbles in other cases."

Willis Blackshear, the Montgomery County recorder, keeps a careful eye on foreclosure filings. Working with an academic and a former mortgage company employee, Blackshear has identified the most active subprime lenders in his county, and in recent months has sent out thousands of letters to their customers, in hopes of alerting them to potential problems before their interest rates are reset and they find themselves unable to make monthly payments. "When you talk about foreclosure prevention, most organizations look to the people to come to them, but most people won't seek help until the problem has basically exploded," Blackshear says. "If you can't get people to come in prior to their loans caving in, what good is it to counsel them after the fact?"

Blackshear has seen a 10 percent response rate to his letters, which "people say is great, but I think it's terrible." He's been able to refer many borrowers to "money mentors" who help them qualify for more favorable loans before payment problems get out of hand. He is seeking grant money to step up his outreach efforts and entertains hopes of preventing 200 foreclosures, but concedes that his program is a small-bore solution to a widespread problem. "The funds that keep basic city and county government running are going to suffer until this turns around," he says.

Blackshear uses past lender performance to help decide which homeowners to contact, but that's far from an infallible method. Because of the convoluted nature of mortgage financing, governments often have to spend months simply trying to track down who holds the title to properties once they've been abandoned. A few years ago, Dayton started putting up "shaming" billboards featuring pictures of lending company CEOs, along with their phone numbers, in hopes that angry neighbors would put pressure on them. That had little impact.

John Carter, a housing inspector for the city, then came up with a different approach. He found that the complications of modern lending made it difficult for title-holders themselves to keep track of their properties and the conditions they were in. So he began sending out "nuisance property" lists that lenders can scour to find out about the shape of their own holdings. He makes direct contact with property companies when he knows who owns the buildings that are in the worst shape. Mortgage companies may not be universally cooperative, but many are glad for a tip about a home that can still be salvaged if they take quick action. Some have responded with repairs or cleanups within 24 hours of hearing from Carter. "The bottom line," he says, "is their assets get better attention and we save in money and resources."

Carter's list has expanded to include more than 500 contacts. His e-mail blasts have become must-reading for mortgage companies, and Carter has become an in-demand speaker on the conference circuit, fielding information requests from localities throughout the country looking to copycat his efforts. "Whether it's a broken window or an overgrown lawn, cities have a better chance of abating the problem and getting rid of the nuisance by trying to be proactive and solving problems, rather than slapping on a fine," says Rob Hicks, of FIS Field Services, which performs preservation work for mortgage companies on hundreds of homes per year in Dayton alone.

But all these efforts on the ground—the different kinds of outreach performed by Carter and Blackshear, and even the city's plans to double its demolition target to 300 homes this year, while boarding up another 1,000—are far from enough to keep up with the backlog of 10,000 vacant and abandoned properties. "This is stuff you deal with over decades and generations, and make adjustments where you can," says John Gower, Dayton's director of planning and community development.

GREED WAVE

Maybe it comes easily in a culture shaped by the highs and lows of gambling, but local officials in Las Vegas sound rather casual talking about their foreclosure situation, which is the third worst of any metropolitan area in the country. They see it as a problem that government may need to recognize, but not one that requires drastic action.

As the nation's youngest big city, Las Vegas doesn't have much in the way of old infrastructure or blighted buildings to worry about. There are more vacant properties in Clark County than in Dayton—including more than half of the 25,000 homes currently listed for sale—but while a lot of people have lost money, neither area governments nor the real estate industry appear too worried about the situation. In many cases, it's homeowners associations that are on the hook for streetscapes and payment of special improvement district bonds.

Even as vacancies mount and prices plummet in Las Vegas, property taxes continue to rise, since a state-imposed 3 percent annual cap on increases in residential property appraisal means the appraisals are still catching up to values reached during a once-hot market. "I feel sorry for our property assessor," says Rosenquist, the assistant county manager. "He's getting killed by people who don't understand why their property taxes are going up while property values are going down."

What went wrong with the Vegas housing market is, in retrospect, pretty simple to understand. Housing prices escalated rapidly starting in 2004. The area was pinched not only by the lack of available land—Vegas is surrounded by mountains and federally owned desert—but also by the continuing in-migration of several thousand people every month. Legitimate demand was bound to lead to a building boom and escalating prices. Soaring prices, coupled with easy credit, led thousands of people to get carried away on what Richard Lee, of First American Title Co. of Nevada, calls "the greed wave."

It used to be that perhaps 20 percent of homes in the Vegas area were bought by investors, but in recent years, that share grew to nearly 40 percent. At the height of the boom in 2006, homebuilders bought and sold more than 36,000 new homes, representing an 80 percent increase over recent annual averages.

Too many of those homes were bought by people who didn't have nearly enough personal or rental cash flow to sustain payments and counted on ever-escalating prices to carry them through. Once the run-up in prices came to its natural end, many were caught short. There are entire subdivisions that were purchased by speculators, and some individual investors have up to 40 foreclosed houses to their names. "It was that Vegas mentality," Lee says. "The irrational exuberance Alan Greenspan talked about with the stock market happened here in Las Vegas real estate."

But if many investors mistook a speculative bubble for ongoing reality, that doesn't mean that growth in Vegas has suddenly ground to a stop. The city's core industry of gambling is expanding mightily, with major new hotel-casinos—Palazzo, Echelon, Encore—opening up every few months. The area is providing a home for other newly arrived enterprises—everything from massive furniture and jewelry marts to a new national center for brain research. Project CityCenter, an $8 billion mixed-use development rising in contorted steel and glass on Las Vegas Boulevard between the Monte Carlo and the Bellagio, is expected to generate 12,000 new jobs all by itself.

The Vegas area, in other words, fully expects to build its way out of its current slump. Area population continues to rise and it is simply assumed that in a year or two job growth will translate into people moving into most if not all of the vacant houses. Prices will continue to soften, but in Vegas, this is seen as more of a needed market correction than a crisis for government to worry about.

Rosenquist notes that if county finances continue to weaken, there could be a hiring freeze, but so far layoffs have not been necessary. There has been increased demand on social services, but even amid the depressed housing market, the most challenging problems for local officials remain those tied to the strain growth puts on education, health care, public safety and the courts. "When you grow so quickly," says Clark County Commissioner Rory Reid, "government is in a constant struggle to keep up and provide the services that people expect. And all of a sudden, the revenues we use to run that race are not there."

DAYTON'S DILEMMA

If political leaders in newer markets such as Las Vegas are counting on growth to pull them out of the doldrums, those in places such as Dayton know they can count on no such thing. Most Midwestern foreclosures were caused not by interest-rate resets but by traditional culprits such as layoffs, medical expenses and divorce. "Here, it's much more a result of the economy," says Diane Shannon, of Dayton's budget office. "It's probably bad to lose your second home or your investment property, but here I think the social distress is much more pronounced."

Dayton has a long and proud history as a manufacturing center. The Wright brothers lived here, converting their bicycle business into flight, and Dayton was the birthplace of the heart-lung machine and the cash register. More than anything, Dayton has been an automobile town. General Motors, long the mainstay, recently invested $69 million in a local plant, but GM and its spun-off parts-making arm, Delphi, along with other companies, have let go tens of thousands of Dayton workers. A vacant lot marks the spot in the Edgemont neighborhood where a million-square-foot Delphi plant stood just a few years ago. Around the corner, on the 1200 block of Wisconsin Boulevard, nearly every house has been torn down or boarded up. Even the Pentecostal church has been boarded up. "Little pockets of despair ripple out everywhere," Lovelace says.

There are little pockets of hope in Dayton as well. A local nonprofit group has been building new homes on land donated by the city, training troubled youth in construction trades as an important side benefit. The school district is engaged in a $650 million building program, prompting the construction of a few new homes near each of the fresh school campuses, and helping lure back at least a few students from one of the nation's densest concentrations of charter schools. Dayton's hospitals have been helpful partners in rebuilding not only their own facilities but surrounding neighborhoods as well, in some cases even helping to finance community-based policing.

Just outside the city, Wright-Patterson Air Force Base— already Ohio's top employer—was a big winner in the most recent round of base closures and realignments, prompting hope for growth in contract- and research-related jobs.

Overall, though, there is a recognition that the jobs that are coming in are not only fewer in number but mostly lower-paying than the manufacturing jobs that have been lost either to overseas competition or more efficient mechanization. "We know we will continue to lose population," says Gower, Dayton's planning director.

There was a time when the city's policy would have been to mothball vacant properties, hoping they would be worth restoring and reusing some day. But Dayton officials now admit, as Gower puts it, that "the region is stunningly overbuilt." That's why the city is stepping up its "strategic demolition" and looking to use zoning to encourage concentration of the remaining population in areas with good housing stock.

Like jurisdictions across the country, Dayton now hopes that the silver lining of the foreclosure crisis will be that cheaper property allows for more aggressive and more thoughtful land management. "Part of the solution here is fundamentally rethinking what the vision of the city is going to look like," Gower says. "Part of the reason people here aren't freaked out is because we continue to believe we can turn this into an opportunity."

38

Crackdown

Josh Goodman

Illegal immigration shakes up politics as usual in state capitols.

When the subject of illegal immigration comes up, the states you think about first are Texas and California. Maybe Arizona. But, as of July 1, it is Georgia, a full thousand miles from the Mexican border, that is at the center of the immigration debate in the United States.

That's because SB 529, its new immigration law now taking effect, is the most stringent statute of its kind anywhere in the country. It is the sort of law that immigration hard-liners would like to see enacted on a national basis. Under its provisions, state and local government agencies have to verify the legal residency of benefit recipients. Many employers will have to do the same whenever they make a hiring decision. Law enforcement officers are given authority to crack down on human trafficking and fake documents. In sum, SB 529 touches every facet of state policy that relates to illegal immigrants.

The central question about the law is, obviously, whether it will work as intended and reduce the impact of undocumented newcomers on the state. But an equally important question is whether the political situation that led to SB 529 can be sustained and replicated in other places. The topic of illegal immigration has bedeviled virtually every state legislature and the U.S. Congress for years, without much substantive result. What made Georgia different was a populist uprising that all but forced the legislature to crack down on the undocumented community. If that sort of pressure gains momentum elsewhere, the near future may portend a series of state laws as strict as Georgia's—even if Congress manages to pass an immigration bill of its own. Oklahoma and Colorado have both enacted laws with some provisions similar to SB 529—the question is how many states will follow.

From *Governing,* July 2008.

If Georgia's experience does become a prototype for other states, it will be through the building of improbable coalitions and unlikely rivalries. In many places, the Chamber of Commerce finds itself at war with the Republican Party over immigration; Christian conservatives are unsure whom to support; and union members and African Americans are forced to reevaluate their ties to Democrats.

These rivalries played out in Georgia, where businesses did not want to be deprived of a source of cheap labor. "The concern," says Bryan Tolar, vice president of the Georgia Agribusiness Council, "is that the illegals would still be in the United States, but that we might not have any of the migrant workers—those who are here legally and those who are here illegally." Even more than that, businesses did not want the state to turn them into residency-status enforcers, creating bureaucratic obstacles every time they take on a new employee.

But the Republican legislative majority that created the law felt little obligation to the corporate community. Senator Chip Rogers, the sponsor of SB 529, says openly that he doesn't care whether big business opposes him because of his immigration views. "I blame 90 percent on employers," Rogers says. "They're the ones that are profiting by breaking the law." He thinks many businesses, especially smaller ones, agree with him. They would prefer to hire legal workers, he says, and don't want to be at competitive disadvantage with those that hire illegal ones. He thinks industry groups are out of touch with the views of ordinary Georgians, including rank-and-file Republicans.

Nor did SB 529 owe its success to Christian conservatives, the other pillar of Republican political strength in recent years. Nationally, the Christian right is ambivalent on immigration, conflicted by conservative principles that say lawbreaking should never be tolerated, and Biblical admonitions to provide charity to the "least among us." Some religious conservatives quietly supported SB 529, but they were not major players in the debate that led to its passage.

So who provided the momentum for the nation's toughest immigration law? "It really was the people," says Phil Kent, a Georgia conservative activist who also serves as national spokesman for Americans for Immigration Control. "It was people walking up to their legislators and saying, 'I'm sick and tired of what's going on in my neighborhood.'"

This line, echoed time and again by supporters of SB 529, is part bluster—almost every politician says the people are behind him—and part truth. The reality is that most of the powerful groups in the state, be they conservative Christians and big business on the right or African-American leaders on the Democratic side, didn't really want a crackdown on illegal immigration, but every opinion poll showed that most Georgians did.

FULL-TIME CRUSADER

If there's one person that Kent and Rogers have in mind when they talk about "the people," it's D.A. King, although he is anything but a typical Georgian. Since giving up his career as an insurance agent in 2003, King has been a full-time opponent of illegal immigration. From his home in a peaceful suburban neighborhood in Marietta, with an American flag flying in front and another one in back, King blogs against amnesty, organizes protests, writes a newspaper column and fields questions from reporters. When the legislature is in session, he spends most of his time at the Capitol in Atlanta. "My typical day is 14, 16 hours long," King says. "I work seven days a week if my wife can't drag me out on a Saturday."

Marathon hours not withstanding, there's probably an aspiring D.A. King in most states. What's unusual about Georgia is that legislators cared just as much about his views as they did about the views of Chamber of Commerce lobbyists. Matt Towery, a former Georgia state representative who now operates a polling and political news company, has as good an explanation as anyone as to why this came about.

For 130 years, Towery says, the business community in Georgia happily coexisted with the conservative Democrats who ran the state. But in 2002, Republicans took over the Senate and, in the biggest shock, Republican Sonny Perdue ousted Democratic Governor Roy Barnes. In 2004, the GOP completed its sweep, winning the state House of Representatives. The party now controls Georgia government in a way it has not done since Reconstruction. "When it changed overnight, the business community had a very hard time feeling its way around," Towery says. "Business doesn't have the influence over these new leaders."

Take Chip Rogers, for example. His soft-spoken style belies his populist political roots as a talk-radio host. To be sure, Rogers compromised a good deal with business groups to make SB 529 a reality. The toughest employer-related provisions were reserved for companies that contract with state and local governments, and they will go into effect incrementally. Only businesses employing 500 or more people come under the initial round of verification requirements. Perhaps most notably, the rules apply only to new hires—all those who were on the payroll before July 1 are exempted.

Even with the compromises, though, the fact remains that business in Georgia had to swallow quite a few provisions it didn't want. Rogers and his supporters were in a position of power, knew it and took advantage of it. The corporate community made little effort to campaign publicly against SB 529 and quietly accepted terms their brethren in other states would never have agreed to. "They're just afraid," says Jerry Gonzalez, executive director of the Georgia Association of Latino Elected Officials. "The issue of illegal immigration has gotten so poisonous that the business community is petrified and shaking in its boots."

DEMOGRAPHIC SHOCK

Georgia is, in some ways, a special case. According to the U.S. Department of Homeland Security, its population of illegal immigrants more than doubled between 2000 and 2005, easily the fastest growth rate in the country. "Georgia just saw such a rapid increase in non-English speaking people," Kent says, "burdening the school system, burdening the court system." The percentage change was great enough to fuel widespread public anxiety, while the total Hispanic population was still too small to carry much political weight. That is the perfect demographic scenario for a crackdown, but it is unlikely to occur in the same way in many other places.

In other states, where the numbers are less dramatic, the issue has been slow to gain potency at the polls. Ernest Istook, the Republican nominee for governor in Oklahoma last year, staked his campaign against Democratic incumbent Brad Henry on the immigration issue. His first radio ad was a country song with these lyrics: "If you sneak across the border, there's some help that you can get/ In a place called Oklahoma where you'll never have to fret/ There a man they call Brad Henry has some gifts he'll give to you/ Taxpayer money to pay for college and in-state tuition, too."

It didn't work. Henry trounced Istook, a previously popular seven-term congressman, by a 2-to-1 margin. Republican nominees for governor in Kansas and Arizona

placed similar emphasis on immigration and failed almost as spectacularly.

But when the Oklahoma legislature met early this year, the climate of opinion seemed to be different. Both the House and Senate passed an immigration bill that goes even further than SB 529, although implementation of some of its most important provisions has been postponed until July of 2008. This was a complete reversal: Only four years earlier, the Oklahoma legislature had voted to grant in-state tuition to illegal immigrants.

Oklahoma has not been hit as hard as Georgia by illegal immigration, but it does have some of the same political conditions. Republicans, who have been in the legislative minority for years, are now coming into power: They control the state House of Representatives and are tied in the Senate. And as in Georgia, the new crop of Republican legislators is willing to take on the business community. "Our state Chamber of Commerce," says Representative Randy Terrill, the sponsor of Oklahoma's tough immigration bill, "is an apologist for big business that seeks to employ cheap, illegal labor." Governor Henry, with some reluctance, signed the legislation.

Most other states, even those in which immigration has become a volatile public issue, have been reluctant to move in this direction. This spring, Texas legislators introduced bill after bill to place new restrictions on illegal immigrants, only to see the measures stall after facing opposition from the business community. Overcoming business opposition is simply not feasible in Texas the way it was in Georgia—at least not yet.

It's not only Republicans who have seen their party split over immigration in these states; Democrats are confronting stresses of their own. In Georgia, these stresses are most deeply felt among African Americans, who are generally sensitive to the problems of undocumented workers in menial positions but also worried that these workers are competing with them for jobs and driving wages down. In other states, such as Oklahoma, labor unions experience the same ambivalence. "They were staying out of the fight," says Mike Seney, senior vice president of the Oklahoma Chamber of Commerce.

Michael Thurmond, Georgia's Labor Commissioner, is a black Democrat who has been elected statewide three times even though the electorate is now dominated by white Republicans. "There was divided opinion in the African-American community," he says in explaining the SB 529 debate. "There were some concerned with the economic impact, particularly as it related to jobs. On the other side, there were African-American leaders, elected and otherwise, who identified with a minority and saw in some of the advocacy latent, or not so latent, discrimination and racism."

Thurmond, whose department is charged with enforcing the employer provisions of the law, embodies this tension. He believes illegal immigration is a topic that should be dealt with by the federal government, and during the debate, he urged lawmakers to give smaller businesses more time to comply, a proposal the legislature adopted. But he also called for the legislation to be strengthened in a couple of ways. He referred to exemptions for existing workers as a form of "amnesty" and asked for money so his department could conduct employer audits, money the legislature hasn't appropriated yet. "We looked at the legislation," he says, "and felt like what may have been missing was additional accountability to ensure compliance."

In the end, most of Georgia's black legislators resolved their doubts on the side of opposition. SB 529 passed the House 119-49 and the Senate 39-16, but the Black Caucus voted overwhelmingly against it. Blacks, in fact, cast the majority of negative votes in both chambers.

Georgia's most visible Hispanic legislator, Sam Zamarripa of Atlanta, was in an even more painful position. Bitterly opposed to SB 529—he scornfully refers to Chip Rogers as "Jim Crow"—he nevertheless worked with Rogers to soften some portions of the bill. "Remember the guys on the Titanic who were playing the violin while people were jumping off?" he says. "That's who I was." But his willingness to negotiate led to some significant changes, especially in the language on state and local services. SB 529 requires beneficiaries of these services to prove legal residency, but it exempts prenatal care, immunization, emergency medical care, crisis counseling and soup kitchens. Everyone under the age of 18 is exempted as well.

Zamarripa's compromises were part desperation but also part tactical. "My strategy then and my strategy now," he says, "is to give enough time for federal reform to step in and have the laws of Georgia surpassed." If Congress offers illegal immigrants a way to legalize their status, much of SB 529 will be moot. With the possibility of federal action on the horizon, he tried to give the undocumented community as much reason as possible to stick it out in Georgia until then. Zamarripa did not run for reelection in 2006 and left the legislature this January.

LOOKING FOR CLUES

As the congressional debate on immigration stretches into the summer, states around the country are following it closely for clues to how the politics of the issue are going to play out. But they might be equally prudent to keep an eye on what happens in Georgia, Colorado and Oklahoma.

Until fairly recently, many state-level policy makers took the position that the immigration dilemma could be resolved only at the federal level and that state efforts to move ahead with their own laws would be a futile enterprise. Fewer are making that argument anymore.

In the end, all of the state laws could be preempted by federal legislation, but even if that happens, the states will have had a significant impact on the federal product. For example, one proposal percolating in Congress requires every employer to verify the Social Security numbers of new hires in a federal database. Georgia is already doing that for some government contractors under SB 529. If the congressional debate drags on for several more months, the evidence from Georgia on the feasibility of this requirement will be increasingly relevant to those working on the issue in Washington.

Colorado's legislation, milder than the bills in Georgia and Oklahoma, began going into effect last year. It was a compromise between Republican Governor Bill Owens and the legislature, where Democrats had narrow advantages. The toughest provisions focused on benefits offered by state government, with only a few modest strictures aimed at employers. At the behest of business groups, the legislature rejected a proposal from Republican Representative Al White to require employers to check the federal database for fraudulent Social Security numbers. "They heralded it as the toughest piece of legislation in the country," White complains, "and it didn't do jack squat."

The public perception, however, is that the legislation has changed the immigration climate in Colorado. Word circulated through Spanish-language radio that Colorado wasn't the place for migrant workers to locate. With 49 states to choose from, why would an immigrant without proper papers want to come to the place with what sponsors were calling "the toughest piece of legislation in the country"? That sense was reinforced by a federal immigration raid of a Swift & Co. meatpacking plant in Greeley, Colorado, last December, in which more than 250 workers were arrested. The consensus among those who follow the subject is that there are fewer illegal immigrants coming to Colorado now than before the law was enacted.

There are signs that SB 529 has created a similar perception in Georgia, even though it is just going into effect. Gonzalez, of the Association of Latino Elected Officials, says that home and car sales to Hispanics have declined precipitously in Georgia in recent months, and the reason is that undocumented workers are afraid they may have to leave the state. "Immigrants are making sure that they are able to move at a moment's notice," he says. "The market has completely collapsed." The Georgia Hispanic Chamber of Commerce also cites real estate as its hardest-hit economic sector.

What the longer term consequences of these laws might be is extremely hard to predict. When the Colorado law was under debate, its sponsors hoped it would save the state money by denying government benefits to those in the state illegally, but there is no hard evidence of this so far. At the moment, Colorado farmers are complaining of worker shortages, so much so that the state has been using prisoners as agricultural laborers this spring.

In Georgia, it's too soon to know whether similar worker shortages will materialize. Chip Rogers, the author of SB 529, thinks it's a mistake to dwell on the issue or even on the question of whether illegal immigrants help or hurt the economy or pay more in taxes than they use. "The law is not for sale," he says. "If someone is in violation of the law and they realize that Georgia is going to enforce the law and they make a decision not to be in Georgia because they don't want to abide by the law, to me, that's a good thing."

39

Can It Work?

Laura Tobler and Christie Hager

New England states take the lead in health care reform. Can the new approaches maintain quality and access while reining in costs?

Health reform swept the nation's capitols in 2007 with at least 28 states considering new laws or discussing proposals to change the system—some inching toward the goal of universal coverage and others taking a giant step. Leading the way for this somewhat uncharted course are three New England states: Maine, Massachusetts and Vermont.

Maine led the most recent wave of health reform in 2003. The goal of Maine's Dirigo Health is to contain costs and improve the quality of care, aiming for universal coverage by 2009. Taking its name from the Latin state motto that means "I lead," Dirigo is a statewide plan for improving and changing the health care system. It requires public disclosure of prices for medical services, simplification of administrative functions, reductions in paperwork, and voluntary limits on the growth of health insurance premiums and health care costs. The state also established the Maine Quality Forum to promote better quality of care and DirigoChoice to offer affordable, partly subsidized health insurance to small businesses and those without employer-sponsored insurance.

On April 12, 2006, Massachusetts enacted legislation aiming for near-universal health insurance coverage. The law distributed responsibility for coverage among individual state residents, who are required to purchase health insurance; the government, which offers new subsidies to ensure affordability; and employers, who pay an assessment for uninsured employees. "Health care reform could not be achieved unless we adhered to the principle established in our Massachusetts Constitution of shared responsibility," House Speaker Salvatore F. DiMasi says. "Our commitment to this principle ensured the passage of our health reform bill."

From *State Legislatures,* December 2007.

The Massachusetts law also creates the Commonwealth Health Insurance Connector, which, among other things, assists small businesses and individuals in navigating the insurance marketplace.

One month later, Vermont adopted health reform legislation designed to make affordable health insurance more available, improve the quality of health care and control costs. Two key components of this reform are subsidized health insurance for low-income Vermonters and a statewide effort to improve health care by managing chronic diseases. Employers in Vermont will also be assessed for certain uninsured employees.

With health care reform still high on almost every state's legislative agenda, what have we learned from these three states?

COVERING THE UNINSURED

The foundation of coverage in Maine, Massachusetts and Vermont is an expanded Medicaid and SCHIP program. Each state covers the poorest of the uninsured with these publicly funded programs—beyond levels that are covered in many other states. For people above the eligibility levels, the states created health insurance programs that are publicly subsidized on a sliding scale based on income.

The centerpiece of the Maine reform is DirigoChoice, an insurance plan for businesses with 50 or fewer employees, the selfemployed and individuals. The state projected initial enrollment for this program to be around 30,000 with an overall goal of universal coverage by 2009. To date, the plan has enrolled about half that amount, many of whom were already insured. Although enrollment numbers are lower than the state planners hoped, the DirigoChoice insurance plan has grown faster than any in Maine's history, according to Representative Ann Perry, co-chair of the Health and Human Services Committee.

Maine found that financing health reform can be the Achilles's heel. Maine has struggled with the primary financing mechanism for Dirigo—a "savings offset payment (SOP)" program. The Dirigo board of directors determines the aggregate measurable cost savings in the health care system, which is then filed with the superintendent of insurance, who makes the final determination. Under this system, health insurers and self-funded plans pay a claims assessment that changes each year depending upon this agreed upon savings. The system has been challenged in court and upheld, but the real problem has been in the determined amount of savings, which has been less than projected.

"This year the Bureau of Insurance has determined that Dirigo saved the system around $40 million, which translates into a tax of 1.74 percent that is paid on all health insurance claims in the state," says Senator Peter Mills. That is far less than the Dirigo board of directors was hoping for—they filed for about $70 million—and not enough money to cover all residents eligible for the program. Because of this, enrollment in DirigoChoice has been capped. "The SOP system is withering away, which threatens the survival of this program," Mills says.

DirigoChoice, which has voluntary enrollment, combines individuals and small groups in the same risk pool. It became clear as enrollment began that there would be a substantial demand among individuals for the new insurance product. A few more than 77 percent of the enrollees are individuals and sole proprietors, which makes them higher risk and costlier to cover. Because everyone is in the same risk pool, the small-employer groups help to cross-subsidize the high-cost individuals making their insurance premiums higher than expected.

2008 Brings Hope for Reform

Presidents dating back to Franklin Roosevelt have tried to fashion health care reform, says Ron Pollack, executive director of Families USA. But some conditions exist now that could help move the ball forward.

A leading factor, he says, is the political pressure the 2008 presidential candidates are getting from growing ranks of Americans who have lived the experience of being uninsured or underinsured.

Democratic and Republican candidates alike are promising to improve the nation's ailing health care system. At the heart of most of their proposals is health insurance coverage for the almost 47 million uninsured Americans.

Although health reform platforms existed in past elections, this time the political heat is on. Polls show that Americans want something done about the cost of health care and the growing number of uninsured. In importance of issues, health care ranks second behind the war in Iraq. Nearly every candidate's health platform includes something the states are already doing—making major changes to cover the uninsured, containing costs and improving the quality of health care.

"Small businesses can get insurance on the private market that is less expensive and doesn't come with the requirements imposed by Dirigo," says Mills. In Dirigo-Choice, small employers are required to pay 60 percent of their employee's premium and the coverage is very comprehensive. "The lack of employer participation hurts the bottom line," adds Mills, since funding projections were based on models that estimated more payments from small employers.

"One needs incentives or mandates to make the pool big enough to achieve economies of scale and also include high- and low-risk individuals," says Debra Lipson, senior researcher at Mathematica Policy Research. Which is exactly what Massachusetts did in 2006.

MANDATING HEALTH INSURANCE COVERAGE

Taking lessons from Maine, the Massachusetts reforms include a first-in-the-nation requirement that all individuals aged 18 years and older obtain health insurance, if it is affordable to them as determined by an annual schedule of affordability. A penalty will be imposed for not having insurance by the end of this month—those remaining uninsured will lose their personal income tax exemption, which amounts to approximately $219. For the 2008 tax year and beyond, the penalty is scheduled to increase to half of the premium of the least expensive plan affordable to the individual.

Because research and experience show that a voluntary insurance system will not yield full participation; the mandate was considered critical to reaching universal coverage.

"We knew that we could not make reform work without asking individuals to take some responsibility for making sure they have health insurance," says Representative Patricia Walrath, House chair of the Joint Committee on Health Care Financing, who was a leader in developing the legislation.

To help ensure the success of mandatory health insurance, Massachusetts made other reforms. For example, the non- and small-group markets were merged, which, according to a special commission created to study the impact, is expected to reduce current individual rates by 15 percent and increase small-group rates by only 1 percent to 1.5 percent.

After Massachusetts passed its reform law, Maine soon began talking about reforming its plan. Enter

The Problem of the Uninsured

There are 46.6 million uninsured people in the United States—an increase of 1.3 million people since 2004, according to the Census Bureau. That amounts to about one in every six Americans. Most have incomes below 200 percent of poverty, but they are likely to be employed or have an employed family member. At least half are racial or ethnic minorities.

Why the increase? The rise can be largely attributed to the decline in employer-sponsored coverage because of the rising cost of health plans. Although health care cost increases have leveled in the past three years, the growth rate still outpaces that of inflation and wages, making health insurance premiums unaffordable for many.

"In Massachusetts, many factors contributed to the need for our reform, but the skyrocketing health insurance costs that are prohibitively expensive for our families was the biggest driver," says Representative Salvatore DiMasi, speaker of the House. The uninsured were costing the state about $1 billion each year, he says.

In 2007, most states considering health reform included covering the uninsured as a top priority. Some use public programs, like Medicaid and the State Children's Health Insurance Program (SCHIP), while others focus on private market reforms. Most use a combination of both.

the Maine Blue Ribbon Commission on Reforming Dirigo, created in May 2006. One of the many items discussed by the commission was making insurance more affordable. Recommendations from the commission include a health insurance mandate for people with incomes greater than 400 percent of the federal poverty guidelines.

Taking a slower, more cautious approach, Vermont chose not to mandate coverage unless goals aren't met by 2010. The state created comprehensive and affordable health insurance for uninsured people with the cost dependent on the household income. "If we haven't reached a 96 percent coverage rate by 2010, the state will consider an individual mandate," says Susan Besio, director of Health Care Reform Implementation in Vermont. Currently, 89.5 percent of Vermonters are covered.

THE MASSACHUSETTS CONNECTOR

Another first from Massachusetts is the creation of the Commonwealth Health Insurance Connector Authority, charged with developing regulations to determine the annual affordability schedule and what will qualify as health insurance coverage. "We run a couple of insurance programs," says Jon Kingsdale, director of the Commonwealth Health Insurance Connector Authority. "One is subsidized for the low-income uninsured at or below 300 percent of the federal poverty level. And the other is a group of more than 40 products that are private, unsubsidized health insurance, particularly for uninsured individuals who are going to be buying out of their own pocket."

A big piece of what the "connector" does is organize and create a one-stop shopping center for health insurance. It began enrolling individuals who make up to 300 percent of the federal poverty level in October 2006. After 11 months, there were about 115,400 enrolled, 92,000 of whom pay no premiums at all. Further, uncompensated care spending had decreased by 9 percent, and is trending downward. Enrollment in the nonsubsidized plans began in May 2007, and continues to exceed projections.

Massachusetts has learned that many people with nontraditional work have a very hard time getting insurance. The connector is improving the "portability" of health insurance to help people with part-time jobs, many different jobs or seasonal jobs get coverage. It allows people to combine contributions from various employers to pay for coverage as well as continue with coverage when seasonal work is over.

"If the state's health care system is reformed so that health insurance attaches to individuals and not to jobs—like the connector system—a significant portion of the uninsured will be able to get and keep coverage without the need for additional public subsidies," says Ed Haislmaier of the Heritage Foundation. "That means that the state's efforts to target the remaining uninsured can be more focused on people who need the subsidy to get coverage."

Many states are studying the connector idea to see if they can learn from Massachusetts's experience. Washington passed legislation this year. The Washington Health Insurance Partnership will initially target small employers with low-income workers. The state will provide premium subsidies, based on a sliding scale, for employees who earn less than 200 percent of the federal poverty level.

EMPLOYER REQUIREMENTS

The "shared responsibility" of the Massachusetts reforms includes employers. To satisfy the business community, a provision that would have required a payroll assessment on employers was modified, in a conference committee compromise, into a flat, per-worker, annual assessment. All employers with 11 or more employees who fail to make a "fair and reasonable" contribution to the health insurance premiums of their workers are required to pay a "fair-share contribution" of $295 per year for each worker. Employers are also required to offer a Section 125 "cafeteria plan" to avoid a so-called "free rider surcharge," on any workers and their dependents who receive care through the state's Health Safety Net Trust Fund.

While Massachusetts has a relatively high rate of employer-sponsored insurance, this fair share contribution and other new policies attempt to level the playing field between the majority of employers who offer coverage to their workers and those who do not. Collections started recently. The effects of these new policies during a time when the state is enjoying record high levels of employers offering health insurance will be monitored closely. So far, there's been no ERISA challenge, but the federal Employee Retirement Income Security Act of 1974, raises potential problems. The act preempts state laws that "relate to" employersponsored benefit plans. For example, the Maryland Fair Share legislation which required employers to pay an assessment based on a percentage of payroll if they did not offer certain health insurance to their employees was overturned on the basis that it violated ERISA.

Vermont also included an assessment on employers to help finance the new subsidized insurance program. "Our employer assessment amounts to one dollar per day for each uninsured employee," says Besio. "Businesses have been trying hard to cover their employees—they were at the table when this assessment was crafted."

Maine does not assess employers but the Blue Ribbon Commission recommends that the governor consider the concept.

Vermont's Blueprint for Health

[Driven by the rising costs and high death rates associated with chronic diseases, a public-private partnership called the Vermont Blueprint for Health Chronic Care initiative was launched in 2003. Its goal is to standardize chronic disease management in Medicaid, state employee benefit programs, state-approved employer sponsored insurance plans, and the Catamount Health plans. This is a new approach to managing chronic care that focuses on:

- Supporting public policies that promote healthy lifestyles and effective health care.
- Establishing community activities that encourage healthier lifestyles.
- Encouraging personal responsibility by making self-management tools easily available.
- Improving health care information technology.

Health reform in 2006 broadened and strengthened the 3-year-old initiative by creating implementation timetables and requiring annual status reports to the General Assembly. The program is now in six communities across the state with a goal of taking it statewide by 2011.

For more information, go to: http://healthvermont.gov/blueprint.aspx

—*Melissa Hansen*

IMPROVING QUALITY

Most states working on health reform are including measures to improve the quality of health care. Compared with Australia, Canada, Germany, New Zealand and the United Kingdom, the U.S. health care system ranks last or next-to-last on five dimensions of a high performance health system: quality, access, efficiency, equity and healthy lives, according to a Commonwealth Fund report.

In conjunction with the Dirigo reforms, Maine created the Quality Forum to advocate high quality health care. The forum, according to its director, Joshua Cutler, helps citizens make informed choices by publishing medical information on a public web page. It also conducts research to ensure that all health care meets certain quality standards and convenes health providers to discuss quality goals and standards.

"As a nurse practitioner," says Maine's Representative Perry, "I can see firsthand how the forum has encouraged hospitals to review the care that patients are receiving and make needed changes."

Vermont's reform aims to help prevent and manage chronic diseases through a public-private partnership that includes all commercial and public payers, providers, state leaders, and the business community. Called the Blueprint for Health, the goal is to provide better support for primary care providers th[r]ough coordinated payment reform; care coordination resources at the community level; promote wellness; and improve health information technology through support for electronic health records in primary care settings and medical information sharing across all care settings statewide. Vermont also is trying to increase the number of physicians practicing in rural and hard-to-serve areas through enhanced loan forgiveness and loan repayment programs.

"We are trying to change the way we deliver health care by reforming the payment system to encourage more appropriate care for chronic diseases, prevention and wellness," says Besio, director of Vermont's Health Care Reform Implementation. She adds that "50 percent of Vermonters have one or more chronic conditions and only half of those get the right care at the right time."

And there is some evidence that it may be working. "For the 400 people enrolled in our healthy living workshops, there has been a 60 percent reduction in emergency room use," Besio claims.

Massachusetts's health reform is moving in that direction, too. The Massachusetts Health Care Quality and Cost Council promotes safe, effective, timely, efficient, equitable and patient-centered care. The council has regulatory authority to make resources available to health care consumers and hold providers accountable. Controlling costs and improving quality must accompany any expansion of coverage.

"We consider the work of the council to be critical to the success of health care reform," says Senator Richard T. Moore, one of the major architects of the Massachusetts law. "Unless we can contain costs while maintaining quality care, access to coverage will be unsustainable."

All three states have found the road to health reform to be long and winding with many unexpected bumps and turns. "Dirigo passed with support from both sides,

States Expanding Health Coverage

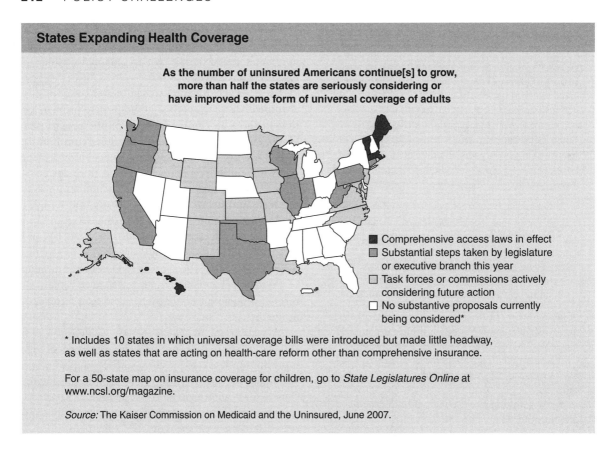

As the number of uninsured Americans continue[s] to grow, more than half the states are seriously considering or have improved some form of universal coverage of adults

- ■ Comprehensive access laws in effect
- ■ Substantial steps taken by legislature or executive branch this year
- □ Task forces or commissions actively considering future action
- □ No substantive proposals currently being considered*

* Includes 10 states in which universal coverage bills were introduced but made little headway, as well as states that are acting on health-care reform other than comprehensive insurance.

For a 50-state map on insurance coverage for children, go to *State Legislatures Online* at www.ncsl.org/magazine.

Source: The Kaiser Commission on Medicaid and the Uninsured, June 2007.

but it has been a partisan battle ever since," says Perry of the struggles in Maine to maintain political support for the new programs. "Don't lose sight of the big picture and the ultimate goal," she warns. "There is a strong temptation to fix one problem in our dysfunctional system with smaller more incremental reforms that may cause a reaction in another part of the system that we didn't plan for and certainly didn't want."

Text Credits

Chapter	Credit
2	Copyrighted © 2008 by the National Conference of State Legislatures.
3	Copyrighted © 2008 by Oxford University Press. Reproduced with permission of Oxford University Press.
4	Copyrighted © 2007 by the National Conference of State Legislatures.
6	Copyrighted © 2008 by the National Conference of State Legislatures.
7	This information has been reprinted with permission of the Council of State Governments.
9	Reprinted with permission of Campaigns & Elections
10	Bullock, Charles S. III and Karen L. Padgett. 2007. "Partisan Change and Consequences for Lobbying: Two-Part Government Comes to the Georgia Legislature." *State and Local Government Review.* 39: 61-71. With permission of Carl Vinson Institute of Government, University of Georgia (www.vinsoninstitute.org).
14	This information has been reprinted with permission of the Council of State Governments.
15	Copyrighted © 2007 by the National Conference of State Legislatures.
16	Copyrighted © 2008 by the National Conference of State Legislatures.
17	This information has been reprinted with permission of the Council of State Governments.

Chapter	Credit
21	Copyrighted © 2007 by the National Conference of State Legislatures.
22	This information has been reprinted with permission of the Council of State Governments.
26	Copyright © 2008 by County News.
30	This information has been reprinted with permission of the Council of State Governments.

Chapter	Credit
33	Copyrighted © 2007 by the National Conference of State Legislatures.
35	Copyrighted © 2007 by the National Conference of State Legislatures.
39	Copyrighted © 2007 by the National Conference of State Legislatures.